Educated Out

Educated Out

How Rural Students Navigate
Elite Colleges—And What It Costs Them

Mara Casey Tieken

The University of Chicago Press
Chicago and London

The University of Chicago Press, Chicago 60637
The University of Chicago Press, Ltd., London
© 2025 by The University of Chicago
For more information, contact the University of Chicago
Press, 1427 E. 60th St., Chicago, IL 60637.
Published 2025
Printed in the United States of America

34 33 32 31 30 29 28 27 26 25   1 2 3 4 5

ISBN-13: 978-0-226-84133-5 (cloth)
ISBN-13: 978-0-226-84135-9 (paper)
ISBN-13: 978-0-226-84134-2 (e-book)
DOI: https://doi.org/10.7208/chicago/9780226841342.001.0001

Library of Congress Cataloging-in-Publication Data

Names: Tieken, Mara Casey, author.
Title: Educated out : how rural students navigate elite
    colleges—and what it costs them / Mara Casey Tieken.
Description: Chicago : The University of Chicago Press, 2025. |
    Includes bibliographical references and index.
Identifiers: LCCN 2024044953 | ISBN 9780226841335 (cloth) |
    ISBN 9780226841359 (paperback) | ISBN 9780226841342
    (ebook)
Subjects: LCSH: Rural college students—United States—
    Economic conditions. | Universities and colleges—Alumni
    and alumnae—United States.
Classification: LCC LC208.8 .T54 2025 | DDC
    378.1/980973—dc23/eng/20241014
LC record available at https://lccn.loc.gov/2024044953

To my mother and father, who taught me to love a good book and to value a good education.

To Veery. I hope I can teach you the same.

And to my third graders. I am so proud.

Contents

1

From a Distance

The first announcement arrived in the mailbox outside my faculty apartment in early May. Inside a small white envelope was a card that read "Congratulations, Class of 2012!" It was covered with photos of a teenager, someone I recognized. She was tall, probably taller than me. She had traded her pink T-shirt and purple plastic barrettes for a long dress and sophisticated heels—but there she was, nearly ten years older than the last time I'd seen her, a mortar board on her head and a diploma in her hand. My third graders were graduating from high school.

I knew the envelope's postmark, too: Vanleer, Tennessee—a place with green hills and old tobacco barns and fences that no longer mark much, a place my third graders used to struggle to find on a map, a place that felt, at once, so familiar and so far. It was there that, just out of college, I began my teaching career. I found my way to Vanleer because I wanted a rural teaching job and the school's principal was willing to hire me; I never imagined that, ten years later, I'd be college faculty, teaching college kids and studying rural education and, from a distance, watching my third graders graduate.

Over the next few years, every May, the mailman would drop a stack of graduation announcements in my box, and more would appear on Facebook. With the photos were notes about their future plans, comments on the lives that awaited them. They were becoming mechanics, vet techs, and linemen, some enrolling at the local community college for the associate degree or trade certificate they'd need. Under their caps and gowns, I could still see my smart, curious eight-year-olds, and I could see these eight-year-olds—and often, their families—in their plans, too.

I also noticed what my kids weren't doing. Few were going to four-year colleges, and none was headed to an elite school—the kind of school where I was now teaching.

I had just been hired at Bates College, a small, wealthy, highly selective, private liberal arts college located in a small city in Maine. At Bates, courses are rigorous, extracurriculars are extensive, and facilities are state of the art. A career office will edit your résumé, and a tutoring center can help with your math homework. Sometimes there's even lobster mac and cheese in the dining hall.

So, why weren't my former third graders enrolling at four-year schools? Why weren't they going to colleges like Bates? I didn't question my kids' plans; their plans were sensible, and the work they would do, valuable. But I wondered whether these plans had been a choice—if they'd had options and what those options were. The resources, the opportunities, the abundances of college were striking, and I wanted all of that—or at least, the *possibility* of all of that—for my third graders, too.

After a few years of teaching at Bates, though, my questions started to change. Bates seemed far from rural Tennessee—really, far from rural anywhere. Busy streets and crowded apartment buildings surround the campus. Its trees are deliberately placed. The school's majors wouldn't be much help in hanging a power line or vaccinating a horse. Its students don't go four-wheeling, and they wouldn't know what to do with a turnip green. On warm spring days, when dorm room windows are open and music spills out, it's not country. I still wondered why my students hadn't gone to a four-year college, but now I also wondered, what if they had?

College Opportunity and Place

College means opportunity, or at least it's supposed to. Admission is taken as evidence of hard work and talent. Graduation is, theoretically, a chance to cash in on that investment, the opportunity for steady employment and future security. It's both high school aspiration and national narrative—the stuff of American dreams—and for decades, policymakers and researchers have preached the benefits and, increasingly, the necessity of a degree.[1] Elite colleges occupy a particular place in this narrative: they're a special destination with the biggest rewards for the best and brightest students. And their benefits are clear. They offer small classes, intensive advising, and robust academic support, and unlike many colleges and universities, they boast high retention rates.[2] Their students develop networks, acquire cultural capital, even find spouses.[3] Their graduates are more likely to land good jobs and enter graduate school, and they earn more—over 20 percent more than graduates of the least selective schools.[4]

But I was beginning to question the "best and brightest" part of that narrative. Not because my new college students weren't talented and smart and determined—they were. But they were also mostly White and wealthy. And despite rural America making up 20 percent of the US population, they weren't rural.[5] "Best and brightest" seemed also to signify something about race and class and geography.

The racial and class inequities of higher education are well documented. We know that, for example, 42 percent of White students enroll in college after high school, but only 37 percent of Black students and 36 percent of Hispanic students do.[6] And while enrollment for students from the wealthiest quintile of families nears 90 percent, it's less than 40 percent for those from the poorest.[7] Study after study makes clear why. Students of color and low-income students face barriers throughout the college pipeline: inadequate college advising, rising tuition, shrinking state aid, racially hostile campuses, mounting debt, and countless other obstacles and costs.[8] These disparities, though intractable, are widely acknowledged by advocates, political leaders, and college administrators, many of whom are working for change.

But so much of this is about who students are and what they have, not *where* they are or how the latter might shape the former. Geography has mostly been neglected as a factor structuring college access.[9] It shouldn't be. Where my rural third graders and my not-so-rural college students are from—and where they are going—suggests that place may actually matter a great deal. I was also beginning to suspect that it isn't just at admission that it matters. Geography might shape it all: who gets a degree, what that degree means, and what that degree costs.

I wanted to know how.

Rural College Attainment

In the American imagination, "rural" exists somewhere between *Little House on the Prairie* and the movie *Deliverance*: poor, White, and either impossibly wholesome or frighteningly backward.[10] Even more recent memoirs, books, and newspaper headlines have done little to demystify rural America, trafficking in stereotypes about hillbillies and assumptions about rural ignorance and, oftentimes, ignoring the structures that shape rural communities and rural lives and rural kids' college opportunities.

I wanted to challenge these stereotypes and explore the relationship between rurality—the land and people of rural places, but also the politics, the economy, the culture, and the social structures of rural places[11]—and college access, college experiences, and college outcomes. Data suggest that there is a relationship. In 2021, for example, 31 percent of rural adults aged twenty-five and older held some sort of postsecondary degree compared to 45 percent of nonrural adults.[12] For associate degrees, attainment is similar: 10 percent of rural adults and 9 percent of nonrural adults had an associate degree. The disparities come with bachelor's degrees. While 36 percent of nonrural adults had earned a bachelor's degree, only 21 percent of rural adults had. And, although a greater proportion of both rural and nonrural residents is attending and graduating from college than in the past, the rural-urban gap in bachelor's degrees has grown over time.

This gap could, of course, reflect the out-migration of college-educated young adults from rural places, and evidence indicates that many of these young people do leave.[13] But studies also show that rural youth across the United States lag nonrural youth in enrolling in postsecondary studies, and when they do go, they attend different types of postsecondary programs.[14] Rural students, compared to nonrural youth, are underrepresented in bachelor's degree programs and at private institutions, and they're overrepresented in associate degree programs and at public universities.[15] They are also less likely to attend selective colleges—schools like Bates—than their nonrural counterparts are.[16] Studies suggest a rural-nonrural persistence gap, too, mostly between rural and suburban students.[17] Ultimately, then, rural students trail nonrural in degree attainment, especially for bachelor's degrees.[18]

The disparities are clear. Rural adults have lower levels of formal education than nonrural adults, and the gap is widening. While a greater proportion of rural youth are continuing their education beyond high school, they still lag behind nonrural students in educational attainment. These gaps are most pronounced for bachelor's degrees, especially bachelor's degrees from selective colleges.

This is usually where the discussion ends, with the "rural disadvantage," a disadvantage so assumed that it has come to seem inevitable. When explanations are offered—especially by television and news media—they tend to blame rural ignorance: rural people simply don't want education.[19] Rural parents often receive the brunt of this blame, with critics faulting them for not "wanting more" for their children.[20] Even practitioners sometimes make these same assumptions. As the director of one rural college access organization told me, "There's no sense of a value of education."[21]

But it's not clear that rural youths' aspirations differ from those of nonrural youth: current evidence is decidedly mixed.[22] And even so, it's hard to choose something you don't know or can't see. Aspirations, though important, might cloud our understanding of the opportunity gaps fueling these disparities, and cultural explanations may be rooted more in stereotypes than evidence. They also tend to overlook a key determinant of college aspirations and expectations: the availability of resources.

Spatial Injustice and College Access

Talent is everywhere; opportunity is not—and this may be especially true in rural places. We know that opportunity is unequally distributed across geography.[23] Some places enjoy more resources, like houses with working plumbing or grocery stores with fresh produce, than others.[24] This asymmetry creates what the urban geographer Edward

Soja calls "spatial injustice," a geography of opportunity that marginalizes the residents of many places, both urban and rural.[25] A variety of factors produce these spatial inequities, including the political and social organization of space, as with, for example, segregation; discriminatory policies and practices, such as redlining; and uneven development, which leads to disparities like health-care deserts and digital divides.[26] Spatial injustice usually reinforces racial and economic injustice, such that the opportunities are most limited in places with larger Black and Brown communities and higher poverty levels.[27]

Geography also influences residents' understanding of opportunities.[28] Individuals learn about resources, like jobs and training programs, and the institutions that offer them, like factories and social service agencies, from their local social networks, in everyday conversations with family and neighbors. This information is based on a community's accumulated experiences with the opportunity structure, and it is deeply influential. It defines values and perceptions—of the "right" decision or the "worthy" goal—and shapes whether and how residents access opportunities.

Studies of spatial inequity tend to focus on urban centers, and few consider the geography of college access and attainment.[29] Yet spatial injustice may profoundly shape college opportunity for students—and for rural students specifically. One way is through local education levels. Parental education is known to predict children's college aspirations and enrollment, as well as the type and selectivity of the institution that children pursue. College-educated parents understand application processes, financial aid forms, and academic requirements, and they're more likely to expect that their children will attend college, to talk with their children about college and financial aid, and to take their children on college visits.[30] But, because degree attainment is unequal across geography, many rural children don't have college-educated parents, and therefore, they can't access those parental supports.[31]

Spatial inequities in wealth may also limit rural college attainment.[32] Family income is a reliable predictor of college attendance for students from all geographies.[33] Given the limited job opportunities and reduced salaries of rural places, rural families have lower incomes than nonrural families, forcing many rural students to either forgo college or take the cheapest college path available.[34]

The geographic unevenness of school resources can shape college opportunity, too. Public schools rely on local property taxes for much of their revenue; because many rural communities don't have the taxable wealth of more affluent metropolitan areas, their schools are often underfunded.[35] Low-income schools are less likely to have resources like qualified teachers, experienced staff, and high-quality facilities that support rigorous academic preparation, all important predictors of aspirations, enrollment, and attainment for rural students.[36] Rural districts also face challenges related to sparsity and distance that can compromise quality; many rural schools lack strong postsecondary counseling programs or, in some cases, any counselors at all, and they're less likely to offer advanced classes.[37]

These disparities extend to higher education. Most US students attend schools within fifty miles of home. According to the sociologist Ruth López Turley, proximity makes attending college "logistically, financially, and emotionally easier."[38] The chance a student will even apply to college increases with each additional school nearby; living close to a college may raise awareness of the benefits of a degree and expand understanding of application processes.[39] Many rural students don't enjoy this kind of proximity, though, because most colleges and universities are located in more populated, metropolitan locations, while vast swaths of rural America are education deserts.[40] Institution type also varies geographically: rural places tend to have fewer four-year colleges and more two-year schools.[41] And most colleges do little to mitigate the distance, failing to send admissions officials to rural high schools to recruit students.[42]

These spatial inequities—the distance of higher education, the underfunding of rural K-12 schools, the lack of parental education and wealth—undoubtedly shaped college access for my rural third graders. But another factor might have mattered, too, one that raises complicated questions about opportunity and choice: the rural economy.

Producing the "Rural Disadvantage"

From cotton to coal, rural economies historically centered on the cultivation, extraction, and processing of natural resources, relying on industries like agriculture and logging and mining.[43] It was often exploitative work, dependent on the labor of enslaved and poor men and women.[44] Typically, this work marked every aspect of daily life, including children's expectations for their adult lives—who they would be and what they would do. And mostly, these expectations did not include college, for work was something learned in the fields or the woods or the mines.[45]

Today's rural economies are diverse. Some sectors are growing, like tourism, clean energy, and prisons.[46] Thanks to the pandemic, remote work from rural areas is also expanding.[47] Traditional rural industries, though, are shrinking. Only 10 percent of rural workers are now employed in the industries that once defined rural economies and structured rural life.[48] Rural work—whether in traditional industries or in newer, service-oriented sectors—is also disproportionately low-wage work, especially for Black and Brown workers, such as jobs picking strawberries or cleaning hotel rooms that don't leave much to live on.[49]

And fewer and fewer people are left to do this rural work. In rural places where industries are failing and jobs are disappearing, populations are also shrinking. From 2010 to 2020, rural America recorded its first-ever decade-long population decline, with two-thirds of nonmetropolitan counties experiencing loss.[50] Much of that loss is due to out-migration, with many rural residents moving to cities, where jobs are more plentiful and better paid.[51] Some, like the sociologists Maria Kefalas and David Carr, argue that rural America is getting hollowed out.[52]

Even with all that change, one thing remains constant: most rural jobs do not require a college degree, whether in a declining rural industry, like farming or mining, or in a growing newer sector, like tourism or prisons.[53] When a degree is necessary, it's often a professional certification or two-year credential—and indeed, for these degrees, there is no urban-rural attainment gap.[54] Bachelor's degrees simply aren't as relevant to rural work.[55]

College, writes the education scholar Michael Corbett, remains "'invisible' training for invisible jobs in an elsewhere economy"— and this is especially true for four-year degrees.[56] Thus, the decision to pursue one can feel fraught, like a choice between education and home.[57] Therefore, it might also be the spatial asymmetry of the economy—which jobs are available where—fueling the rural-urban attainment gap, with rural young people just calibrating their plans to their local context.

And perhaps this is as intended. Even as rural economies change and restructure, the country remains dependent on its rural industries to feed, fuel, entertain, and imprison. These rural industries are economically and politically necessary, and so rural workers are necessary. Rural youth become rural workers; limiting their education keeps them rural and working and cheap. The rural attainment gap, then, is more than an unfortunate statistic; it's what sustains these industries. Rural youth—my third graders—aren't supposed to want to go to college.

Those Who Go

Despite all this, though, some rural students do go to college. This "invisible minority" often pursues a degree for practical reasons—specifically, employment.[58] Those from places marked by poverty and economic decline may be especially motivated to earn a degree, and although some hope to return home after college, most recognize the challenges of finding work there.[59] Their parents often support college aspirations; they may not be able to help with completing applications or navigating admissions, but they can offer more general support, like high expectations and conversations about careers, that promote college-going.[60] Communities, too, can support college-going, with dense networks that expose students to careers and keep students "on track" for college.[61]

Less is known about these rural students' college experiences.[62] A couple of studies suggest that they face challenges during college, such as difficulty adjusting and shifts in their identities, and they're disproportionately likely to take on debt.[63] They also have resources to rely on, including families and communities that encourage them to persist.[64] But it's not clear how they navigate those challenges, use those resources, or understand those years. We also know little about their plans after college, how those plans might change as graduation nears, and what their degree means for them and for their families and communities.

So, as much as I wanted to know why my rural third graders weren't going to college, I also wanted to know about those who do go: What's college like for them? What's it like for their parents, the ones with so much at stake in sending them? Did these families make the right choice? How *does* geography shape college opportunity?

This Study

I knew that, to answer these kinds of questions, I needed to go to the students themselves, students from the hard-to-find places, students who could tell me what college opportunity meant for them and their families. I was interested in the outliers, the rural students who find themselves on the unlikeliest of college paths: pursuing a four-year degree at an elite liberal arts school. Their experiences, I believed, would offer a unique perspective on college access.

This kind of "studying up" has a long tradition in anthropology and sociology: in examining the upper reaches of the opportunity structure—like elite colleges—"studying up" can shed light on the processes that create and maintain inequities across the social hierarchy.[65] Although some college experiences may be specific to elite schools—such as navigating a culture of wealth—many are rooted in barriers to access and inclusion that exist across higher education, like soaring tuition and distant campuses and rural invisibility. This focus on elite education is also a useful counterpoint to recent attention to rural community colleges. The educational and community benefits of these schools are well documented, but the overrepresentation of rural students in associate's degree programs—and their underrepresentation in bachelor's programs and at elite schools—may be an indicator of a kind of place-based educational sorting.[66] The economic and social benefits of an elite degree, deserved or not, are real; thus, rural students' paths to and through elite schools can offer insights critical for both understanding spatial inequity and expanding opportunity.

The study focuses on nine students—all from rural places, all first generation, all entering an elite liberal arts college that I call Hilltop.[67] Using students' addresses and parental education levels from their applications, I identified every rural, first-generation student from the classes of 2018 and 2019 as they entered Hilltop. (See the methodological appendix for details on research design, including definitions of "rural" and "first generation.") This process led to a few important realizations. Hilltop, I discovered, has very few rural, first-generation students. Before I began the study, administrators at the school had guessed that the student body likely contained "quite a few" or "a lot" of rural, first-generation students; after all, they explained, Hilltop is located in a mostly rural state with a comparatively low rate of adult educational attainment. But in reviewing students' addresses, I found that these estimates were inaccurate, and quite so: an overwhelming majority of Hilltop's students are from cities and suburbs, and its few rural students mostly have college-educated parents. Only 1 percent to 2 percent of Hilltop's incoming class is both rural and first generation—a very small proportion.

The confusion about these students is telling: like most other colleges, Hilltop doesn't identify students by urbanicity or rurality. It counts states and countries represented, but it doesn't track place in ways that could indicate students' access to resources that support college matriculation or persistence. I also learned how broad the "first generation" and "rural" labels are. "First generation" includes families with very different educational histories, from no formal education to associate degrees, and "rural" encompasses farmland, ski towns, coal country, tribal land, and soon-to-be suburbs. These are elastic, imprecise categories, capturing students with exceptionally diverse backgrounds and experiences.

I sent a letter to all eighteen of the rural, first-generation students whom I identified in Hilltop's incoming classes of 2018 and 2019, inviting them to participate in the study. I knew it was a big ask—a more-than-four-year commitment of time and trust—and in return, I offered to serve as an informal adviser as they navigated their college years. Nine accepted. I then followed these nine students from the summer before their first year at Hilltop to the fall after their graduation, using the qualitative method of portraiture.

A kind of human ethnography, portraiture is often employed to explore people's experiences and how they make sense of them.[68] It typically relies on in-depth interviews and observations; the researcher questions the data for meaning and then renders the understandings in "portraits."[69] This method was a deliberate choice. I was interested in students who defy the odds—and portraiture avoids the social science tradition of documenting failure. I knew that our conversations would likely involve sensitive topics—and the method requires that the researcher build trusting relationships with participants. I wanted to investigate the influence of home and college on students' experiences—and the approach focuses on understanding participants within their contexts. Portraiture is a generous method, one that would accommodate the complexity of studying college students.[70]

I purposefully interviewed the students at specific moments each year. The first round of data collection happened the summer before they started at Hilltop, once in early June, soon after they'd committed to attending Hilltop, and again in late August, right before they would leave home for their first semester. I then followed up with the students at regular intervals: three times during that first year, twice each subsequent year, and once the fall after graduation. I planned the conversations for times that were especially important or meaningful, like soon after registration for courses or during Senior Week. Each time we talked, I asked about the same topics—classes and majors, extracurriculars and jobs, roommates and friends, families and hometowns—and from there, our conversations wandered into a variety of other issues: campus events, their classmates' clothing, the 2016 presidential election. Sometimes I raised a question that research suggested might be relevant or timely, such as whether they felt homesick or how they'd changed since their first years on campus, and occasionally, they'd bring questions or issues for us to talk over. Typically, we met at Hilltop to talk, but over the course of the study, I visited most of their homes. We kept in touch more informally, too— they'd email looking for advice, or I'd reach out just to say hello. I also attended many campus events, like convocation and graduation, and for some background on Hilltop's recruitment practices, I joined its admissions staff for a few high school visits, campus tours, and on-campus admissions activities.

I also interviewed the students' parents, once the summer before matriculation, once the summer after the first year, and once following graduation. Our conversations covered many of the same topics as my interviews with students did, although we focused on their understandings, as parents, of their children's experiences. I sometimes served as a resource for them, too, fielding questions about college processes or structures.

After more than five years of interviews and observations, I then drew on those conversations and events to write four "portraits" of these students' college experiences, each representing a different period of their time at Hilltop. These portraits center the students' stories, those that best represent the portraits' themes or, occasionally, highlight important nuances. I tell the stories mostly using students' words, perspectives, and experiences, although I also incorporate parents' voices to add background or detail. Their stories are stitched together with my analysis, including ties to the experiences of other students who are also underrepresented on college campuses.

After I completed the portraits, I returned to the question that motivated this study: How does place matter to rural students' college access and experiences? Again, I looked for patterns across the students' stories, as well as divergences, and consulted the literature on other underrepresented students, seeking to better understand how geography shapes opportunity, both during and after college.

The narrative I tell in this book isn't the narrative these students would tell about themselves. I focus on the themes that I heard across their stories—and not the more specific and varied experiences that mark them as individuals. But in this telling, I try to honor their voices, their wisdom, and their faith that, with some change to policy and practice, education can level the inequities of society.

Introductions

This is a study of opportunity and place. It is also a study of a college and nine of its students.

Hilltop

Hilltop College is among a rarefied bunch of colleges known as "elite schools." These schools are relatively small in number: only about 10 percent of colleges are selective—that is, attracting many more applicants than they have spots—and an even smaller number are highly selective.[71] They are also expensive, with average 2019 annual tuition nearing $75,000.[72] Helped by much-publicized school rankings, though, they remain in high demand.[73] And it's mostly the wealthy who gain entry. Nearly three-quarters of students at the most selective schools come from families in the top quartile of wealth; those in the bottom quartile make up only 3 percent of enrollment.[74] This isn't surprising. Wealthy families can afford the boarding schools that feed elite colleges; they can pay for the private sports camps and weekend SAT prep courses that make an application competitive; and they make up the ranks of college legacies, another admissions advantage.[75] Elite colleges need these students: it's only with large numbers of full-pay students that they can finance their abundant offerings and provide aid to even a limited number of low-income students.[76] While the nation's college population has radically shifted, then, students at elite schools remain mostly affluent, mostly White, and mostly urban and suburban.[77]

Hilltop is no different. The college, located in New England, was founded as a seminary during the 1800s. It quickly lost its religious affiliation and became a college, one known for admitting students without regard to race or religion. Today, Hilltop is more recognized for its academic excellence. It regularly ranks among the *US News & World Report*'s top twenty-five liberal arts colleges, and its acceptance rate is less than 20 percent. The vast majority of its students are from out of state, and nearly 10 percent are international. The school's inclusive history features prominently in its mission statement and on admissions materials, and it informs several policies, including a test-optional admissions process and a commitment to fully meeting admitted students' demonstrated need through financial aid. But other aspects of admissions and campus life are less inclusive. Tuition is steep—Hilltop routinely ranks as one of the country's most expensive colleges—and, as at many small private schools, admission is "need aware": that is, Hilltop considers students' ability to pay when making admissions decisions. More than half of the school's students receive no financial assistance, and the same proportion graduated from private high schools, often exclusive boarding schools. On campus, it's assumed that students have money for travel and incidentals: dining halls close during breaks, the residential life website lists laundry delivery services, and many courses have "supplemental" fees. Students and faculty sometimes argue that Hilltop's inclusive mission is more aspirational than actual.

Hilltop's campus sits atop a hill in a residential area of Millston, an old mill city with a struggling economy. The city is small—tiny to most of Hilltop's student body but decidedly urban to these nine rural students. A large historic quad, crisscrossed with walking paths and lined with towering trees, lies at the center of campus. In the fall, large piles of fallen leaves cover its green grass; in the winter, it's blanketed with snow; and in the spring, students' hammocks stretch between trees. Academic and administrative buildings surround the quad, and beyond that sit dorms and athletic fields. The architecture is classically New England: pillars and cornices and bell towers. The stately campus feels sheltered, a little insulated, a small green oasis tucked among the crowded row houses of a weary city.

The Students

The nine students are all rural, all first generation, all enrolled at Hilltop, but they are a diverse group. Seven have hometowns in the Northeast, two in the West—not surprising, given Hilltop's New England location. Seven identify as White, one as Latina, and one as biracial Asian and White—also not too surprising, given rural America's mostly White demographics and its substantial racial gaps in access to education.[78] Seven are men, and two are women—and this is a little surprising, as research suggests that female rural youth are more likely to enroll in college than their male counterparts.[79]

Four of the students attended their local public high schools, two lived in towns without high schools and choiced into nearby suburban or urban public schools, two attended semiprivate academies with their tuition paid by their towns, and one had a full scholarship to a local private school. Four qualified for SAT and application-fee waivers, and they all received financial aid from Hilltop. Their parents' education levels vary from eighth grade to associate degrees, and their parents mostly have blue-collar and working-class jobs, such as waitressing or long-haul trucking. They are also from different kinds of rural places, some filled with ski resorts and second homes, and others marked by abandoned factories and empty barns. But their hometowns do share one characteristic: wages are low, and jobs are limited, especially jobs for young college graduates.

Over the years, I came to know these nine students intimately. I interviewed them over and over and over again. I heard from them between interviews. I talked with their parents. I visited many of their homes, met loved ones, learned intimate details about their friends and how they spent their Saturday nights and what they hoped for and feared. I witnessed some of their best moments: the high of acceptance to Hilltop, the joy of new passions, the thrill of graduation. I also saw the hard ones, when they were stressed out or depressed or lonely. I learned their strengths and talents, their soft spots and edges. And they saw all of mine, too.

Oftentimes, we connected easily. I am White, like most of the students. I live in a rural place, and I've been a rural teacher. I'm a graduate of an elite college, and currently, I work at one. But we differed in some important ways. I'm a professor, not a student. My own childhood was suburban, not rural. And I'm not first generation. My parents, one from Chicago and one from rural Indiana, were, but *I* didn't have the experience of being the first in my family to go to college. Their path to and through college was not mine—and I had a lot to learn.

Ours was a long relationship, considerably more complicated and committed than most research interactions. Despite our differences, it sometimes felt like we were growing up together. They began college, relationships, careers. I began a marriage, tenure, motherhood. I can't imagine nine individuals I'd rather grow up with. They are smart, witty, and thoughtful—and their stories show this. Yes, they taught me about college survival and success, about elite education and access, about educational inequity and place. They also taught me about courage and grace, and for all of that, I am grateful.

Here, I share their stories. I tell them through four portraits, each a separate chapter: applying, entering, persisting, and leaving. I then look across their experiences, examining how geography shaped their college opportunities and how it likely shapes the opportunities of other students who are also underrepresented on college campuses. I conclude with recommendations for making college opportunity more spatially equitable.

For these students, attending an elite college is an act of resistance: "kids from here" aren't expected to go to an elite school, and they have little help getting there. When they arrive, they learn that many college opportunities aren't available to them, that belonging is often provisional, and that after graduation, they can't return home. They make it—all are now Hilltop alumni—but for them, the costs of college are high.

I began this study in 2014, at a moment of college skepticism—a moment that now, one pandemic and a few culture wars later, doesn't feel so momentary. But in the early 2010s, after many decades of strong public support for higher education and widespread efforts to push youth to college, enthusiasm for college was waning.[80] Polls showed that Americans' faith in the value of higher education was dropping. Newspapers and magazines began running headlines questioning its value. "Some say bypassing a higher education is smarter than paying for a degree," the *Washington Post* declared. The *Wall Street Journal* described "generation jobless," an entire cohort of college graduates unable to find salaried work. The *Atlantic* reported that "Americans are finally starting to ask: 'Is all this higher education really necessary?'" Researchers were asking the same questions, with some concluding that, no, college isn't for everyone. Even college faculty were speaking out, debating the value of the very institutions that employed them. And legislators were putting all the doubt into policy, dramatically cutting funding for their university systems—so much so that some states seemed close to abandoning the college enterprise entirely.[81]

This skepticism wasn't new—since the founding of the nation's first university, critics have questioned the worth of a degree.[82] But the intensity of the doubt was. College tuition had been climbing for years; by the time these nine students began Hilltop, it was reaching staggering heights. From just 2000 to 2012, the cost of attending a four-year public university had increased by 54 percent, and at private colleges like Hilltop, tuition and fees surpassed most families' annual income.[83] Meanwhile, a crater of college debt was swallowing students and families: by 2012, student debt had topped $1 trillion.[84] And, critics argued, students weren't getting much for all that money.[85] Many jobs, even in growing sectors like technology, still didn't require college-level training; meanwhile, plenty of recent graduates were struggling to find work. The quality of instruction didn't appear to be improving, and many students were spending years in college without significant academic growth. Elite colleges were receiving the brunt of the attacks, with critics lambasting tenure-protected faculty, bloated administrative staffs, and sheeplike students.[86] College was no longer an education system, the critics claimed; instead, it had become an expensive, elaborate, unnecessary system of credentialing. It was time to stop pushing our kids to college.

Then, in 2016, the debate grew a little more complicated. The election happened, and rural America became a focus of attention. Suddenly, as the *New York Times* put it, colleges discovered the rural student—and specifically that the rural student wasn't going to college.[87] Now, it was the rural attainment gap that was making headlines, and story after story ran through the statistics: limited aspirations, lagging enrollment, few degrees.[88] Many advocates began to argue that rural students should go to college: it would be good for them, they said, and good for their communities. So, quite unexpectedly, a new, very rural college push began.

Sometimes, though, these college debates didn't seem to be about the students. Critics' arguments—that college isn't important, that degrees aren't necessary, that elite credentials shouldn't matter—are cloaked in populist rhetoric, but they function to exclude. Questioning the value of a degree serves to protect that value: applicants are deterred, reform is delayed, and access remains restricted. Limiting access also helps to ensure a population of low-skill, low-wage rural workers. The college doubt, then, might just be about maintaining an undereducated, exploitable workforce and protecting the American economy.

But the new focus on rural access also seemed self-interested. It arrived in the wake of the election, just as many liberals were trying to make sense of Trump's strong rural support. Clearly, they argued, Trump and his policies weren't going to help rural America. So why were rural voters voting for him? Well, maybe it came down to education—or its lack.[89] Maybe that's what rural America's lagging attainment rates really mean: rural voters simply don't know better—and college can change that. Thus, the college push may be nothing more than an effort to change rural voters, making sure another Trump isn't elected—and "fixing" rural America.[90]

For rural students, though, this college debate isn't some sort of political or economic strategy. For them, it's immediately and enormously consequential, with effects that will reverberate across generations. They're also the ones who, if college grows even more exclusionary, will find their access to it most limited.

Not every rural child needs a college degree, nor, for that matter, does every urban or suburban child. But it needs to be an option—the chance for new skills that bring higher wages, for an economy that doesn't require exploitation, for a public that isn't so divided—an option that doesn't cost so much.

2

Applying

COLLEGE HOPE

When Henry was sixteen, he hiked Mount Abenaki.[1] The mountain is remote. Uninhabited timberland stretches to its north and west, and its southern and eastern slopes descend into dense forest and, eventually, green pastures, small towns, and a rocky shoreline. The climb up Abenaki is long and hard, most of it above the treeline.

The hike was organized as a tribute to soldiers killed in combat, including Henry's brother, a twenty-year-old US Army corporal killed in Afghanistan. As they climbed Abenaki, each hiker carried a rock to symbolize a lost family member or friend. Holding his, Henry thought about his brother.

It was also during this hike that Henry learned about Hilltop College, an elite liberal arts college in a city several hours south of Abenaki. An officer—one of the few Hilltop graduates to enlist in recent decades—overheard Henry talking about his hope to attend college and suggested that Henry look into Hilltop. So, between windswept peaks and family memories, Henry also began to think about Hilltop.

Henry tells me this as we sit in the quiet, sunny living room of his mother and stepfather's home. He's wearing a gray T-shirt and shorts, his White skin tan from working outside at a ropes course all summer. He offers me a glass of water when I arrive, and I immediately think of my third graders; like them, he's been raised to be polite. The house, a small ranch built by his stepfather, is tucked away on a dirt road, six miles off a state highway clogged with the cars of summertime tourists. Tall pines tower over it, and its wooden porch is ringed with Henry's carefully tended bonsai trees. Inside, school portraits line the walls. Two dogs lay at our feet as we talk.

Henry was a good student in high school. He lived with his dad then, in Petersburg, a small town growing smaller, where sawmills have closed and incomes dropped. He earned mostly As, played tennis, and was active at his public school and in the community, and his teachers and guidance counselor pushed him to go to college. They pushed everyone. "It's been kind of forced down our throats since elementary school," he says. The type of college didn't really matter, nor, it seems, did the school's fit with a student's goals. It was more about getting a degree—any degree—which, they said, would mean "a better job." "They just didn't want to see us end up stagnant," he explains. I ask what "stagnant" looks like: "Staying in Petersburg your whole life. That is not something I want to do." Those who go to college, he says, don't come back.

His mother, an office manager at a lumber company, and stepfather, a mason, encouraged college, too. They weren't that involved with Henry's college search; they didn't have college degrees, and "he did a lot of it on his own." But they did talk about college, especially different kinds of schools and the jobs each might lead to. The timber industry is shrinking rapidly, and summer tourism doesn't offer many good jobs; college, especially a four-year school, would give Henry options. Henry's father, though, didn't want him to go. He hoped Henry would choose trade school or join him at the lumber company where he works. To him, the liberal arts are impractical.

Henry went on a couple of college tours with his high school. Yet Hilltop, despite its relative proximity and strong academic reputation, was never a destination. He also doesn't remember seeing Hilltop admissions representatives at his high school. But after learning about Hilltop on Mount Abenaki, Henry, his mother, and his stepfather drove down and took a tour. He liked the campus, and his mother and stepfather did, too. To Henry, the campus seemed "down to earth," and his mother and stepfather found it less "snob-drawn" than some of the other elite schools in the state. So, with his application fees waived, he submitted early decision and was accepted.

For Henry, focusing on Hilltop made sense. He wanted to stay near his family, and his high school girlfriend—whose parents did attend college—was applying, too. He liked the breadth of courses offered at a liberal arts college like Hilltop, especially since he wasn't sure what he wanted to do. He did have some reservations about Hilltop, and they linger: career paths are less defined in the liberal arts, and he worries about the cost, even with the school's financial aid. His mother and stepfather share those concerns. "Try to focus," his stepfather advises him, "so you are not having all these years of tuition payments not going towards what you want to do." They know "it's a lot of pressure"; still, they're "very proud" he's going. They even drove down to campus and bought bumper stickers for the truck.

One thing they seem to understand, though, is that going to college—and maybe to Hilltop specifically—portends change. College, Henry's mother tells him, is a little like entering the military: it changes you.

Hilltop, with its careful hedges and manicured athletic fields, is a world away from bald-faced mountains and military tributes. But somehow, it's the place that Henry and eight other rural, first-generation students land as they pursue a college degree. I wondered how—how they got to Hilltop when so many other rural students don't.

Like Henry, these students all aspired to college; that, I learned, was never a question. Their goals were shaped by many of the same factors: the push of a parent and a weak rural economy, the pull of educational opportunity and a welcoming campus. The supports they relied on to realize these aspirations, though, varied. While those attending private schools or public schools in well-resourced, metropolitan districts could depend on their schools for help with planning and applying, the others had to find resources elsewhere, patchworking a much less comprehensive system of support from colleges and family. But they all got in, and they enroll, and they are excited—hopeful for the career and future that an elite college promises, a little unsure of what that eliteness means.

College Aspirations

The decision to attend Hilltop was a careful one for these nine students. For years, their college aspirations were nurtured; this decision was not theirs alone. They were pushed to college, as many rural and other underrepresented students are, anxiously pushed by their parents, their schools, even their communities.[2] They were also pulled to an elite liberal arts education at Hilltop specifically, to what they hoped would lead to a more stable, more promising future.

Pushed to College

When blonde-haired, blue-eyed Amelia was little, she would tell people she wanted to be a dentist *and* a wedding planner. Her high school pursuits reflected her dual interests. "All day I would be the most studious science student," she tells me. "And then I would go after school and spend hours figuring out what color balloons would be at homecoming." By the end of high school, though, her plans to be a dentist—or maybe a genetics researcher—were starting to prevail. It was expected that she'd be going to college: her grades were high, everyone knew her name, and she was both the student body president and the valedictorian of her public high school. She wasn't like most other students at her high school, who wanted to stay in their hometown the rest of their lives and were "satisfied with that." The town's mills and tanneries are closed, families have left, the only store is a Dollar Tree; she wanted to "move on." So, when the fall of senior year arrived, the guidance counselor didn't ask Amelia if she'd be applying to college; she assumed her applications were already filled out. And they were—twelve of them.

Amelia's parents, especially her mother, started talking with her about college early. They began making good money at the shipyard, nearly an hour from their home, right out of high school, her mom as a welder and then, after having Amelia, an accountant, and her father refueling nuclear reactors. But they know that today, middle-class wages just aren't possible without some kind of degree: the shipyard no longer hires uncredentialed workers, and the area's other industries—logging and milling and tanning—are shrinking. So when Amelia spent first grade as "the worst student ever," her mother stepped in. She explained that, after high school, "it wasn't going to be like it was for her"; "there weren't going to be jobs that . . . make $20 an hour." After that, Amelia got "motivated." Her parents' pressure continued throughout high school, as they tried to ensure she didn't make the "same mistakes" they'd made in high school. They asked their college-educated coworkers for guidance—How do you get into college? Is an elite degree worth it? What's a good major? But they couldn't help much with Amelia's applications, so instead, they just pushed her toward college and, they hoped, toward a more secure future, one with plenty of jobs, good wages, financial stability. They knew she'd likely leave the state, and that was all right. Their faith in this path was unshakable: when Amelia suggested taking a gap year between high school and college, her mother, afraid Amelia would get distracted and never go, wouldn't hear of it.

Amelia tackled the applications by herself. Her high school wasn't much help, and her friends—those going to college—weren't applying to the kinds of schools she was. She also didn't tell anyone, even her parents, when she started hearing back from schools: their hopes and expectations were too much to manage, and the anxiety that filled the long weeks between learning of acceptance and hearing about financial aid could be overwhelming. For a while she tried to get comfortable with the possibility of a more affordable state school, but then she finally heard from Hilltop and, that same day, received her financial aid package: "It just kind of felt right." Hilltop was small and a "junior Ivy," and its location in a small, manageable city appealed—"I could not fathom having to use the subway." It was also close, just about an hour and a half away: she wanted to stay near home, and she suspected that her mother "would have had a mental breakdown" if she were any farther. When she finally shared the news with her parents, they were "ecstatic."

So Amelia spends her summer getting ready, rereading the classics, and perusing medical case studies, thinking they might be useful background for her college classes. Her friends joke that it seems like she's already left. And maybe she has. "Not a lot of people around here went to college," she explains, "so when there are kids that want to achieve more than Littleton"—her hometown—"they are definitely outcasts." She worries about the academic rigor of college, even though she tells me, "I don't remember the last time I didn't get an A+ in a science class." Her parents also worry about Amelia's safety on an urban college campus. "Living in a rural area, she is not real street smart," her dad says; "she wouldn't know what heroin looks like," her mother adds. But mostly they are excited. They're happy for Amelia to attend a school where "the majority are going to be there to learn." And so is Amelia: "My high school was such a big part of me the last four years . . . I'm excited to see who I am without them."

Parents' expectations are a critical source of college motivation, and much research suggests that both rural parents and parents without college degrees have lower educational aspirations for their children than urban and college-educated parents.[3] Not Amelia's parents, though, or most of the others. These parents are, of course, a select group: I chose their children to participate in this study after they'd applied and committed to Hilltop. But still, the parents were a major reason these students got to Hilltop; their college advocacy was consistent and unwavering. "Go to college," they told their children again and again. These messages were rooted, implicitly and explicitly, in their experiences. Most of these parents have struggled to find work, some have relied on public aid, and several hate their jobs. They've all watched rural industries decline, worried about money, feared for their children's futures. They believe that life would have been different if they had a degree, and so they pushed their children to college.

Some of them hope their children will return home, or nearby, after college. But most of them understand there's a chance—a good chance—that a degree will take their children far from them. "We raised the kids to fly away from the nest," Liliana's father tells me. Ethan's is more direct: "There's nothing here," he says. "I don't want him to come back," his mother adds. The students will have to leave. Departure, it seems, is the price of opportunity—and mostly, the parents know that.

Only one parent—Henry's father—isn't sold on college, especially elite liberal arts schools. According to Henry, he's concerned that a pricey liberal arts degree won't translate into lucrative employment, and his doubt has a consequence: he won't help pay for Henry's education, which will create considerable debt for Henry. Henry's father is also the only parent working in a traditional rural industry—timber. It may be this tie that keeps him from wanting college for his boy; he still hopes, like many rural fathers do, that his child—his son, specifically—will follow in his footsteps, working in the woods or at the lumberyard or, at the very least, working with his hands.[4] The other parents, though, don't have these same economic and cultural ties. They're freer to want college for their daughters and for their sons, to be bumper-stickered college advocates.

Another push to college came from school.[5] The students' teachers and counselors expected college. The "go to college" message was consistent, if vague, mostly couched in assurances that a degree would lead to a "better job." These students were bright, with good grades and strong extracurriculars, and so, like Amelia, it was assumed they'd go. But according to Amelia, Henry, and the other public school students, their high school counselors weren't talking about elite schools. Students are expected to go to college, but local schools, big universities, community colleges—not small, selective, private schools like Hilltop. Even with all the college talk, then, expectations felt low, especially for the public school students.

As other researchers have also found, the students' rural communities shaped their aspirations, too, though more indirectly.[6] The industries that surrounded many of them growing up—timber, farming, manufacturing—are changing. Some, like shipbuilding, now require a degree, but most are simply struggling: mills are shutting down, factories are closing, jobs are disappearing. Even in rural tourist towns, jobs are scarce—at least, the students tell me, jobs that can support a family and sustain a career.

And so this economic context also pushed these students to college. It informed their parents' and teachers' urgent go-to-college messaging, and it shaped the students' own experiences: their parents have lost jobs, their friends have moved, their schools have closed. They've all worked blue-collar jobs, too, stocking grocery shelves or washing floors or folding jeans at Old Navy, and they know they don't want a lifetime of that work. They want a "good job," and for that, they have to go to college.

Like their parents, most of the students also seem to understand that this "good job" will require living somewhere else. "There's nothing to do," Sylvan tells me, "unless you leave." They know, at

least implicitly, that college means a more permanent kind of departure.[7] For some of the students, this leaving seems just an inchoate
understanding. But for others, it is instead a fervent hope. This hope
runs counter to some research, which shows that rural high-achieving
youth are among the most attached to their rural hometowns.[8] Ethan,
Daniel, and Hunter, though, are decidedly not attached. They tell me
about the cities they want to live in after college, places with jobs,
places that are "more civilized" and "more vibrant." A few also fear
"getting stuck" at home, trapped in low-wage work in their "small-
world hometowns." For them, it's not just that they can't return; they
don't want to.

But all these students, no matter how attached they are to their
home communities, have, for years, been told to leave. College, then,
isn't just about getting a job. It's also about getting out.

Pulled to Hilltop

Hunter can't wait for college. "I want to learn more about the things
that I am interested in," he says, and "Hilltop hit me as a place where
I could actually really see myself being successful." He already knows
that he won't return home after graduation; he wants to "travel the
world" and "live in a big city." He's ready to leave his small mountain
town: both of his parents have talked with him about college "since
he was a baby." "'You will go to college,'" his mother remembers. "It
was whispered in his ears."

I'm sitting with Hunter's mother and father on Hilltop's campus,
where they've just arrived to drop him off for orientation, and as we
talk, it quickly becomes evident that the motivation behind their
advice differs. For his father, a neatly dressed man with piercing blue
eyes, it's economic anxiety. He explains, "I always thought that, if I
ever had a child, a son in particular, I would like him to step better
than me." I ask what he means by "better." More formal education, he
clarifies, "something that would give Hunter a professional edge." He
attended trade school but left without a degree; now he's a long-haul
trucker. Youth today "don't have as many chances to go from labor
to management to improve themselves like we did. . . . Once Hunter
became an adult, there was really no choice; he had to attain some
sort of education."

Then Hunter's mother speaks up: "I have a totally different point of view." She worked in entertainment and lived a "gypsy existence" for years, singing and dancing and waiting tables, before unexpectedly getting pregnant with Hunter and staying home to raise him. Her flowing black skirt and dramatic curls are a stark contrast to her husband's crisp button-down. "To me, I want him to find his passion," she continues. "I want him to . . . have the joy of finding something that he loves and being paid for it." College, she says, "is his first step into his life, and he can be whoever he wants to be. He can create himself here."

Hunter's mother has a more classical view of the benefits of a liberal arts curriculum: education should expand your mind and transform the whole person. She thinks Hunter, a tall, bespectacled White kid who loves languages and swims competitively, belongs at a small school with rigorous academics and strong athletics. For Hunter's mother—and for Hunter, whose aspirations seem to align more closely with his mother's—going to college is less about the push of a weak economy and more about the pull of opportunity. Her vision is still tethered to a career—"finding something that he loves and being paid for it"—but she also appreciates the personal growth and exploration that the liberal arts offer, while her husband and the rest of the students' parents focus on the occupational and economic benefits of a college degree. But whatever their reasons, Hunter's parents agree on one thing: Hunter's going to college.

They worked hard to make these college aspirations a reality. Their small town, nestled deep in the Rockies, has high poverty, a rickety economy, and according to Hunter, "a lot of pot shops." After three years in the local elementary school—a school that Hunter calls "underdeveloped"—Hunter's mother moved him to a small private school. For middle and high school, she drove him an hour down the mountain to a stronger, more resourced city system. Hunter's father worked long hours driving across the Midwest to support Hunter's eventual college tuition.

After an early application and a deferral to regular admission, Hunter heard he was admitted to Hilltop—and with good financial aid. His parents were thrilled. They loved the school. "It was just a feeling," they explain, a "psychic connection" they didn't get at the other, "more yuppie" schools. Hunter was thrilled, too, in his calm and understated way: "I was ecstatic, I guess you could say."

They have their moments of doubt. "Is Hilltop as fair and as nice as it seems?" his father asks me. "Or is it just camouflage?" They've heard about "kids whose parents helicopter them in and out." They've been preparing Hunter for this, telling him, "Remember, you are not a rich kid." Mostly, though, they're confident in Hilltop and Hunter's readiness. "I think he is going to take to it like a duck to water," his mother says. "I think he is ready to swim off."

These students weren't just pushed to college by their families, schools, and communities; they were also pulled. These factors, the ones that drew them to an elite liberal arts college and to Hilltop, specifically—making them outliers among their rural peers—mattered more later in the process, as they applied to schools and made enrollment decisions.[9] Although the forces pushing them to college were grounded in anxiety and fear, these influences were more about hope and possibility.

One draw—the one that so appeals to Hunter's mother—is a liberal arts curriculum. This is somewhat surprising; research finds that many first-generation students and their parents take a more practical, career-specific approach to further education.[10] The students and parents vary in their understanding of what, exactly, a liberal arts education is; most don't know anyone who's attended a liberal arts college. But they do know that liberal arts colleges offer a "well-rounded" curriculum, "an education in various aspects and not just in one field." "It's like you have this whole platter in front of you," Daniel's mother explains; "they want you to try everything." They also describe it as the best option for students who are undecided about their occupational goals—most of them, at this point. In that sense, then, the liberal arts *is* the practical choice; it's how they will find that rewarding, remunerative career.

The students also sometimes note Hilltop's academic reputation as part of its appeal. For some of the students, like Amelia, their Hilltop application was one of many applications to highly competitive colleges, whereas for Hunter and others, Hilltop was their single "reach." They all know that it's a "good school," though. Most are familiar with the *US News & World Report*'s rankings and recognize that Hilltop is among the top liberal arts colleges. Several also looked

at other data, like postgraduation employment numbers and acceptance rates at graduate schools, that hint at Hilltop's academic status. But they don't usually talk about Hilltop's selectivity explicitly.
Their references to its academic caliber are mostly vague acknowl-
edgments of its "academic reputation" or the "opportunities" and
"connections" it promises.

More important than either curriculum or reputation is the "communal feel" of the campus. The students visited Hilltop and "fell in
love with it," and so did most of their parents. They describe a "sense
of community," a kind of interdependence many first-generation
students value.[11] Hilltop feels "welcoming," "accepting," and "open-
minded"; "you feel like you're a part of it as soon as you walk in,"
Sebastian says. Some tell me about its history. The school has always
admitted students of all races and religions, they explain. Daniel says,
"The history of acceptance and its founding by abolitionists and just
its entire history matched up with what I believed in." Others mention its racial diversity, specifically: Hilltop's campus, though predominantly White, is more diverse than most of their hometowns—except
for Liliana, they all live in overwhelmingly White places—and they
like this about the school. The students and parents also repeatedly
characterize the school as "down to earth," and they cite this unpre-
tentiousness when distinguishing Hilltop from its "snobby," "yuppie"
neighbor Riverside—another elite college nearby, one with a slightly
lower acceptance rate and a much larger endowment. For these students and parents, Hilltop is the better choice because its values—as
least as advertised—match their own.

Hilltop's location, at least for the families from New England, is
also a draw. Seven of the nine families live in the region, anywhere
from a thirty-minute to four-hour drive from campus, and this proximity matters, as it does for most any student choosing a college.[12]
Despite the students' desire to leave their hometowns, they don't
want to go far. They're emotionally close to their families, and they
want to remain physically close. Sylvan, for example, only looked
at in-state schools: "I wasn't trying to run away from home," he
explains. Nor did their parents want them far. They like being able to
get to campus for a quick dinner or a football game; they, too, want
to maintain their closeness to their children. They also like the security that comes with proximity. As Amelia's parents tell me, Hilltop is

"close enough where if she needs a rescue, we are right there." For Liliana and Hunter, though, the higher education options are much more limited—the West has fewer options—forcing them to look farther from home, and Hilltop's distance is their largest concern.[13] The city of Millston, where Hilltop is located, also brings mixed feelings. Most of the students like it: it's a real city, with "more culture" than home, but it's not too big—and there's no subway. A few of the parents are more hesitant, concerned about "safety" and "trouble" in the city.

A final factor—perhaps the most necessary factor—pulling students to Hilltop is financial aid. All the students need financial assistance, and most need quite a bit. The students knew these constraints. As Ethan's father explains, Ethan "was well aware that we didn't have any money and we can't afford checks for ten grand or borrowing money, because I'm not going to stay in debt . . . until I'm seventy." Generous aid offers, then, were an important focus of their college searches and, because Hilltop meets students' full demonstrated need, a major reason they chose the school. Liliana's father tells me: "We don't have to pay a lot of money at this college. . . . It was good, good financial aid." Not only does Hilltop's financial generosity make enrollment possible for these students; it also contributes to its "down to earth" aura: its aid "speaks volumes for Hilltop."

I notice what the students and families don't mention, things that often attract students to schools like Hilltop. They aren't going to Hilltop for the posh dorms or the nice gym. They don't care about the good food. They don't talk about professors or academic programs. Sometimes, it seems they don't know much about Hilltop—a reflection, perhaps, of first-generation families' unfamiliarity with college or just an indifference to the more aesthetic aspects of elite education.[14] It is a "good school," with "good financial aid" and "a good vibe," and that's enough.

I also sense that the parents are a little surprised to find their children heading to an elite school—and maybe even more surprised that they actually support it. Their friends' and neighbors' children don't go to elite schools: elite schools are expensive and uppity. The sticker price is probably the largest concern. "That is a huge thing for kids in a rural area," John's mother tells me: they go to community colleges and state schools not only because these schools are closer and more career focused, but also because they assume they can't afford private schools—a belief held by many first-generation families.[15] Most of these parents made the same assumption; when they received their aid packages, they were "shocked" to learn that private colleges can offer assistance that can drop tuition well below public schools' costs. They still worry about debt, but as Sebastian's father says, "You have to go; you have to get through it one way or the other." And although there are the "kids whose parents helicopter them in and out," Hilltop "just felt right."

It's also hard to deny this: the school promises so, so much.

Sebastian definitely does not want to be a lifelong grocery store employee—actually, that's exactly the kind of work that he hopes to avoid with a Hilltop diploma. Like most of the students, though, he needed "to make some cash," and so he'd planned to spend the summer bagging groceries. So, when he's laid off a few weeks before summer's end, it "stings a little bit," and he finds himself "checking the bank account every day." But he's happy for the extra time with family and friends before he says goodbye.

Relationships are important to Sebastian. Even though his town, an old mill town named Barrington, is sometimes called "Boringtown," he appreciates its familiarity. He attended the local public schools until tenth grade and then, with his tuition paid by his town, switched to a small, semiprivate academy near his house, graduating with kids he had known since kindergarten. "The same thing with my family," he says. "We're all really close, we all live close by." That kind of closeness "is a big reason why I chose Hilltop, because . . . I heard that it was like a family and you're not on your own."

Like the other students, Sebastian reports that college was an expectation "from the day I was born." He was a good student, and his parents told him, "You're going to get a good education." They hadn't gone to college, and, he says, "they knew what a blown opportunity that was." After talking to them, I see that college wasn't so much a "blown opportunity" as a nonexistent one. Both of them, his Asian mother and his White father, were raised in rural New England by single mothers without much money. "We were on welfare," Sebastian's father explains, "so we both obviously don't want that for our kids." He is a production manager at a local power company, and Sebastian's mother waitressed for most of his childhood; they wanted more for Sebastian and his sister—more money but also more satisfaction. His mother remembers coming home from work and telling her children, "Oh my God—go to college, love what you do." Despite his parents' consistent reminders to think about the future, by the time he applied to colleges, Sebastian had "no idea" what he wanted to do, so they decided that "maybe the liberal arts schools would be good." He looked up the top liberal arts schools in New England. They visited about ten, and "Hilltop was beautiful." It is close, about two hours from his parents and one from his grand-mother; it's not in Boston or New Haven or one of the big cities— "that's never really appealed to me"—and, he says, it's "small enough that I could keep that communal feel." And the financial aid was "great": "I was . . . shocked at the deal they gave him," his dad says. Hilltop was actually his second choice, but now he's glad he didn't get into his first choice, Riverside: it's "a little pretentious." His parents are excited, too: "This is the school," they tell him, "that . . . you can do whatever you want. This is the place."

Sebastian agrees: "This is the place." It's a "fantastic school," one that's "friendly, warm, welcoming, diverse." He knows "the aca-demic stuff will be good," and, he assures me, "that's obviously why I'm going." But he's also excited for the social life, the connections, the personal growth: "If I can meet people, if I can learn how to act around people, if I can better myself, that's what I'm looking for-ward to the most." He admits that he doesn't know too much about Hilltop, but "why not graduate with little debt and an impressive résumé? . . . A degree . . . from a really good liberal arts school, it kind of covers everything"—and, hopefully, saves him from a life-time of grocery bagging and layoffs. So, even with all the goodbyes, Sebastian is excited for Hilltop.

College Applications

Why these rural students are going to Hilltop is clear; given the many barriers to access, how is less readily apparent. With the students' permission, I ask Hilltop for their college applications. I don't get them until after we've met and talked, after I've visited their homes and spoken with their parents, after I've started to know them as college students. And as I read through them, it's jarring to see their complex selves rendered in tiny application fields. But I do get a better sense of who they were as high schoolers. I can also see this: their applications are strong.

Each contains page after page of high school activities: National Honor Society, student newspapers, debate teams, bands and orchestras, varsity sports, student governments, and community service. These are standard-issue extracurriculars, nothing like the more lavish opportunities of larger and wealthier schools, but they speak to the students' involvement and well-roundedness. Most of the students also worked long hours at jobs, some during breaks and others throughout the year. Their essays are engaging—not as polished as those edited by private college counselors, but still, thoughtful and strong. Nearly all the students were ranked within the top tenth of their graduating class, and their transcripts contain A after A after A.

But the applications also indicate something about these rural students' access to Hilltop: across the group, it's uneven. I notice that their applications differ in some important ways. These differences seem tied to their high schools, where they're located and whether they're public or private, and they suggest markedly divergent application processes, too. Certainly, other factors also shaped their paths to enrollment—outreach from colleges, parents' support, their own motivation and drive—but mostly, it's their high schools that make for such different applications.

School Support

Liliana's private high school is small, with only eighteen students in her graduating class. She enrolled in ninth grade, supported by a full scholarship. She knew that the school—one of three in her wealthy, "touristy" mountain hometown—offered many resources, and she engaged them all, playing lacrosse and competing as a debater and joining Model United Nations.

For Liliana, too, college was always an "assumption." Her parents, immigrants from Mexico, didn't have the opportunity to complete middle school, so they pushed her and her brothers to college, she says, "in order to be able to live life like we want." They explained

that, with a degree, "there are more opportunities economically."
She agrees with her parents, but for her, the desire is also more personal: "Being Hispanic, being Mexican, I think there is always these
negative stereotypes of being uneducated and having to work in construction or housekeeping"—her parents' own jobs in her segregated
hometown in her very White home state. She continues, "I think it
has always been a goal of mine to prove people wrong, and college
would do that." And her private high school supported these aspirations, encouraging her and her classmates to pursue academically
competitive colleges.

Liliana and her parents credit her school's college counselor for Liliana's acceptance at Hilltop. Liliana hadn't heard of the school until
her junior year, when her counselor suggested that she consider it.
He also recommended Hilltop's Preview program, during which first-
generation students and students of color can visit the campus, attend
classes, and participate in special admissions programming: for low-
income students like Liliana, Hilltop covers the cost of travel—in Liliana's case, three flights and a bus ride. At first, her parents said no. It
was just too far. But her counselor convinced them, explaining that
the trip didn't commit her to anything. And so she went, and she loved
it—"she was so happy," her father remembers. Liliana liked its "community feeling," and its diversity appealed to her, especially coming
from a high school in which she had been one of only three students
of color. She learned that Hilltop offers good financial aid, and, while
she plans to be premed and eventually join Doctors without Borders,
she is interested in a variety of majors—neuroscience, international
politics, and Spanish—and appreciates the "options" of a liberal arts
curriculum: she wants to find what she's "passionate about."

Liliana returned from Preview to intensive college counseling.
She had an adviser who met with her class weekly throughout junior
year and senior year. Together, they worked through the Common
Application, wrote essays, prepared for standardized tests, and built
their résumés. College nights, fueled by pizza and advice, provided
more time and support to finish the applications. Liliana applied early
to Hilltop, and then she and her counselor met with her parents to
finalize the financial aid paperwork. By graduation, all her friends had
been accepted to college—and Liliana was going to Hilltop, with full
financial aid.

Although the distance still concerns her parents, her dad says, "I want to see her happy. I don't want to stop nothing. . . . I don't want to stop her dreams." He adds, "I hear this college is really good." And Liliana is confident, "more excited than worried." With the support of her high school and her family, she is ready for Hilltop.

Liliana, Sebastian, and Sylvan graduated from small private or semi-private schools, Liliana from a local private school that she attended on scholarship, and Sebastian and Sylvan from semiprivate academies they went to as local, publicly funded students. And I can see that in their applications: more robust college-prep coursework, more extensive extracurriculars, more refined essays.

Their schools also invest considerable resources in college advising. They have large counseling staffs, information nights on the dos and don'ts of applying, sessions for filing financial aid forms, and college fairs featuring dozens of institutions, including elite schools. College admissions officials visit their schools for smaller, more intimate meetings to talk about their institutions and their opportunities. It's not surprising, then, that these schools' websites proudly tout the places their students have been admitted, lists filled with Ivy League schools and competitive state universities and wealthy liberal arts colleges.

Liliana, Sebastian, and Sylvan confirm that their high schools were key to their successful paths to Hilltop. Liliana and Sebastian received plenty of "one-on-one help" from school counselors, while Sylvan relied more on his Advanced Placement teachers, who encouraged him to take rigorous classes and then helped him develop "a short list of good schools" to apply to. Both Liliana and Sylvan also depended on their counselors to access financial aid and scholarships; as Sylvan's mother explains, "The school got him a ton of stuff." And all three had lots of peers—from full-pay families with college-educated parents—who were exploring and pursuing elite colleges, creating a kind of college herd effect.[16] For them, then, their high schools both expected and supported an application to an elite school.

John's Hilltop application was not an expectation, at least not at his local public high school. His town is small, once made up of farms and orchards, and lines of trees still stretch across green fields. Today, it's becoming a bedroom community for the state's capitol, and its mostly White residents—like John's family—commute out. Educational attainment is low: few residents have college degrees. John's teachers and guidance counselors were committed to changing that, and they encouraged college-going—but not to schools like Hilltop. And they weren't always helpful. When I ask his parents about his school's counselors, his mother replies, "I wish our guidance had given more guidance," and his father adds, "There was not a lot of information." They arranged some campus tours and financial aid nights—and "they are nice," his mother reports—but she says, "We just learned it from experience." None of his teachers told John about Hilltop. "It's kind of strange," he says, "you don't hear about it much, and it is so close," less than thirty minutes away. Even after he was accepted, the low expectations lingered. "When one of my math teachers found out I got into Hilltop," John remembers, "she chuckled. She couldn't believe it." He adds, "That stuck with me. I was like, 'I'll prove you all wrong.'"

Most of John's friends are going to a local nonselective private college focused on preprofessional training, to nearby community colleges, or to the military. The sticker price of places like Hilltop scares off families, and his father shares that "they will settle and maybe do a two-year degree, just to get into a trade and go to work." Even John didn't really understand the differences between public universities and private liberal arts colleges until long after he'd applied. "No one I know went to a liberal arts school," John explains.

But John did have one major asset in his path to Hilltop: football. "Hilltop actually was never even on the radar," his mother explains, "because he never thought he would get in. . . . We don't know if he would have gotten in here without football." It was Hilltop's coach who approached John, told him about the school, invited him to a football game and campus tour, and encouraged him to apply. When John's early application was deferred, he reached back out to him, and he told John to submit additional materials showing rising grades and new awards. John did, relentlessly, ultimately getting into his "dream school" and receiving a good financial aid package.

John's parents were also important to his Hilltop admission. Both earned associate degrees later in life, but they encouraged John and his brother to pursue four-year colleges. "They really wanted to push us both," John explains. "That is pretty much why I'm going to college." His parents felt forced into work at a young age, his father doing maintenance for a power company and his mother as a social worker for the state, without much time to explore options or develop skills or find work they enjoyed. They wanted John to go to college to find something he loves, not "just to get a degree." They did offer a warning: "You are going to have loans, so you do have to pick something that you are going to make money." But Hilltop's reputation and academics put to rest any fears about employability and money, "just because of the school itself, as good as it is."

And so, despite having little support from his high school, John is on his way to Hilltop, helped by athletics and his parents' motivation. He is thrilled: "Hilltop just has so much to offer. I have grown up around it and rode by it since I was a little kid. It is just kind of surreal that I am actually going here." He's ready to prove everyone wrong.

Four of the students—John, Henry, Amelia, and Daniel—attended their local public high schools, schools with fewer resources and less college support than the private and semiprivate schools attended by Liliana, Sebastian, and Sylvan. These rural public schools offer relatively few of the advanced classes, like International Baccalaureate or Advanced Placement, that provide strong college preparation and signal academic quality, especially to admissions teams at elite colleges.[17] The students also report having received little help with the SAT—no tutors, no coaching, no practice exams—and their scores show it, with all four asking that Hilltop, an SAT-optional school, not consider their SAT I scores as a part of their applications. Their schools' support as they searched for information about specific colleges was also weak: although staff pushed higher education, they didn't talk about different kinds of schools, types of admission processes, or levels of academic competitiveness. Their counselors didn't—or couldn't—tell these students about liberal arts colleges or how to find a school that fit them or their aspirations. And later, as the students worked on their applications, there were no pizza nights or essay edits. With few classmates pursuing private, selective liberal arts colleges, these students also missed out on the camaraderie and support of friends struggling together through similar deadlines and forms. There were some resources: Henry's and John's schools took students on a few college tours, and Amelia and Daniel both had an honors-level teacher who believed they could—and should—apply to selective schools and offered advice. But even that limited guidance was the exception, and mostly, these schools lacked clear and consistent advising structures, supportive teachers were scarce, and guidance counselors provided little assistance. These students, then, learned about and applied to Hilltop in spite of—not because of—their high schools.

Ethan and Hunter had a slightly different experience. As a result of local school choice policies, they were able to choose a public school to attend, and both opted for high schools in larger districts, Ethan's in a wealthy suburb and Hunter's in an affluent, growing city. Their schools, financed by strong property tax bases, could provide more resources than the rural high schools that John, Henry, Amelia, and Daniel attended. Ethan's school, for example, offered eighteen Advanced Placement courses, and Hunter's had twenty-six—many more than the rural schools, and even more than the private and semi-private schools. Both found their counselors to be helpful, especially Hunter, whose counselor provided critical guidance after his Hilltop application was deferred to regular admission. Colleges also regularly send admissions representatives to their schools, and Ethan's school has a robust advisory system, with meetings and information sessions beginning early in high school. And the majority of students at their schools—students with college-educated parents—pursue college, including selective liberal arts schools, so they had classmates and older friends to turn to for advice, giving these students a much more thorough support system than those attending rural high schools.

College Contact

Hilltop was also a resource in the college admissions process, although its supports, like those of the high schools, were unevenly offered. The most robust assistance came through athletics: both John and Hunter were recruited to Hilltop as varsity athletes, and for them, recruitment was critical to learning about, applying to, and quite possibly getting accepted at Hilltop. John never would have considered

Hilltop without the encouragement and outreach of Hilltop's football coach, whereas Hunter heard about Hilltop from an older teammate who attended. Their athletic abilities also made their applications more competitive, and Hilltop's coaches do play a role in admissions decisions (though a far smaller one than at schools more focused on athletics)—influence that might have been especially useful for John and Hunter, both of whom were deferred during early admission.

Hilltop offers other, less comprehensive forms of outreach, too. One is Preview, a three-day admissions program for first-generation students and students of color—an event that, though open to all nine of these students, only Liliana and Hunter attended. Through Preview, prospective students spend two nights in the dorms, sit in on classes, participate in an admissions interview and campus tour, and engage in special events. The visit concludes with a final dinner held in a cavernous room usually reserved for faculty meetings. At the Preview dinner I joined, nervous students wearing suitcase-wrinkled shirts and dresses not warm enough for a New England spring sat at elaborately set tables. The evening included remarks on the school's history of inclusion from Hilltop's chief diversity officer, a rousing speech from a Black, first-generation alum, dessert, and then a student-led talent show. The evening—and the entire Preview program—seemed designed to showcase Hilltop's diversity and inclusiveness and, ultimately, to boost admissions across underrepresented groups. And for those who attend, the program works; both Liliana and Hunter cite the "sense of community" they felt during Preview as a major reason for applying.

Hilltop also engages in off-campus recruiting through college fairs and admissions visits to high schools. Hilltop admissions staff regularly attend college fairs, even, occasionally, those held at rural high schools. I tagged along for a couple. At these fairs, folding tables are packed into a high school gym, each with an official or two from some kind of institution of further learning or training—the US Army next to a big state university next to a cosmetology school. These nine students, though, never saw anyone from Hilltop at the college fairs they attended, nor did they describe college fairs as all that useful. High school visits are quieter, more intimate events, but Hilltop staff target private schools and wealthy urban public schools, schools where they know the guidance counselors, schools where interest is higher and questions are more relevant. I quickly learned why Amelia, John, Daniel, and Henry never encountered elite college admissions officials at their rural public high schools: there's little reason for them to trek out to rural schools when events in more accessible, better-resourced places yield more—and more competitive—applicants.

Family Resources

Daniel and his twin brother, Greg, began researching colleges "quite young." They were curious and motivated, their mother Jackie explains, and a little competitive. By nine, Daniel was telling her that he wanted to go to a "really well-known, good college." By junior year, each "could rattle off" a list of statistics about their favorite schools: endowments, average financial aid awards, employment rates of graduates, even crime and safety numbers. "They did so much research," Jackie explains, "and they did it on their own." They had to: she didn't know what to look for or how, and his guidance counselors weren't too helpful. "Had my kids not been in their office all the time and asking them, 'What do I do? And do I send this? And can you send this?' I think they wouldn't . . ." she trails off, then simply states: "They needed to advocate for themselves."

Daniel and Greg weren't entirely alone in this process. They had a high school teacher, a tie-wearing, lawyer-turned-history-teacher, who had a "huge influence on them," Jackie says; "he really encouraged them to get the best education possible." It was this one teacher who urged them to take AP classes and, later, helped Daniel with his essays and recommendation letters. He also pushed elite liberal arts schools, telling them that it "doesn't matter how much debt you get in to get the best education you can . . . you're going to do better in the long run"—advice that, Jackie admits, worried her. But, she says, after considering the job placement rates of Hilltop and Riverside, where Greg is enrolling, "it makes sense."

Daniel and Greg's parents, especially Jackie, also played an important role in getting them to college. Daniel remembers them telling him, long before high school, "You need to go to college to have a good job." Their father has an associate's degree, their mother a GED; they divorced when the boys were young, and she and the boys moved north, where she had family. Daniel and Greg witnessed where limited education and low-wage work leave a person: they saw their rural town's mills close, its economy collapse, their mother struggle. "There's nothing here anymore," Daniel says; the town is "slowly depleting." He's a White kid tired of his White town, ready to leave for a "more vibrant community."

Jackie organized college trips for them, two sets of visits that brought them to nearly twenty campuses across New England. They left some of these visits "intimidated" by the people they met. They were "way advanced, real academics," Jackie remembers, and "everybody in the room was fairly well dressed and affluent"; later, Daniel and Greg told her that she "should get a new wardrobe." Even so, after these visits, Daniel was set on Hilltop. It's a "better college," he says, with strong financial aid, a "history of acceptance," and "values . . . matched with mine." He also likes that it's located in a city with "more culture," and the liberal arts appeal: he wants to "find a concrete passion [to] build off of and hopefully form a professional career from." With his application fees waived, Daniel submitted his application early decision. It was deferred. After getting "paranoid" and scrambling to submit applications to twelve other schools, he was accepted and granted substantial aid.

Now, as the last summer before college ends, he's excited to meet new people and try new things and explore new subjects—and he's a little nervous, too. He worries "about keeping up with the academics": he knows that about half of Hilltop's students attended private schools, whereas he's "coming from this area, from a public high school." His background, he realizes, will be different from many of his classmates'.

It's Jackie who tells me the details of Daniel's path to Hilltop as we sit outside their house and watch the town's remaining paper factory belch steam over the green hillsides. I'm surprised by Daniel's thoroughness; he comes across as pretty mellow—not one to submit thirteen college applications. But perhaps I shouldn't be. He was, after all, a stellar high school student. And he is very ready to leave this town.

One support that all the students could access—regardless of their athletic ability or their high school's resources—was their family, and this support was critical. Their parents talked about college, early and often. Most were a consistent source of motivation and encouragement as students applied: they set high educational expectations, and they believed their children would fulfill them. Some of them, like Daniel's mother, drove their children to visit campuses and nagged them about college deadlines. These parents preached college, they pushed college, they prayed for college; college wasn't just the students' hope—it was also their parents'.

But the parents couldn't offer much concrete information or advice.[18] "We don't know how to do this," they said—a refrain I would hear often over the next four years. They couldn't help with applications, and they didn't understand the variety of college options. I notice the things they don't seem to know about small, elite liberal arts colleges: that there's a health center on campus, for example, or that, unlike larger schools, these colleges hate to keep students longer than four years. "In some ways, he's parenting us," Ethan's parents confess, "because we don't know." Although they did play a larger role in securing financial aid, they found that process opaque and confusing, making them feel like "complete idiots trying to figure it out."

As desperately as they wanted college for their children, then, these parents couldn't provide much help. These rural students also didn't have the legacy connections, the savvy guidance counselors, or the private college coaches of many students admitted to elite schools; they didn't even have the community organizations that can be so helpful in getting first-generation youth to college.[19] If these students were actually going to go—to defy the expectations, to challenge the stereotypes, to build a "better future"—they had to make it happen.

And they did: they got in. So now, after all the aspiring and preparing, the researching and applying, the deciding and committing, it's time to wait for September—to wait and to wonder what, exactly, comes next.

College Possibilities

These students' paths to Hilltop are marked by determination and strong credentials. They also had parents who pushed them to college and did their best to support that pursuit. They received generous financial aid: fee waivers, private scholarships, and tuition assistance from Hilltop, anywhere from eight thousand dollars, for Amelia, to a full ride, for Liliana. They had other, more circumstantial factors that mattered, too, like the advice of a tie-wearing teacher or a mountaintop conversation with a Hilltop alum.

Whatever the exact reasons, these students are now on their way to Hilltop. And they're excited. They're hopeful that a Hilltop education means a good career and maybe even a way out, for that is what the school's reputation and selectivity seem to promise. But they also enter a little uncertain, not quite sure of the meaning of such eliteness.

College and Career Ready

I visit Sylvan and his family at the end of August, just a few days before orientation is set to begin. Sylvan, a White seventeen-year-old with a quick smile, has been busy even though he hasn't worked his job at the local deli for two weeks: instead, he's in the middle of forty hours of mopping. The "sentence" comes after he and a friend were caught sneaking into his old high school—a semiprivate academy that he attended as a local student, tuition covered by his town—through a window; they just wanted to see if they could do it, he explains. But they set off the alarms, and the school offered forty hours of maintenance work in lieu of trespassing charges. So now he's spending his last couple of weeks at home mopping, sweeping, and vacuuming classrooms. He's ready to leave: "especially with having to work on the maintenance crew, I know that I want a college degree."

Not that he'd been unsure about college before this week—he'd always assumed he'd go. His parents "didn't have that opportunity": his father, unable to afford college, joined the military, and his mother had some health issues that prevented her enrollment. His older siblings, who "hated" school, also enlisted. But Sylvan excelled at academics, and so his parents pushed him to college. Sylvan "saw what a lack of education does for you," his mother says. "He wants a good life . . . [and] he knows that just doesn't come—you have to earn it."

Sylvan's career plans also require college. When he was little, his teachers called him smart and told him, "You could be a doctor!" And for as long as he can remember, that's what he's wanted to be. His mother is a nurse—she got her associate's degree when Sylvan was in high school—and his dad, a veteran of the US Air Force, is a respiratory therapist at the local Veterans Affairs hospital, where Sylvan volunteered during high school. After that volunteering work, plus a job shadow and a career advisory class—all required by his high school—Sylvan became even more convinced that medicine was for him. His goal for college is pretty simple: he just wants "a degree." Then he qualifies this: "the correct degree so that I can continue with my career path. I hope to do well enough in college to . . . attend a medical school."

Sylvan always figured he'd go to one of the few selective liberal arts schools in the state; he's close to his parents, he knew that an out-of-state education would likely cost more, and he wanted a school strong in the sciences that would allow him "to be educated in other areas as well." Hilltop, he discovered, has a 97 percent acceptance rate for those applying to medical school, and it seemed "more community-oriented" than other liberal arts schools. After talking with his AP teachers and attending a few school-sponsored college application and financial aid nights, he applied early decision and was "very, very excited" when he got in. His parents were a little more measured in their response—they were excited, but they knew enrolling would depend on the financial aid he received. Ultimately, his package was good, making Hilltop affordable, as long as, his mother says, "none of the cars will break down in the next four years." And so Sylvan accepted.

Now, a week before orientation, Sylvan tells me that he's feeling "pretty separated from this place"—a small fishing town that, each summer, gets crowded with tourists; he's "just waiting to get to Hilltop." He didn't go to the meet-and-greet for in-state students—it was held at what "looked like this huge, huge house," his mother explains, and "we didn't think we would feel comfortable there"—but still, he's looking forward to Hilltop. "I'm excited," Sylvan says. "This is me actually going to college and starting the career path that I want."

As these students perch on the edge of college, I ask them what they hope to get out of it. Employment, they tell me. All of them, no matter their interests, link college to career. The specificity of their goals varies. Four of them enter Hilltop knowing—or thinking they know—what they want to do: Sylvan, Amelia, and Liliana want to pursue medicine, and Ethan plans a career in law. The others—John, Henry, Hunter, Sebastian, and Daniel—are undecided, hoping that Hilltop's liberal arts curriculum will help them find a career that interests them and pays well. But no matter their level of occupational certainty, securing a career is their motivation for going—and their parents' motivation for sending them. And their college searches, filled with research on schools' job placement rates and questions about preprofessional programs, reflected this intention. For them, Hilltop is not an end unto itself; it is a means to an end—a career.

This focus on careers comes, at least in part, from home. As the parents talked with their children about college, they imparted messages, both implicit and explicit, about careers: today's jobs require a degree, education leads to more career options, attending a "good school" means economic security and job satisfaction. These lessons are an acknowledgment that times—and rural economies—have changed; that, as Amelia's mother told Amelia, "it wasn't going to be like it was for her"; that livable wages require college and, quite possibly, an urban adulthood. These parents also want their children to have a particular kind of employment: a *career*, not just a job. A career means money and security, including the ability to pay back college loans. For the parents, it also means options, like choosing a path, weighing offers, and having flexibility, and it means "passion," loving what you do. The parents want for their children what they didn't have.

The students listened to their parents: college will give them "a good life." Sometimes I hear in the students' goals and their parents' hopes a desire for upward mobility specifically. Except for Henry's father, these parents don't want their children to follow in their footsteps, nor do they want them working in their towns' traditional industries. Their children don't want that either. None hopes for a parent's job or a friend's parent's job, and for those with specific career plans, these goals imply class climbing: they want to enter medicine and law, careers that require more education and bring greater compensation than their parents' jobs. Wealth, I notice, is never named as a goal, nor is status—at least not directly. But both the parents and the students seem to understand Hilltop, at least vaguely, as a route to a better—or at least more secure—future.

And this is exactly why they worked so hard during high school: for the reward of admission to an elite college and its promise of a better life. They sat at the top of their high school class, they served as student government leaders and community volunteers, they earned athletic and academic awards. Then they spent long hours on their applications, penned essays both articulate and poignant, and doggedly filled out financial aid forms. Admission at a place like Hilltop, they know, is earned, and they earned it. These students enter Hilltop eagerly, confident they belong.

Occasionally, though, I see moments of doubt.

An Elite Institution

Ethan is hot, his cheeks pink against his White skin. He's in the midst of packing, and the floor of his living room is covered with small piles of stuff: towels, a shower caddy, extra-long twin sheets—the unmistakable supplies of a rising college student. Just a few weeks before orientation, he's in full preparation mode. He finished working at the local farm when strawberry season ended, and soon he'll stop driving the half hour to his job at Old Navy, too. He already registered for classes; now he's debating whether to order his textbooks used online, which risks them arriving after classes start, or to buy them from Hilltop's bookstore, which costs more but ensures he'll have them right away. He's also got some questions about the all-class "recommended read." He hasn't finished it, and he's not sure if he will—or whether he should. Hilltop's first-year website, he tells me, says "that it's not required, though it's just kind of a norm that people read it, and I'm still going to read it, hopefully on time. Also, I don't know if it's one of those things that's, like, should I get it done? Is it OK if I'm still reading it when I come in? Am I supposed to read it? You know what I mean? It's not a summer assignment, like for high school when they were like, 'Read this over the summer, take notes, come in the first day, and we'll start discussion.'" He's not looking for my advice; he's got his opinions—often quite a lot of them, I'm learning—and they're well reasoned. He concludes that, even though the book is only "recommended" and Hilltop should be clearer in its expectations, he'll read it.

This is also how Ethan went about his college process: motivated and informed. He started early, during his sophomore year, when some older friends began looking at schools, and over the next three years, he would spend hours on College Prowler and College Confidential and colleges' websites. He developed a list of variously competitive schools that cover accepted students' financial need, and with fees waived, he submitted his applications—all while also taking AP courses and working at Old Navy and playing in several bands and orchestras. Although his suburban high school offered "a lot of support and help and resources," the advice was kind of generic and not so useful for the schools he was applying to—and, besides, he really didn't need it. His parents weren't too involved, either. "We supported him emotionally and whatever we can financially, but really, this is his deal," his mother, an administrative assistant for a pharmaceutical company in a small nearby city, tells me. They did what they could. They moved to their rural town—then a tiny, affordable farm town, now an expensive destination for well-heeled retirees and commuters—when Ethan was young because it offered school choice for high school, which would allow them to get Ethan, who was already "really smart," into a strong suburban school with accelerated classes. They encouraged college from an early age, and they talked with him—a lot—about financial aid, especially after his father lost his manufacturing job and remained out of work for nearly three years. They still don't understand exactly what a liberal arts college is, but they love Hilltop. And they know it's a "good school," or at least a competitive one: "How do you rate . . . schools . . . other than how hard it is to get in?" "Being where he is intellectually," his mother says, "he didn't want to settle."

Well aware of the *US News & World Report* rankings, Ethan is excited for Hilltop, too. It's a "good college," and it's close—about a four-hour drive—but not too close. When he visited, he felt like he was "already part of the community." He's still deciding exactly what he wants to do, but right now, he plans to study politics, go to law school, and then "live somewhere a little more urban, a little more civilized." He knows, "I really don't want to go back to normal life, if that makes sense. I don't want to come back here and work at Old Navy still." He's excited for "the college experience—aesthetic things . . . like waking up and being in ivy-covered buildings and all of that kind of stuff." And going to Hilltop, specifically, to "a higher caliber college, . . . [is] kind of a pride thing." So he's excited, for the ivy, the dorms, the "higher caliber."

But still, he worries a little. "I'm not sure about it," he begins, "but I think . . . the typical Hilltop student has a different upbringing than me." He continues, "There are preppy people, which I'm excited about in some ways because I think it will be nice to meet those people because I've never really hung with that crowd. . . . But I guess in some ways I'm more nervous about that: . . . there's going to be a lot of people who are different than me."

Even though the students feel like they earned their place at Hilltop, they occasionally seem to question what, exactly, does earn entry. Sometimes the students suggest that they may be "different" from "the typical Hilltop student"—"preppy people," Ethan guesses, whom he hasn't really spent time with before. And Daniel knows that he is "coming from this area, from a public school," whereas many of his future classmates will come from much wealthier schools and more urban places. The parents, too, sometimes hint that wealth might be related to admission: "There is going to be one or two that is there because mom and dad have a lot of money," Amelia's father tells me. This doubt is usually fleeting, mentioned briefly before reaffirming their faith in the educational sorting system. But in these moments, I hear students and parents trying to make sense of Hilltop's elite status.

Hilltop is not open to all who seek admission; it is, by design, exclusionary. Its primary—or at least most explicit—basis for exclusion is "merit": academic record, extracurricular talent, and intellectual promise. Its admissions process also serves to signal Hilltop's academic worth and its status as a "good school." So, to the extent that they recognize Hilltop's elite status, the students and parents mostly understand eliteness as an indicator of quality, which will translate into a strong education, a good career, and a more secure future. It's what will ensure that these children "step better" than their parents.

But eliteness is also about wealth: the institution's wealth and the wealth of the student body. Hilltop is a private institution with high tuition and a large endowment—not as large as some peer institutions', but much larger than most private and public schools. These resources allow the school to meet 100 percent of admitted students' demonstrated need, enabling these nine students to attend. The financial calculus behind this "generosity," though, is also in part what makes Hilltop elite: the school must balance the financial needs of those requiring assistance with the tuition of full-pay students. Hilltop can accept only as many financially needy students as it can pay for, putting these students—including these nine rural, first-generation students—at something of a disadvantage and giving their full-pay counterparts an edge. Through admissions, then, Hilltop does not just exclude on the basis of talent or academic promise; it also excludes on the basis of wealth. "Merit" is, at least in part, a question of ability to pay.

The parents and students don't seem fully aware of this aspect of eliteness or what it might mean for them and their experiences—or, for that matter, any of the other, even more hidden factors that determine exclusivity, like attending a high school that admissions officers visit. Only Ethan directly acknowledges the relative affluence of the student body; a few others note that most Hilltop students probably attended private or prep schools. The parents' comments are more frequent, if somewhat coded, like Hunter's mother's admonishment to remember that he's "not a rich kid." These remarks are often a little derisive or anxious, indicating an understanding that their children will spend the next four years surrounded by wealth and maybe, as Henry's mother suggests, come back changed. But mostly, these families are attracted to Hilltop because it feels "welcoming" and "down to earth"—for its inclusiveness, not its exclusivity.

At the end of our conversations, several parents ask me a version of the question Hunter's father also puts to me: "Is Hilltop as fair and as nice as it seems? Or is it just camouflage?" I'm never sure how to answer. These students did their homework; they know Hilltop's statistics, and their first impressions are important. And I have no doubt that these students are qualified to be at Hilltop and that Hilltop is lucky to have them. But I also wonder whether, after a few weeks or months or even years, Hilltop will feel as open and welcoming as it does this summer.

3

Entering

FAR FROM HOME

Hunter's mother cried all the way home. In August, she and Hunter's father drove the two thousand miles from their rural mountain hometown to Hilltop to drop off Hunter. They stayed a couple of days, attending some of the parent sessions and sightseeing on the coast, and then suddenly, it was time for parents to leave. "There was no lingering," his mother says, "just that quick, clean cut." They got in the car and took "the scenic route" home—three thousand miles of back roads this time, three thousand miles of tears.

Hunter didn't cry. He unpacked, spent a few days completing orientation, and then left for his Freshmen Summer Orientation (FSO) trip, a three-day excursion led by juniors and seniors that takes small groups of first-years off campus to explore the area, get to know classmates, and acclimate to college life. He loved his trip, doing community service and hiking, and when we meet up a few weeks into the semester, he's feeling settled in. He's already made "a best friend" and found a group of first-years to hang out with—all members of the swim team, perhaps because, even though they're not in season, they still practice for two hours a day. He's doing well academically, too. His "work ethic" has improved since high school, and he's happy to find that classes "aren't . . . overflowing with work." Playwriting is his favorite—"you can be really creative with what you do." So, he concludes, "Yeah, I can't really think of anything that is all that hard about the transition."

Hunter and I talk again in December and then in May. As his first year ends, he's finding a "good path." Although the second semester was a little rockier than the first, the workload has remained "manageable," and he is getting by with Bs in "almost" everything. He also takes his first art class at Hilltop and loves it. Because he's still interested in psychology, and it holds more career potential, he's planning a double major in psychology and studio art. He's grown closer to his teammates and is making friends quickly, much more quickly than he did in high school, and he has a girlfriend now, too. It is hard to be so far away from home, and even with financial aid, he knows that tuition payments are difficult for his parents—but, he says, "I really love it here. . . . I just think I'm a really good fit."

Hunter is a good fit, and to me, his transition to Hilltop seems pretty easy: he's involved, managing classes, making friends. But every once in a while, he says something that suggests otherwise. When telling me how much he enjoyed moving in, for example, he mentions that he and his roommate "didn't really hit it off, so we are not that talkative." Or when he talks about his second-semester classes, he names only three: he dropped a fourth, it turns out. He also shares that it's hard to return to campus after breaks. And that spring, when I ask if he thinks everyone should go to college, he gives an uncharacteristically vehement response. He's changed his mind: "I don't really think it is for everybody now. . . . Sometimes freshman year can be rough because you have to find your footing, and you don't really know what you want to do, and you kind of get laid by the wayside by all the work."

But it isn't until later that summer, when I talk with his mother, that I begin to see how much I've missed. She's direct. First, there was his roommate—"the roommate from hell." Hunter, she reports, "hardly spent any time in his room at all, except to sleep." Then there were classes: "He definitely fell off the wagon second semester." And then emotionally: "I think the homesickness and the stresses, they all really hit him." In the middle of the semester, he called and told them: "I have to come home. I have to get out of here." They swallowed the cost of the ticket and flew him home for spring break. It was the right decision. "He got a nice breathing space and went back more able to deal with all the new situations." But, she concludes, "college is such a different atmosphere."

Hunter finishes his first year and looks forward to his second. He finds friends and settles into academics and stays close to his parents. He remains grateful to be attending Hilltop. But after listening to his mother—and listening more closely to him—I wouldn't call his transition into Hilltop easy.

This is a pattern I notice across these students. Their initial descriptions of those first few weeks and months of Hilltop are mostly positive, filled with stories of friends made, experiences enjoyed, and classes loved. They seem to take to Hilltop, as Hunter's mother predicted, "like a duck to water." But as the year wears on, their reflections on the transition into Hilltop change. Their early evaluations give way to more sober assessments, and parents' appraisals often confirm—and sometimes expose—the challenges of the year: loneliness, isolation, and the uncertainty that comes with a place so unfamiliar. They're far from home—and, it seems, getting farther.

So, yes, the students all make it through their first years. But it isn't easy.

Like a Duck to Water

These students enter Hilltop feeling ready and hopeful, and my conversations with them that first semester reflect their excitement. John "loves" his dorm. Liliana's FSO trip was "amazing," and Sebastian's was "awesome." Ethan's Western Political Theory class is "really, really interesting," and Amelia is delighted that her biology class begins with genetics, which is her "favorite thing ever." They tell me about late-night conversations with hallmates and classes on topics they've never before considered. They're excited to be at Hilltop, a little awed, and eager, and they want to succeed—to do well, to fit in, to be happy—because they chose this school, and it chose them, and they want those choices to have been the right choices. And with the help of some important supports, they mostly do feel successful.

Fitting In

The students describe a smooth academic transition into Hilltop. They were prepared for their college studies, they say—no matter whether they attended public schools or private schools. Several report less homework and easier grading than their high school teachers had warned. They also notice—and appreciate—their classmates' focus. Back home, the students' academic talent was sometimes a social liability, especially for those attending rural public high schools. But at Hilltop, Amelia explains, everyone is here for the academics.

The students generally avoid the kind of exploration advertised by liberal arts admissions officials and enjoyed by their classmates, instead taking classes in disciplines that are familiar, ones they know from high school. But they like these classes, and by the end of the first year, they are settling into majors. They continue to tie their coursework to career plans, and these careers—practicing medicine or law or owning a business—are also familiar, recognizable and respected in their rural hometowns. The students are spending the year as they'd hoped: they're developing their interests and planning for work. And they're doing it well. They report mostly As and Bs in their classes. Academically, it's hard to argue that the year is anything but a success.

Socially, the year seems to be a success, too. "Everyone is just as nice as I expected," Sebastian reports, "which is really cool, getting random 'hellos' and 'how you doing?'" They're glad they're "meeting entirely new people," and the White students appreciate the school's racial diversity—"not just all White people," like at home. They find other first-years to spend time with, eating in the dining hall, decorating Christmas trees, and playing hockey. About half happily attend the parties that dominate Hilltop's weekend scene, drinking and enjoying new freedoms, and the others spend their Saturday nights "babysitting" drunk classmates, watching movies with floormates, or going home. Each of the students has at least one close friend by the year's end, most with many more, and these relationships prove a key support—one of many—during this first year.

Supported

John's year at Hilltop doesn't begin with an FSO trip, a campus orientation session, or a floor meeting. He doesn't spend nights sleeping with six other first-years in a tent in the woods, or afternoons crowded into a classroom learning about the risks of alcohol poisoning, or evenings getting to know his hallmates in his dorm. Instead, he does football: morning walk-throughs, lunches with his teammates, afternoon practices, nightly team meetings. By the time classes begin, he has seventy-five football-playing friends.

Football continues to define John's first year, even after the semester starts. He gets out of class each day around 2:30, does homework until 4:00, has practice from 4:30 to 7:00 p.m., eats with his team, returns to his dorm to finish homework, goes to bed, and then wakes up and does it all again. He likes it this way. "If I had the rest of the day," he admits, "I would procrastinate." He also likes the community that comes with football: "It is fun to be a part of something." He grows particularly close to a few other first-years on the team and even finds another teammate, Nick, who, like him, is "not really into the partying thing." On weekends, he and Nick hang out and watch TV—and play football, with games nearly every Saturday throughout the fall.

In November the season ends. "It was a little bit rough," John reports—they won two and lost six—but "it was really fun." Football continues into winter and spring, though, with conditioning and lifting and meetings. When I talk with him as classes are winding down for the year, he's wearing his usual Hilltop Athletics T-shirt, and he tells me that he spends most of his time "definitely with guys on the football team. . . . We have our little group." With football, then, comes his "little group," some "structure," and a lot of support.

As consuming as football is, John also stays closely tied to home, both emotionally and physically. His high school girlfriend attends a nearby community college—and midway through the year transfers to a four-year school with a strong nursing program—and he spends weekends with her, too. He talks to his parents regularly, at least twice a week, and during football season, they drive the half hour to attend his home games, cooking burgers and hot dogs for the team afterward with the other football parents. They also come to Millston once a week during that first semester to take him out to dinner, just to give him a break from "dorm room life," and throughout the year, he brings his laundry home—as do all of the students living within two hours of campus, likely motivated by rumors of the abuse inflicted upon the Hilltop laundry machines by drunken students.

For John, this support—from home and from football—seems to work. "I love it here," he tells me again and again throughout the year. He loves his dorm, his courses, and his classmates. He learns "way better from these professors" than his high school teachers, and he likes the liberal arts curriculum: he's "not entirely sure what to specialize in, so just getting a lot of options is good." He appreciates Hilltop's academic focus, compared to the schools his high school classmates attend, where "football is put on a pretty high pedestal over education." Adapting to the simultaneous demands of collegiate athletics and coursework was a challenge, "but I'm very comfortable now," he says in December. "I have come a long way."

By May, he is certain: "This is definitely the school for me." Despite the "options," he has focused, choosing a history major and considering teaching or law school after graduation. As classes slow and the year concludes, he's waiting tables at a restaurant near home, working weekends to make "a little extra money" for books and his eventual loan payments. He's busy, but "it hasn't been too tough," he says. And just in case he wasn't clear, he tells me again, "I love it here."

A variety of resources make the students' transition to Hilltop "manageable." The two varsity athletes—John and Hunter—enjoy the most comprehensive system of support: athletics offers resources, like tips on good professors, and develops skills, like leadership, that are important for navigating college.[1] As John and Hunter wear Hilltop gear and compete for Hilltop wins, they also grow more attached to Hilltop, and relatively quickly, both feel like "Hilltop Huskies." Athletics gives (nearby) parents an easy way to get involved, too, and John's regularly spend time on campus. Perhaps most critical, though, is the community—the friends, the mentors, the caring adults—that athletics offers. For underrepresented students, finding community is

essential to a successful first year, and it might be especially important for rural youth, who are often coming from small places with
dense social ties.[2]

Other kinds of extracurricular activities also provide support,
though less encompassing. Sebastian and Sylvan join a cappella
groups, which offer friendships and institutional connection. Liliana
signs up for the club hockey team, and Ethan joins an improv comedy troupe: like a cappella, these activities structure their days and
introduce them to new people. These relationships also provide information about Hilltop and its opportunities that helps them navigate
campus.

Another source of support is home. For Sebastian, Liliana, and
Sylvan, all graduates of private high schools, hometown friends'
attendance at schools like Hilltop helps normalize the challenges of
the first year. Through group texts and visits, they share their experiences and learn about others', which, Sebastian says, shows him "I'm
not alone in this." For the others, conversations and visits with high
school friends at public institutions, with larger classes and wilder
parties, often remind them why they chose Hilltop. And even though
Sebastian's long-distance relationship is troubled, John and Henry are
supported by hometown girlfriends—John's at a school nearby and
Henry's with him at Hilltop—and for them, these relationships are
grounding and familiar.

Family is especially important, as it often is for underrepresented
students.[3] The students are close to their parents, and they remain
close, relying on them for everything from advice to inspiration to
laundry. They communicate with their parents regularly through
phone calls, Skype, and text messages, and although their families
don't understand all the details, they listen. The students also don't
want to disappoint or disrespect their parents, and so they work hard
to get good grades and make it to a second year. Visits home are an
important part of the transition, too. The students with families who
live within an hour or two of campus regularly go home—a couple
of them nearly every weekend—sometimes for a specific purpose,
like a weekend job or a family gathering, and sometimes just for an
"escape." Those farther from home say visits, though infrequent, give
them the "breathing space" to survive the year. These visits are a time
to hunt, hike, or fish; to return to the mountains and waters of home;

to simply be alone.[4] Home, then, is a refuge—even for those who'd been ready to distance themselves from their hometowns.

Hilltop also provides some resources to support students with the transition to college. FSO trips, required for all students except fall athletes, help them learn about Hilltop and meet their new classmates, building connections that often last well beyond the trip itself. All first-years are assigned an academic adviser through a mandatory first-semester writing class, although these advisers serve only until students declare their majors, and the advising, it seems, is sometimes weak. Several of the students, like other first-generation students, grow close to the campus staff, such as custodians and dining hall workers—"some of the nicest people I have met here," Henry notes.[5]

In addition, the school has an array of formal, on-campus support systems that students can engage: a writing center, tutoring programs, faculty office hours, and a career center. There's also a multicultural center that provides programs and services for first-generation students, including workshops on study skills and dinners with first-generation faculty. But aside from an orientation session for first-generation families that Hunter's parents attend, the students don't use these resources. They don't need the support, they tell me— an assessment that, years later, most revise. I also suspect that the White students feel like the multicultural center and its resources aren't meant for them. Hilltop's mental health center is the only student-support service that any of them regularly accesses that first year: I connect Sebastian to counseling in the winter, and he continues to see a therapist during the spring.

So, although the students mostly avoid formal programs, they rely on other resources—varsity sports, extracurricular activities, and home—to support their transition into Hilltop. And these supports work. All the students make it, with (mostly) good grades and new friends and optimistic reports, to sophomore year.

Below the Surface

But these happy stories grow less happy as their first year wears on. The students' confidence that their high schools prepared them well wanes, a few tell me they're lonely, and I begin to see some of the

costs of that first year: stress, isolation, and doubt. These are challenges that other first-year rural and first-generation students also
face—and for a couple of the students, they are particularly acute.[6]

Floundering

By any measure, Sylvan's first year is an academic triumph. Taking
challenging premed classes that, whether by design or outcome,
"weed out" students with weak preparation or interest, he emerges
with a 4.0. He didn't expect to do so well: Intro Chem was hard, and
during our first conversation that fall, he reports that, having come
from a small high school, "it's weird having a teacher who doesn't
know me by name at all." But he gets all As that fall semester and
the next one, too. When we talk in May, he still can't believe it: "First
semester I got a 4.0, and I was incredibly surprised by that. So I was
like, 'Yeah, that is never going to happen again,' and then it ended up
I still have a 4.0. I don't know how."

Even so, "I do love Hilltop," he tells me. Latin is "absolutely fantastic," and he adores his professor: "She is a nut case. She is hilarious."
He still wants to enter medicine, and he's planning on a biology or
biochemistry major. He's working at the campus bookstore, and he
returns home occasionally for a bartending gig, which helps make
finances "manageable" for him and his family. He sees his parents
regularly, during his bartending weekends or when they make the
thirty-three-mile drive down to campus and take him out to dinner.
His parents can't be a resource when it comes to classes—"he is way
smarter than we are," they say, "so we weren't much help there"—but
still, he reports, "I'm liking our relationship." He's making friends,
too, during his FSO trip and in his classes, and by May, he has a "best
friend" he'll room with next year. Weekends are "fun" and usually
involve some drinking. And our conversations are upbeat and entertaining, with him often offering witty asides to my transcriptionist.
Sylvan appears well adjusted and happy.

But over the course of the year, the hints that he's not so happy
grow more frequent. He's often stressed out, and he doesn't feel
like he deserves the grades he's getting. He has a falling out with
an FSO friend and then a classmate, and he spends a lot of time
alone, although he's quick to say, "I don't mind it." His roommate's

messiness and drunkenness are beginning to irritate him more, and he no longer uses the water fountains on his floor, after learning that someone "regularly gets drunk and pees" in them. When I ask him how well he "fits" Hilltop—a question that I routinely ask the students—he always answers, "This is definitely the place for me." But then he usually offers a qualification: "I'm not quite at the college level," or "I don't understand these people around me," or "There is still that nagging feeling that I am not interacting with as many people as I should be." By the year's end, his doubts are piling up.

Then, during our final interview of the year, halfway through a discussion about classes and roommates, he admits this: "I actually got into a great deal of trouble." It happened back in March, when he invited his friends from home to campus so they could all go out to a college party together. He had a "weird desire to go fairly hard," he tells me, and then continues:

> I have no memory beyond 10:30 that night. I woke up at [the hospital], . . . didn't have my phone, none of my friends were there, and I didn't know what was going on. Apparently, while very, very, very, very intoxicated, I got my friends kicked out of a party because [the hosts] said that they had to take me home. . . . After that, apparently, I was violent and emotional, so my friends didn't know what to do. I was crying on the floor. I literally kicked the TV off of my dresser. My knuckle still hurts because my walls are concrete in my room. . . . It was very scary, and I don't want to really fuck up like that again. So that was my big event.

He shows me his hand; a month and a half later, it's still bruised. He hasn't gotten his hospital bill yet, but he knows it'll take him a while to pay it off. As we talk more—and as I hear from his parents that summer—it becomes clear that he had entered that weekend upset. He had just learned that he hadn't received the dorm adviser job he'd applied for, and, he tells me, "all the freshman . . . that I knew were applying got it." Sylvan's parents explain that he "has never really been in a situation where he didn't get something he thought he would get." He'd also just been denied entry into a course he'd really wanted to take: an unpaid bill led to a registration hold, and even though his mother, after figuring out the issue, went to the bank, withdrew cash to cover the payment, and then drove down to Hilltop to hand deliver it, it was too late and the class was full. "Suddenly," his mother says, "he was floundering." She continues, "I thought his friends coming up would cheer him up, and it seemed to have the opposite effect." He learns from the experience, they know, but his mother also learns something: "He is not as straight as I thought he was. . . . It was a shock."

The incident unsettles all of them, and me, too: not so much the drinking itself—"people do stupid things," his dad recognizes—but what it might indicate. Maybe the As and the friends and the cheerfulness are all covering something, whether depression or doubt, some sign that things aren't going as well as they might appear to be.

Sylvan's "big event," as he calls it, is a pretty dramatic signal, but I hear this, to some extent, from all the students: below the happy stories are tougher, scarier, sadder stories. These stories often involve stressful classes, bad roommates, rowdy parties, and disappointment. Hilltop isn't what they'd hoped, or harder still, they're not what they'd hoped—that is, Hilltop material.

Sometimes, with their cheerful first reviews, I think that the students are trying to convince themselves that they are OK, even if they occasionally worry they aren't. They don't want to disappoint anyone—not their parents, not their friends and neighbors, not me, not themselves. Like Sylvan, these students haven't failed at much, and to fail now, when stakes are high and expectations higher, is terrifying. The pressure to succeed is overwhelming.[7] Back in their small rural hometowns, everyone knows that they're the kid who got into the "good school." They can't not finish.

Other times, though, I suspect that they just might not see the challenges, or they might not see them as challenges. Their fierce desire for success might blind them to some of the costs of the transition, and they don't realize that their classmates might not be encountering the same difficulties or experiencing the same consequences. They simply think that this is what college is.

Stress

Amelia's parents are worried. It's the summer after her first year, and her grades are fine: all As and Bs, no Cs. "All we ask is that she does her best," they tell me, and they try to reassure her, "You stayed afloat, and your head stayed above water." It's clear they're proud. But they know she's under pressure: no one wants to be known as a premed dropout. Good grades came easily to Amelia during high school, they explain; everyone knew her, and they knew she was smart. At Hilltop, though, "it wasn't so easy." It was a "culture shock," her mom says, to go from being a "big fish" at her small high school to being "a nobody" at Hilltop.

The year started well. "Bio might actually be a breeze," Amelia tells me that September, and sociology looks like "a lot of fun." But when I see her after her first chemistry test, she looks on the verge of tears. "The stuff on the test . . . was not exactly what we had covered in class," she explains; it required application, not simply memorization—something she wasn't ready for. It's a similar story with her winter biology course, a premed requirement and notoriously difficult "introduction" to the biology major—a class that "is supposed to kill you." She shows up to class after the first test, and the room is half empty; everyone with a 75 or lower in the class, she later discovers, was encouraged to drop, and she's just grateful not to be in that group. She holds it together until mid-March, and then it's a "slippery slope" until the end of the semester.

By May, she has mono, and when we meet, she's pale and coughing. She seems tired of her science classes, and although she's still planning to be premed, she's considering a psychology major. She was stressed for much of the semester, she acknowledges, and concerned about her grades, worried that they won't get her into med school. And she knows that her parents, especially her mother, worries, too— about the stress and what it's doing to her confidence. But that's just what college requires, and, she says, "my mom doesn't really get that." So Amelia just puts in the work, and her grades end up fine— "not what I used to get in high school," she says, but "now I get a B+, and I feel the same joy that I felt when it was an A."

It's her new friends that help get her through the year. "I was scared coming here," she admits, but "I'm definitely making some good, genuine friends here, because in high school, people didn't really understand why I wanted to get good grades." At Hilltop, people get it. She's particularly close to her hallmates. They hold laundry tutorials on the proper use of bleach, they do homework together, and they talk about being homesick. Sometimes they spend Friday nights making popcorn and watching movies, or if they go out, Amelia is the "mom of the floor," making sure everyone gets home safely.

But it's not entirely easy socially, either. As the year concludes, Amelia's frustration with her roommate is growing. They are very different; her roommate is a partyer with little interest in academics, and, Amelia says, "she stole her dad's credit card number and charged four hundred dollars onto it and didn't even think twice." The biggest issue is her roommate's messiness: dirty laundry, a smelly closet, mold in the refrigerator. Amelia is also growing tired of the weekend scene, explaining that "parties just smell like beer and desperation at this point."

So Amelia goes home, driving three hours round trip nearly every weekend by year's end—for a clean bedroom, for a quiet place to study, for, as her parents put it, a "rescue." She needs it. She can't fail out.

At the beginning of the year, when I ask about academic readiness, most of the students tell me that their high schools prepared them well for Hilltop. But over the course of the year, this question begins to yield a different answer: on second thought, they weren't so prepared. By spring, I'm hearing that they weren't trained for the depth of analysis required on tests, weren't prepared for the rigor of the science classes, weren't equipped with the necessary critical-thinking skills. Most of these students, from both public and private schools, now think they weren't ready for Hilltop, a feeling shared by many first-generation students.[8] And for rural students, this doubt may be heightened: research suggests that rural students are less prepared than their urban counterparts.[9]

They mostly struggle alone. When they leave class confused or fail important assignments, they don't reach out to faculty. They don't visit the writing center or sign up for tutoring. They don't contact their academic advisers. The supports are there; Hilltop makes the academic assistance available. But they require that students reach out, navigate unfamiliar campus systems, admit they're struggling. To the students, these supports are a sign of weakness—a failing rather than a resource they're entitled to—and so they don't ask for help. And they don't have the resources at home—the savvy parents to suggest a resource or proofread a paper—that their continuing-generation classmates do.

This underpreparation is consequential. Some see the impact in their grades; their grade point averages never recover. It also shapes their courses of study. Liliana's weak science and math background, for example, means a D+ in her first-semester chemistry class and the end of her premed plans. For others, it's more about the stress. They worry about academics: Sylvan describes periods of "absolute hell" in his science classes, Ethan tells me about all-nighters and piles of deadlines and mounting anxiety, and Amelia is "stressed 95% of the time."

Mostly, they locate the problem individually, within themselves. Henry tells me that he's not good at taking notes, John knows he needs to participate more in classroom discussions, and Sylvan admits to procrastinating. They often blame themselves: "I could have done a better job managing," "I'm not a math person," "I got cocky." Sometimes the parents look to the students, too. Amelia's father, for example, explains that "her being valedictorian, maybe her britches were bigger and she thought, 'Well, this is going to be easy,' but by no means, we know it is not." The problem isn't their high schools, small and resource-limited. It's not Hilltop and the preparation and initiative—or even the entitlement—it assumes. Instead, it's them. And so they just work harder.

Isolation

Daniel is a tough read. He usually shows up to meet me—sometimes early, sometimes late—although occasionally he forgets. He's apologetic then; it's nothing personal—appointments just aren't his thing.

He never volunteers much information, but his responses are frank and surprisingly funny. I'm not sure where I stand with Daniel, though he does seem to like my dog, Lulu.

Throughout his first year, our meetings are much the same. He wears a plaid button-down shirt and jeans—and if it's cold enough, a pullover—and our conversations are short. I take few notes; I just want to keep him talking. Lulu learns that, if she nudges him with her nose, he'll pet her, and she does, again and again and again. His classes, he tells me that fall as he strokes Lulu's ears, are "manageable," and he reports feeling "very prepared," even for his math and science courses. His winter term is harder, and he learns that he should only take one math class a semester—"I'm just not a math-oriented person." But he does "fine," ending the year with As and Bs and thinking about a possible major in psychology. Socially, too, the transition into Hilltop was smooth, he says. His FSO trip was "really fun," and he spends time with his roommates, mostly watching Netflix. He joins the Outing Club for a few activities and attends the badminton club for a bit, but he doesn't get too involved; he's "kind of focusing on work." He mentions a few challenges: one of his roommates doesn't sleep, and he hasn't met too many people. But aside from a few oblique references to an "interesting experience" in his dorm room, he reports that "pretty much the year has just progressed fairly normally."

As with Hunter, it's only when I talk with Daniel's mother that summer that I get a better understanding of his first year. She is as detailed as Daniel is plainspoken, and she is angry. She begins, "We started the year with very positive thoughts and big dreams, and moving into the dorm was the first slap in the face, like, 'How are they ever going to live in these tight little quarters—four kids—and study?' . . . Then within the first two weeks . . . he was approached by two drug dealers." This happens at a party one of the first weekends of the semester; two men try to sell him ecstasy. She doesn't hear much from Daniel for the next few months—"he doesn't talk much"—but she realizes that "something was going on when he came home for a break." She continues: "It was mostly the roommate situation. That was difficult because the roommates were partiers, and the one roommate"—the insomniac—"was doing his prescription drugs, crushing them and snorting them." This roommate, she explains, "had a very privileged life"—spending his time trading stocks, ordering food from restaurants, and snorting his prescriptions—and "that was probably hard" for Daniel, who relies on considerable financial aid. Harder still is when the resident adviser finds drugs in their room, and all the roommates receive a disciplinary strike. The year gets worse: "He came home at Christmas, and I could see that he was a different kid." It's not just the roommate. His floor is "out of control," too, and academically, he's struggling to find a major and "doesn't have a lot of help." Then, in March, he asked his mother to pick him up for the weekend: he needed to come home. "The low point," she tells me, was taking him back to Hilltop at the weekend's end, "watching him walk in that door and knowing that I wasn't sure it was the right thing to do." But, she says, "it is a lot of money and you don't want him to quit."

They spend the summer debating whether Daniel should return. He tells his mother, "It was like I had a really bad piece of pie, and I don't want to go back for another bite." And she's confused: "I don't know if I should be saying, 'Don't go,' or 'Try again.'" She's proud of him for making it through the year, and he's gained confidence. But she also worries that he's growing more "negative," that "he feels trapped there," that he's "sad." She feels a little guilty, too, like "maybe I influenced him on that college." They decide to give it another semester.

Their stories of the year are different, though not inconsistent, and years later, he's more open with me: his first year was hard, and he wondered whether he'd chosen the right school. As he prepares to return to Hilltop for a second year, I wonder about the impacts of this first year—and what it means for the rest of his time.

The year's challenges are not just academic; they're also social. The students are often lonely in those first months, when homework and friends and clubs have not yet filled all of that unstructured time, and for some, like Daniel, the loneliness continues. They miss home—their family, but also its beauty and space and leafy quietness. They rarely venture into Millston, and several seem surprised by its sprawl. They are also much more anonymous at Hilltop—"a nobody," as Amelia's mother puts it—than they ever were in high school, a challenge other rural students face, too.[10]

Another issue, I learn, is the party scene. The students had understood that parties would be a part of the Hilltop social scene; what surprises them is the extent—maybe it's not academics drawing everyone to Hilltop—and how comfortable their new classmates seem to be with all the excess and indulgence. They share stories of drunken property damage: sprinklers activated in the dorms, water fountains used as urinals, feces found in laundry machines. The partying also leads to random sexual encounters, and the openness of this hookup culture is uncomfortable. Several students are completely new to drinking and parties: "I had never tasted alcohol," Amelia admits, "and was just like an innocent little deer being cast into the world of college"—a world that she finds, frankly, shocking. The students vary in their responses to the Hilltop party scene. Amelia, Liliana, and John carefully limit their drinking and mostly avoid parties, which they find unnerving and, for Amelia and Liliana, unsafe. For most of the year, Sebastian also doesn't drink; this changes after his first a cappella tour. The others participate more fully from the start, attending parties and drinking and, for some, occasionally using drugs. All of them, though, denounce the irresponsibility and disrespect associated with partying, especially the dorm damage; this wasn't how they were raised, and they wonder what it says about their classmates.

Nearly half the students—Daniel and Amelia, as well as Hunter and Sylvan—also encounter difficult roommates. The specifics of the issues vary, but most include messiness and extensive drinking or drug use. These tensions, I later realize, profoundly shape the students' first years. They only rarely lead to explicit arguments; more often, the students adapt by trying to ignore the dirty laundry and moldy refrigerators, spending more time out of their rooms, and living with the anxiety of possible disciplinary sanction for the presence of contraband material. But this leads to frustration, lost sleep, a feeling of displacement—and maybe, as Daniel's mother notes, some envy, because so much of their roommates' negligence and partying is funded by their substantial wealth. And their parents are left worrying, unsure how to advise their children.

The students mostly weather these challenges. With the support of new friends and the respite of home, they survive the uncertainty, the parties, and the roommates, and they arrive at their second year wiser, more informed—"smarter," Ethan tells me. Even Daniel, whose transition might be the hardest of the group, returns for a second year—and a third and a fourth—and settles in, finding a good roommate and joining the rugby team and choosing a major.

But the year also raises questions, and those, I find, are more lasting.

Questions

As I learn about the harder moments of college, I hear the students struggling to figure out Hilltop and their place in it and what, exactly, this education will mean for them and their families. I also hear them struggle with what it means to be rural at Hilltop. Some of the students—and most of the parents—are worried about the degree and whether it will actually lead them to a career. Most worry about relationships, too, trying to make sense of their changing ties to family, to friends, to home. They wonder where—and perhaps whether— they belong.

These questions don't resolve so neatly. They're hard because they bring doubt, and as Sylvan tells me, "I didn't want to doubt that this was the right place." And this doubt lingers.

A Little Bit of Direction?

During February of Sebastian's first year, I get an email from him. He tells me that he's filling out transfer applications, explaining, "I am extremely happy at Hilltop, but I fear they might not have the major I want to study." He'd like to meet and "talk some technical stuff out." We sit down a few weeks later. He says he likes the people at Hilltop, but he's learning that he wants to major in communications, like his sister and some hometown friends, and possibly go into radio or some kind of performance. He shares his application with me; his essay focuses on his love for pop culture. "I need to create," he writes. "I want to write, express myself, and entertain." He concludes that he needs to leave Hilltop to pursue communications, a major that small elite schools like Hilltop don't have.

When I'd talked with Sebastian a few months earlier, he was still planning on a math major. But when we meet in February, he is taking more music than math courses, and he dropped linear algebra, which was "not going well," midway through winter semester. Sebastian seems unsettled: he fidgets in his seat and doesn't seem to know what to do with his hands. He asks if I'll write him a letter of recommendation—I assure him that I will—but it's clear he's mostly come for advice: should he stay? This isn't my decision to make, we both know; it's his and his parents'. I ask if he's talked with them about transferring, and he says he's spoken with his father, who worries about what a move might mean for financial aid. Sebastian also remembers how excited his father had been when Sebastian got into Hilltop.

Hilltop's lack of a communications major is not the only issue, I know. Sebastian often reaches out to me between our regular interviews, and we've had some long conversations about his transition. He always begins with everything he loves about Hilltop: entertaining his FSO tripmates with campfire songs on his guitar, the friendliness and "random hellos" on campus, joining a band and an a cappella group, "how much pure talent there is here." But then, quickly, we're talking about the hard parts. Frequently, it's long-distance relationships: we're both in one, and his hometown girlfriend is now enrolled at a college in New Haven. Their relationship is rocky, and it's not getting better. They see each other every few weeks, meeting up back home, but even when he's on campus and busy with rehearsals and performances, he feels a little removed: he'll go to parties, but he doesn't drink, and he's preoccupied with how his girlfriend is spending her weekends. "I want to be 100 percent here but can't," he says. And he worries: "Maybe I don't fit in here." Things at home are hard, too, with his parents in the middle of a divorce and Thanksgiving their first holiday apart. He mentions feeling depressed; several times I suggest that he sees a counselor, and eventually he does.

I submit Sebastian's letter of recommendation in mid-March, and I don't hear from him again until May, when I contact him to find time for an interview. As soon as I see him, I can tell something has changed: he's calmer, less fidgety, smiling. He never submitted his transfer application. He's taking a rhetoric course, loving it, and thinking about a major in the discipline. He talked with one of his roommates—a prep school graduate with plenty of "confidence" and "charisma"—who reminded him of all the long-term benefits of Hilltop, those that are less related to one's major: "Hilltop has these connections that are really important, and that is why it is a pretty prestigious place here. It is not just the diploma; it is them setting stuff up for you and the gateways into the world." His relationship with his girlfriend ended—much to his relief, it seems—and after spending a "really, really fun" spring break on tour with his a cappella group, he now drinks, with some eagerness. There was no reason to leave.

When I talk with his father that summer, though, I can tell that he still has doubts. He's excited that Sebastian decided to stay at Hilltop: the financial aid is good, it's a great school, and it's close to home. But, he confesses, "I just kind of looked at the whole first year . . . and I don't know where he's going with it." He is apprehensive about Sebastian's possible rhetoric major—"I . . . don't know what he can do with that"—and he fears that a career in media "just might still not be realistic." So while Sebastian is excited for his second year, his father is concerned, hoping Sebastian will "find a little bit of direction."

During the year, a few of the students occasionally question whether they chose the right school. For Daniel, the concern is mostly social, tied to isolation and loneliness, but for others, like Sebastian, it is at least in part academic and occupational: they wonder whether they should have chosen a different college with a wider variety of more "useful" majors. Hilltop has fewer majors than state schools and community colleges, and its majors are decidedly not vocational in nature. With most—in disciplines like English and anthropology and classical studies—it's hard for the students to understand how those courses translate into an actual job, especially any of the ones found back home. They're also mostly alone in their struggles to connect coursework to careers. Their first-year advisers are more concerned with academic requirements than employment, and they won't be assigned a major adviser until they officially declare a major, typically not until halfway through their second year. Right now, their professors are encouraging academic exploration, not focus. Cast a wide net, they're saying: indulge your curiosity, embrace uncertainty, worry about a job later. But their hometown friends and siblings—whether studying at a university or community college or already out in the working world—are stepping into much clearer, more defined career paths. And the urgency of finding that career hasn't changed; at home, the mills are still closing, the fields are still fallow, the families are still leaving. These students need the assurance of a clear career path, and some aren't finding it, and so they're worried.

Their parents are even more concerned, and they tell me about these concerns, often at length, as we talk the summer after the students' first year. They wanted their children to finish the year with "a little bit of direction"—specifically, a useful major tightly yoked to a "realistic" career path—and most of them aren't seeing it. Yes, they supported a liberal arts education during their children's search for a college, but after a year of enrollment, they want proof of concept: the reassurance of a major and the prospect of a job after graduation. They worry, like Sebastian's parents, about a degree that doesn't get used, and they feel like their children "do 'not have a lot of help.'" By summer, then, they're anxious and frustrated.

Despite the mixed messaging and limited guidance, the students do focus their studies—well before most of their Hilltop classmates—and all end the year with plans for a major and a career. Although the specificity of these plans varies, they're listening to their parents and finding that direction. But the parents remain concerned, and I suspect that some of their children feel pressured, caught between the exploratory ethos of an elite liberal arts college and the occupational imperative of their rural contexts. This question, about the utility of their degree, isn't resolved.

A Gap between Us?

The students remain close to their parents throughout their first years: they call for advice, share stories, visit. But these relationships shift a little, as they do for other rural and underrepresented students, and some new tensions emerge.[11] Majors and careers are sometimes a source of these tensions, although parents mostly try to give their children the space to choose a path and the students work hard to find one. But the students are learning that college is an experience their parents don't have, and they can't understand the minutiae of academic life and campus culture—the timeline for declaring majors or the difficulty of switching roommates or the stress of finals week. "My parents not having gone through the college experience," Amelia says, "it was like kind of a gap between us."

The parents describe some new disagreements with their children, too. Some are political, tied to the fast-approaching 2016 presidential election, emerging arguments about issues and candidates and platforms. Occasionally, they worry about the wealth of Hilltop students and the risk of their children getting a "little rich snobby" attitude. "You are not a rich kid," they remind them; "don't be no snob."

For some of the students, relationships with hometown friends are also growing tense. Most of their friends are attending nonselective colleges, large state schools, or community colleges, or they're working or serving in the military or still figuring out what's next. These nine students, though, are on a "different path"—a carefully curated path of elite admissions, small classes, and rigorous academics. Over the year, the differences between the paths become clearer, and there's less to talk about, more silence, some distance.

It's March, and the snow is melting, finals are coming, and a shaggy beard covers Henry's face. Henry isn't talking to friends from home much anymore. I'm surprised to learn this: Henry had stayed in close touch with his hometown friends. But he explains that, recently, one of these friends—one who's not attending college—reached out. He was heading to Florida and wanted to see Henry before he left. Henry couldn't; he was "slammed" with deadlines and studying that weekend. A week later, he received a text from the friend: "Are we friends anymore?" In this friend's estimation, they weren't, and then he said something that's been eating at Henry. Henry scrolls through his phone to find it: "Apparently my things that I'm doing are more important to me." But, Henry asks me, shouldn't he be prioritizing himself?

Relationships with home friends have been weighing on Henry for a while. Back in September, when I asked him about the hardest part of the transition into Hilltop, he responded, "Trying to forge new relationships and cutting ties with old ones." For Henry, the difficulty isn't just about making time for his hometown friends, although that's certainly part of it. It's also about what's "important," which way of life—college or not—is better and why and what it means that he's chosen a different path than most of them. I know he thinks about his dad and his desire for Henry to enter trade school or work with him at the lumberyard. I wonder, too, if he's thinking about his mother's prediction, worrying whether college is changing him. Henry has a pretty good first year. He enjoys his FSO trip, gets along with his roommate, makes some new friends, and earns As and Bs. He enjoys his courses, especially his art classes, and he's finding that the "workload is not that bad." By year's end, he's the only one to still think that his high school "did a great job of getting us prepared for college." For him, the doubts are about Hilltop. He's concerned about majors—none interests him—and he wonders whether he should have chosen the state school, which has more options. This question continues to bother him, even as, after dismissing art as impractical, he begins to plan for a psychology major. When I talk with his mother and stepfather that summer, they echo these concerns: "He really doesn't know what he wants to do." They worry about the courses he has taken his first year—"Holy shit, man, we are not paying $62,000 a year for you to take art class," his stepfather remembers telling him—and feel like he's not getting any guidance from his professors. By the spring, Henry's doubts have grown beyond majors. He hasn't made a lot of new friends: he's spending more and more time with his hometown girlfriend, who also attends Hilltop, and he's also going home quite a bit—"more often than I think I should, as society says." His mother reports that he gets "antsy" from "the atmosphere down there," and he tells me that he's tired of the typical "fratty" college guy: "Everybody is the same person. It is all about who can drink the most and who can have the most sex." He misses home.

Whenever Henry and I talk that first year, he updates me on his hometown friends—who has dropped out of college or found a job or gotten pregnant. He acknowledges that some of them are making "bad choices," and with a bit of guilt he tells me, "I feel like I'm in a better position than most." But at the same time, back home, "there is just all sorts of stuff happening. How am I supposed to feel about it? . . . They are starting their lives and things are happening, and I'm kind of stuck here in neutral between high school and life." Occasionally, he wonders what things would have been like had he taken that job with his father: "I would probably be still living at home, but maybe I would feel more like an adult. Maybe I would have moved out and took an apartment and started life. But that is not what happened, and here I am."

Maybe who's better off is not so clear.

For some of the students, these new silences and tensions don't matter much: they don't change their relationships with their parents or hometown friends. But for others, like Henry, they do. They lead to occasional arguments with friends and family and, sometimes, complex emotions: relief, guilt, even a little envy. They bring hard questions about who to prioritize—oneself or one's family and friends. And sometimes, they seem to hint at their increasingly divergent lives.

Fitting In?

The year also leads to questions about them and their place at Hilltop. During their first few weeks on campus, they felt—or perhaps hoped— that they could belong at Hilltop, surrounded by similarly smart, equally motivated college students. Some months into the year, though, it's the differences they're noticing. Most of the students tell me at some point that first year that they're "in the minority," that they feel different from the other Hilltop students. They're struggling in their classes—and their classmates aren't. They're avoiding the weekend scene—and their classmates aren't. They're worrying about tuition—and their classmates aren't.

For the most part, these differences are merely observations, things they've just noticed over the year. But occasionally, these differences are confusing—"I don't understand these people around me." Some of them are even troubling—"maybe I don't fit in here." Sometimes the differences send them home for a break, to escape "the atmosphere down there." And I notice that the language they use to describe these differences is personal and, usually, negative: these are *their* deficits, flaws and shortcomings specific to them.

Liliana's parents and her younger brother come to drop her off at Hilltop in September. This is their first time in New England, and after unpacking and hanging Christmas lights in her dorm room, they spend the weekend "doing touristy stuff": going to the beach, eating lobster, and visiting Boston. The goodbye is quick, as her parents and brother rush to catch their flight, and then it's many months until December, when Liliana finally returns home. During that first semester, she has a long list of things she misses about home: October snow, her mother's Mexican cooking, the mountains, burgers made with elk her family hunted. By May, she's beginning to feel a "large division" in her family: they don't understand college or her college life. Still, though, she misses them, and she knows that they miss her. Her dad cries every time she calls home. It was hard to leave her at Hilltop, he says, but "that is life. She is happy, and I am happy for her dreams."

I can see that Liliana is trying to be happy. Academically, she struggles her first semester, mostly with chemistry, a large, lecture-style, premed requirement. The workload increases "at an exponential rate," and by the end of the semester, she has abandoned both the premed track and her anticipated neuroscience major: she "didn't enjoy" the classes. But academics improve in her second semester. She focuses on Spanish and politics courses, loves them, and plans to double major. The social transition is similar. It's hard first semester: she has friends, but they like to party and she doesn't, so she often finds herself alone. But in the winter and spring, she joins the club hockey team and makes friends who are, like her, "academically . . . inclined," and they spend most of their weekends off campus, hiking and exploring beaches.

And Liliana does seem more comfortable over the course of the year. But she makes one observation repeatedly, from our first on-campus conversation in September to our last one before summer: Hilltop isn't as diverse or inclusive as she expected. This had been an important reason she chose Hilltop, especially as a Latina from a place as White as her home state. When she visited during Preview, she "did see a lot of diversity" and "was super excited," but she says, "now that I'm here it is not as diverse as I would think." "The diverse population is still a subsection," she continues. Most of her friends are White. And "inclusion is a little weird"; in the dining hall, "I will sit at a table and I will be the only ethnically diverse person." Also, she explains, as a first-generation student, she's "in college for academic reasons and not necessarily the social weekend reasons"—the drinking and the parties aren't for her. Actually, it sometimes seems like much of Hilltop isn't for her.

I notice, though, that she stops short of calling out Hilltop's exclusivity. Instead, she focuses on managing her expectations and "breaking social norms"—on surviving. And if she has any critique, it might be about the students of color: they're the ones who "sit together" in the dining hall, and "when they talk about race on campus, they blow it a little bit out of proportion. . . . It is almost like a victimization." She doesn't seem to connect her dining hall observations to her struggles in chemistry or her discomfort with the weekend scene or the "large division" in her family. It's Liliana that needs to change—Liliana, and anyone else that doesn't fit in.

That first year, the students rarely mention the privilege of Hilltop's student body. About three-quarters of Hilltop's students are White, between 50 percent and 60 percent receive no financial aid, about 95 percent have parents with bachelor's degrees, and the vast majority are from urban and suburban places: they are a relatively homogeneous, relatively privileged group. Yet the students rarely talk about any of this. Liliana notes the lack of racial diversity occasionally; she's the only one to readily identify as a student of color. When I ask about race, the others might mention the school's Whiteness, but Hilltop is more racially diverse than most of their hometowns, and more frequently, that's what they see. They also don't notice the segregation Liliana does; "it's nice coming here," John says, "and seeing all of the different cultures interacting together." And across the group, comments about being the first in their family to attend college are relatively rare—I suspect they're even less common among their friends and classmates.

I also notice that they rarely talk about place. They don't talk about what it means to be a rural student or to have mostly urban and suburban classmates or to attend an urban college. They don't talk about it with me—although they did before Hilltop began, and they will in the coming years—and they don't talk about it with their friends. Their rurality comes up only if I ask, and my questions don't get me far. I suspect they think it's irrelevant—but I think they don't yet know what to say.

They are more aware of the relative wealth of their classmates, but this, too, I know only because I ask; it's not something they usually volunteer. Their classmates don't either. In general, they report, Hill-top students don't talk about money. You can tell who has it, though. It's everywhere: in their Canada Goose jackets and their L.L.Bean boots and their family vacations to Italy.

They see this wealth, but, they say, it doesn't have much of an effect. As Sebastian tells me: "I'm sure some of the people I've met and have come in contact with are wealthy, and they haven't acted differently. They're just as friendly, just as cool, and, you know, it doesn't even come up." Yes, their classmates are wealthy—but it doesn't matter. Only Ethan seems to think it might.

The worst moment of Ethan's first year happens on a weekend in the fall. His parents had just gotten paid, and they put a hundred dollars in spending money in his bank account. He uses it to rent a car and go shopping with a friend. That night, they meet up with more friends for dinner out. They stop by an ATM, and Ethan tries to withdraw another twenty dollars. "It was so embarrassing," he explains: "Insufficient funds." He overspent by only fifty-one cents, and the error is due to a recent change to his account; it now requires a minimum balance. But he has to call his parents, in front of all of his friends, to ask them to deposit a dollar. He feels guilty, too: "They had just put so much money in my account."

I notice how careful Ethan is with his money and how often he talks about it. He works at the campus coffee shop for textbook and spending money, and he keeps his job at Old Navy back home so that he can pick up hours during breaks. He knows exactly how much he's making and how much he can spend and whether he can stretch a paycheck until summer when he can make more. He knows when his tuition bills are due and when his loans should appear in his account, and if they're late, he's in the financial aid office asking about them. He knows, too, the burden these mounting costs put on his parents: "We don't have a cushion." This financial pressure shapes his coursework, keeping him from dropping a work-intensive, upper-level course his first semester because he can't return the books, and perhaps even more, it colors his social life. "To have a life outside of academics, you need to spend money," he tells me.

He's surrounded by money at Hilltop. The campus, he says, "is so wealthy, so incredibly wealthy." His classmates' wealth isn't exactly a secret, but for the most part, it's kept quiet. It's something you discover, he says, when you see a photo online "of them with their dad after the Super Bowl with confetti falling on the floor of the stadium"—that's how you know.

In the fall, he just notices the wealth and occasionally tells me about it. But by May, he acknowledges that, with all the money and privilege, it was "stressful" when he first arrived—it was a kind of wealth he'd never experienced at home. I remember back to our interviews over the summer, when Ethan mentioned that Hilltop was full of "preppy people" with a "different upbringing" from him, and then our September interview, when he told me, "I feel like in some ways I'm different from a lot of people." There's a "Hilltop person," he explained. "It's aesthetic. . . . The way people carry themselves, the way people talk, and the way people dress is homogeneous." And, he said, "I don't know if I'm that person yet." He didn't connect this "aesthetic" to the culture of wealth at Hilltop, but I later wondered whether that was really what he'd been worrying about over the summer and experiencing during the fall: feeling out of place among so many rich kids—rich kids, he notes, from Manhattan and Greenwich, Connecticut, and the Boston suburbs.

By year's end, though, he reports, "I feel like I can fit in and do just as well as anybody else." And he is doing well: he joins an improv comedy group and auditions into the orchestra, he decides on a politics major and earns mostly As, and he makes friends and seems busy. The work has been stressful, but it's worth it: "I'm actually actively getting smarter from what I'm learning here." He's excelling in what feels like a "foreign land," and he's proud of himself for that. He's proud of his grades and his extracurriculars and also, I think, his ability to fit in—to become that "Hilltop person."

Later that summer, his mother also talks about the "very wealthy people" at Hilltop. Ethan "has always gravitated toward that sort of lifestyle," and she's OK with that. But, she says, "we are not smart enough, rich enough, or classy enough for Ethan right now." And that "is a change."

So Ethan sees the wealth at Hilltop—and, it seems, he also wants to have "that sort of lifestyle." What I'm not sure he recognizes, at least right now, is its costs, to him and to his family.

And so the students end the year, all still Hilltop students. For the most part, supported by teams and clubs and family and campus staff, they end with majors and friends and good grades, with their fears of a shameful return home unrealized. They also close the year with some questions—and some doubts—but these they try to ignore. Instead, they focus on fitting in, and mostly, they do.

Their faith in Hilltop also remains intact. They continue to believe, as Hunter's father put it, that Hilltop is "as fair and nice as it seems." It's fair and nice, and they belong—at least, they think they do. They seem to trust that, if they continue to work hard, get good grades, and fit in, they'll earn a Hilltop degree and everything it promises, just like their classmates. Then, any costs may be worth it.

4

Persisting

DIFFERENT WORLDS

"A lot has happened," Ethan says as we sit down to talk during the May of his junior year. He's wearing a blue T-shirt that's splattered with paint, likely from his past two summers painting dorm rooms, and I notice that he's lost a bit of his fresh-faced youthfulness. He seems older, a little world-weary. And he's right: a lot has happened.

First, there was the 2016 presidential election. As a politics major, he followed it with great interest. He was disappointed by Trump's win, but not surprised: back home, he'd watched the yard signs go up, seen the flags flying, argued with his Trump-supporting dad. But Hilltop took Clinton's loss hard. "It was very clear how people felt," he says, "how seriously and negatively people took it, rightfully so." Then, right around the same time, his father lost his job. It wasn't as bad this time, not like when Ethan was a kid; instead, he found work pretty quickly, holiday temp work that turned into a permanent position at a small factory. But still, it was "hard and scary." Actually, Ethan says, after winter break, he almost didn't come back to Hilltop.

It certainly wasn't academics that made him reluctant to return. His academic record is stellar—including three A+s that spring—and he loves his classes. He's been nominated by the politics department to write a yearlong honors thesis his senior year, and he's planning for law school.

His reluctance to return to Hilltop, he explains, was social—and financial. "Hilltop isn't that fun when you're living paycheck to paycheck," he says. He was "bored-sad." His friends are "overwhelmingly . . . rich," and he can't match their clothes, their vacations, their weekend plans, or even the semesters abroad that many Hilltop students take. He tries to keep up, but he's developed "champagne taste on a beer budget," and it's making him a little "jealous"; he's never been around so many wealthy people before. He's also often stressed out about grades. He knows that he wasn't prepared for Hilltop like his prep school classmates were, and even a couple of years into Hilltop, he has to work hard for those good grades—so hard that his friends sometimes tease him for being "neurotic."

And so, he tells me, "I feel like I am different than a lot of my friends." He lists the differences, a list that I suspect he's been cataloging for a while. His friends are all twenty-one, and he's still twenty. He doesn't have money, and they do. They've all traveled, and he hasn't. "It is fine," he says, "but it is the comparative thing, and that is hard." And then he adds one more difference: "Like being gay—that is another thing, and I have been sort of hyperaware of it."

This is the first time he's told me that he's gay. His parents don't know, and I'm not sure his friends do either. But to me, this disclosure isn't the most surprising part of his story. What I can't believe is that he almost stayed home.

I'm surprised because I know that Ethan is feeling disconnected from his parents. There are the political differences, and all the arguing. With his father, he says, "it gets dirty," but he argues with his "more moderate," Clinton-supporting mother, too. She thinks Ethan "needs to tone it down," but as Ethan tells me, his parents just don't get it; his father especially "doesn't understand things critically in a lot of ways." They also don't understand Hilltop, what he's studying, all the intellectual language and academic jargon. "It has always been clear that I am academically more gifted than my parents," he says, but those differences are magnified "having received a college education." He's similarly disconnected from his hometown, where most residents are less educated, conservative Trump voters. For years I have listened to Ethan's fears of "getting stuck" at home—college, for him, is a way out. Why would he want to return to a place that, for so many reasons, could feel closeting?

But Ethan has complicated feelings about his parents, his hometown, and Hilltop. He knows that his opportunity to attend Hilltop is a product of his parents prioritizing education in a way that their parents couldn't. He recognizes that, as much as he wants the expensive clothing and lavish vacations of his wealthy peers, their wealth is a problem—an indication of the economic inequalities that disadvantage families like his and, sometimes, keep his father out of work. He understands that his parents' inability to understand his experiences may be more about Hilltop's "exclusionary" language than any failure of theirs. Also, in the aftermath of the election, he has noticed a lot of "scapegoating" of rural America—of people like his father; Trump, he's quick to point out, had plenty of support outside of rural areas. And as often as Ethan complains of home, as often as he tells me he wants to leave, being from where he's from "is something to brag about," with its green fields and snowy mountains and rolling rivers.

Ethan returns to Hilltop. His mother really wants him to "stick it out," and if he'd stayed home, he would have had to start paying back his loans. So he does "stick it out," through the jealousy, the stress, the otherness—"it ended up being fine." But Ethan's critical capacities have grown, and his sense of who he is and who he wants to be is clearer. He has less patience for the rural scapegoating and the rich kids who don't need "a real job." Despite everything he has accomplished and will accomplish during his time at college, he's less sure he belongs at Hilltop—and also maybe less sure he wants to.

Ethan is the most critical of the nine students; he's quick to notice gaps between rhetoric and reality, between his classmates' apparently easy existences and his own, more sharply lived Hilltop years. But I also see his experiences reflected in the other students'. They're all successful, both academically and socially, and they're developing clearer plans for graduate school and jobs and careers. But as their second year turns into a third and a fourth, they're also feeling more different, more marginal.

For the students, it's the 2016 election that seems to highlight the precarity of belonging at Hilltop. They're not entirely sure what to make of the postelection narrative about rural America. The distance between home and Hilltop—and, increasingly, between home and them—seems wider, but it also sometimes feels as if there's a distance between them and Hilltop. They don't always have full access to a

Hilltop education; they're outsiders, even if they're not always sure why. And with this comes some disillusionment—like Ethan, they're a little less sure they *want* to belong at Hilltop.

As they complete their Hilltop years, the doubt that marked their first year seems only to have grown. They "stick it out," but their confidence in Hilltop, and everything that a degree from Hilltop suggests, is fading.

The Politics of Belonging

The 2016 presidential election happens during the fall of Ethan, Sebastian, and Daniel's junior year, sophomore year for Amelia, John, Henry, Hunter, Liliana, and Sylvan. It is a topic in most of my conversations with the students throughout 2016 and, with some of them, for many months afterward, too. It is also a topic of conversation on campus and, of course, nationally. I notice that, as the students try to make sense of the election and its aftermath, they also seem to be trying to make sense of Hilltop—and, perhaps more importantly, their place at Hilltop.

The Election on Campus

To Sebastian, Hilltop's reaction to the election is ironic, even hypocritical. The election, he explains, "show[ed] us how separated we are from the rest of the country—thinking there is no way someone like Donald Trump can get anywhere and then 50 percent of the country is backing him. It is like, 'Oh, we really are not as progressive as we thought we were.'"

In the spring of 2017, Sebastian seems a little edgier than usual. We talk about the election for a while. First, he clarifies his vote: "I didn't vote for Trump; I am by no means a fan of him at all. I think he is an idiot and a boob." But he confesses, "I got a sick enjoyment of waking up the next day, wandering outdoors, and just seeing everyone so upset. It was tangible. There was an energy: it was so upsetting and just beaten down and gray. It was so bad. Everyone had their heads down. It was like, 'Oh, get off your high horse.'"

I ask him why he thinks Hilltop isn't progressive. On campus, he explains, "people have strong opinions," which he likes: "Take a stance on something, understand it, and then formulate because that is how you be a person." What he doesn't like, though, is "when you have one opinion and it is constantly being reinforced. . . . You get this pretentiousness. It is the sense that my opinion is more valuable than anyone else's. . . . We have this opinion that we are so progressive and we are so far ahead, that we are great, as long as you shut out half the country." So when Sebastian tells me that Hilltop isn't progressive, he's not referring to progressive politics; instead, he's saying something about dogmatism. At Hilltop, people stand for "freedom for all and equal rights for all—as long as you agree with me." Hilltop isn't just liberal; it's also, he feels, a little narrow-minded.

It's hard to pin down Sebastian's personal politics: he entered Hilltop planning to join the Republican club; his junior year, he tells me he's "pretty middle ground . . . maybe a little more left-wing"; and by graduation, he calls himself a Democrat. What's clearer is what he opposes—campus groupthink—and why: he finds it "pretentious" and exclusive. And even though he begins to identify as a liberal himself, it also becomes clearer that he feels like he's among those excluded, at least sometimes. While he says that he is usually "completely at home and very happy and comfortable" on campus, he describes times, mostly during his first year or two, that he felt "completely rejected by Hilltop." When I ask him how well he fits in on campus, he points out: "I am not a rich perfect kid that can pay my tuition, and I'm not an outspoken liberal, so it is tough." For him, class and politics are inseparable—and he has neither his classmates' wealth nor their liberal ideologies.

His parents don't either. They are "right wing"—Sebastian thinks they voted for Trump—and they're definitely among the "half the country" that Hilltop would "shut out." They struggled from welfare to working class: they "grew up pretty poor," Sebastian explains, and "got their jobs for us," for him and his sister. And although Sebastian rarely talks about it, they're also a mixed-race family from rural "Boringtown," USA—and I wonder how that matters, too.

Regardless, he does know this: that Hilltop "is a whole new realm for my family"—a realm of wealth and liberal politics and, they all hope, opportunity.

The 2016 presidential election emphasizes an uncomfortable reality: that belonging at Hilltop is conditional. The students' politics vary, from leaning right (Henry) to far left (Ethan), and so do the election's impacts. A few regard Trump's election as an interesting-but-faraway event, but for others, it is both consequential and personal, dividing families and threatening safety. But one reaction is shared: the election shows them that Hilltop, a place that advertises its openness, can in fact be pretty intolerant.

Even before the election, the students noted Hilltop's liberal lean. Colleges are liberal places, they explained to me—some even assumed that the "liberal" in "liberal arts" was a comment on campus politics, not a description of college curriculum—and, when they had searched for colleges, they read that Hilltop, in particular, was "incredibly liberal." Once they arrived, they agreed. They aren't surprised, then, when Trump's win is greeted with sadness and anger. The students describe the campus mood much as Sebastian does: "upsetting and just beaten down and gray." Classmates cry. Some faculty cancel classes; others suspend lessons to process the election and its results. In the following weeks, Hilltop students and faculty organize on-campus protests and join in local and national events.

Whatever their personal political beliefs, most of the students find the campus's apparent lack of political diversity problematic. They all recognize that there are at least a few conservatives on campus, but they are "marginalized," which, Liliana explains, creates a "one-sided discourse." "People just flock to people that they agree with," Sebastian reports. "You are constantly telling each other, 'You are right,' which villainizes the other side." All the agreement makes for lazy thinking: "strong opinions," Daniel says, without a lot of substance. It also means that students don't learn how to disagree. "College is supposed to be a time of enlightenment and openness to all sorts of different ideas," Henry notes, "but the thing about Hilltop and possibly liberal arts generally is that, unless you agree, you are kind of shut out." This kind of political silencing just gets worse after the election. Daniel reports: "If you say something that doesn't have the right politics, people are definitely going to jump on you pretty quick about it." It's not a problem for him—"I'm not usually the person saying something like that"—and Ethan appreciates the silencing: "Hilltop is a place where I think it is a good thing that people that support Trump . . . aren't encouraged to speak." But it keeps others, like Henry, quiet: "I almost feel like I have to walk on eggshells," he says.

No matter their own politics, most of the students also note the irony that Sebastian points out: Hilltop is not as open-minded as it's made out to be. Conservative viewpoints largely go unexpressed, and liberal ideologies often go unquestioned. A certain political elitism—a rich-kid, liberal "pretentiousness"—exists on campus. And so the election makes something clear for the students: not everyone belongs at Hilltop.

The "Rural Vote"

Henry's description of election night is much like the other students': "We were all in the common room . . . , and nobody was rooting for Trump. . . . We started to watch the polls come in and swing in his favor, and people were having fits. . . . Waking up the next day, clearly there were many upset feelings about it. That day was honestly like somebody had died." The entire reaction mystified him, and it still does. "I understand that this election carried certain implications," he explains, "and people certainly have their reasons to worry about the outcome, but in my opinion, we have had [many] elections and we are still here and everything is still fine. It is probably not going to be that bad." Henry is careful to tell me that he "voted on everything except president"; he is a registered independent who "lean[s] conservative," with some "liberal ideas that hardcore conservatives wouldn't agree with." But on campus, he typically keeps his politics "secret": "Conservatives are often the butt of everybody's jokes at Hilltop, and . . . I don't let people onto that, that I don't always agree as much as everybody here does."

While Henry generally—if covertly—finds himself right of campus, he's often left of home, especially his father. His dad, he explains, "is very opinionated and . . . has become more conservative in recent years." It's become "hard" to talk to him about politics. He gives the example of Trump rolling back net-neutrality policies. "My dad thought it was great because it was an Obama thing . . . [but] I'm like, 'What are you, nuts?'" The strength of his dad's opinions actually reminds Henry a little of Hilltop: "a refusal to compromise and to see an issue in the middle."

Henry shares one more memory of the day after the election. He went to his psychology class, which started with "almost a moment of silence." Then the professor began talking. She "was flabbergasted at how [Trump] could have been elected and just couldn't understand what happened, why there's such disconnect between academic—I think was the word that she used—and rural areas." How did academia let this happen? she wanted to know. The presumptuousness of this irritates Henry: "What do you mean 'academia let this happen'? Sure, people make uneducated decisions pretty frequently. But is that academia's job? I'm not really sure. I feel like it's your own job to educate yourself." He does agree with her on one count, though: "100 percent right that there is a disconnect there, that academia . . . kind of forgets the rural area." But he's not surprised: "If you think of a typical Hilltop student or maybe even a faculty member . . . they don't really know what it is like to be from a rural area because that is not where they came from."

During his first year, Henry worried about changing: his mother had told him that college was like the army and he'd come back different, and a hometown friend suspected his priorities had shifted. But by sophomore year, Henry seems more self-assured. Hilltop hasn't changed him; after graduation, he still wants to "live on a mountain with tons of land and forest." "I don't feel like I'm assuming the iden- tity of the majority," he tells me. He keeps that quiet, though—and maybe that's just the price for being a rural kid at an elite school.

After the 2016 election, a narrative emerges: rural America elected Trump.[1] The students now have something to say about rurality— and sometimes a lot. They, too, talk about rural voters. Some tell me about their families' enthusiasm for Trump, while others describe their parents as rural Clinton-voting outliers, and they all mention the Trump signs they pass as they drive home. They typically characterize "rural voters" with the same generalities heard in the media—White, uneducated, racist, and Trump-supporting—even though their families and neighbors don't match many of these stereotypes.[2]

The students seem unsure of what to make of this rural election narrative, its assumptions, and its effects. Mostly, they seem to agree that rural voters played a role in getting Trump elected—they saw the Trump yard signs, the Trump bumper stickers, the Trump billboards back home, and a few of them, like Henry, know their parents voted for Trump. Some feel that the rest of the narrative—about Whiteness and racism and a lack of education—is accurate, too, at least part of it. Sylvan, for example, explains: "The whole national narrative about rural America being uneducated and bigoted and racist, I saw a little bit of that in some of the people I grew up with." Henry tells me about the kid he graduated with who had "two Confederate flags off the back of his Chevy pickup truck." And John says, "I think in a lot of ways that people are right when they talk about rural America being a little ignorant to the rest of the country." The White students, I know, haven't thought much about racism, at least as it relates to their hometowns; this new narrative forces them to see what they hadn't seen before.

But as we talk more, they sometimes offer some qualifications. Bigotry is not a rural trait, specifically: plenty of rural people are tolerant and open-minded, and John thinks "it's wrong to put them in a box." And people confuse the mostly White demographics of many rural places with racism, Henry explains, thinking "because we're racially homogeneous, then we must be racist." They also note that the reasons for Trump's support in rural America are misunderstood, arguing that issues like gun rights, not racism, motivated voters. Henry and Ethan are the most directly critical of the election narrative. Henry doesn't like its arrogance—and the arrogance of those telling it—while Ethan questions rural voters' supposed impact: "If only poor rural people voted [for Trump] in this election, Donald Trump would not have won. People, do you know how to do math? There is just not enough people there to make him win. The Greenwich, Connecticuts, of the world got him the votes that he needed." The students, then, seem to both participate in and reject what Ethan calls the "scapegoating" of rural voters.

Not only are students unsure of what to make of this narrative; they also seem to struggle with whether they can, or should, locate themselves within it. Sometimes, they distance themselves and their families from it. Some tell me about their Clinton-supporting relatives or note, as John does, that, while "my parents live in the boonies . . . their mindsets aren't inclined that way." Others, like Amelia, separate themselves from hometown friends: "They're all Trump supporters; I have a hard time relating to any of them anymore." And Henry just keeps to himself.

They're also cautious about the "rural" label. Identifying as "rural," once irrelevant, has become fraught. Sylvan tells me, "People being more open about hate-filled opinions has made it hard to be like, 'Oh, no. The way that you paint rural America is completely wrong.'" If you claim your rural roots at Hilltop, are you also outing your racist beliefs or uneducated parents or vote for Trump? The students, already hesitant to publicly identify as rural, seem even more guarded, suspecting that rurality, specifically, doesn't belong at Hilltop.

Far from Home

The 2016 election also highlights a growing distance: the distance between home and Hilltop. For many students underrepresented on college campuses, home and college seem like entirely separate worlds.[3] These worlds operate according to different norms, values, and assumptions—a separation that can be particularly acute for students attending elite schools.[4] These rural students feel that divide, too, and some of them grow more judgmental of home.

John had a good summer. He's just beginning his junior year, and with his usual understated enthusiasm, he's catching me up. He lived at home and worked his familiar job at a nearby Mexican restaurant— "pretty fun as always"—and he lifted weights and ran to stay in shape for football. But a "cool event" happened, too: "My whole family went to Disney World, which was fun. My girlfriend that I have been dating since eighth grade—I proposed to her at Disney. It was a pretty awesome summer." They won't get married until after graduation, but he explains, "I just know what I want, and I didn't feel the need to wait."

Admittedly, I'm a little surprised to hear his news—in general, undergraduates aren't a very committed lot. I ask how it feels to be back on campus, among people for whom marriage is a very, very distant prospect. He acknowledges: "It is just so different from my friends. A lot of them don't have girlfriends. But . . . I kind of took my own road with everything and thought it was the right thing to do." Maybe I shouldn't be surprised; John has never been too beholden to the standards of Hilltop or, for that matter, the expectations of his hometown. These two worlds—Hilltop and home—are markedly different from one another. The political differences are obvious. He explains, "When I take the drive home"—just thirty minutes—"I will see people who have made their own personal billboards of Trump. . . . During the election, you would be made fun of for being a Clinton fan. But here [at Hilltop], it is the complete opposite." His hometown friends' postsecondary paths are different from his, too. His best friend joined the military and deployed to Iraq; several other friends didn't go to college. Classmates who did mostly attend state schools or trade schools, like his girlfriend, or they're enrolled at a local, nonselective private college, which, his mother explains, "is like Greenville High School all over again." He sees class differences, too, between the "wealthier, middle to high class" students at Hilltop and his "blue-collar, working-class" high school classmates. And at Hilltop, he points out, "all of my friends are from Boston, one from Florida. They've never experienced rural America."

I ask him about this, if he feels like he lives in two separate worlds. He does. "I almost feel different in each world, you know what I mean?" He continues, "There's very different people at Hilltop than at home, just different goals and aspirations and everything." Mostly, he's comfortable with this. Yes, he misses his fiancée when he's at Hilltop, and when he's at home, he can't attend campus events. But, he says, "I'm able to appreciate both sides."

For John, Hilltop is a "whole different way of life." The others tell me this, too: Hilltop and home are "completely separate." The election made apparent the political divides—divides that separate the students from their hometowns and, sometimes, from their families. But the students are also learning that there's a geography to the distance separating home from Hilltop, one measured not so much in miles— although, for Hunter and Liliana, the mileage is considerable—but instead, in whatever complicated and contested space exists between rural and urban America.

This space is not just political: there are also "very different people" with "different goals and aspirations and everything." At home, few people have bachelor's degrees. The students' parents don't, and most of their hometown friends won't either. They work—or they're preparing to work—rural blue-collar jobs, mostly in trades or service. But the people at Hilltop are different: they're college students and graduates, academics, future urban white-collar workers, and these students are, too. As Amelia's parents put it: "She's different than us. Her work ethic is—ours is physical, and hers is mental." These students wanted something different, and for the most part, their parents wanted them to have something different. So they chose Hilltop—to use their heads, not their hands.

Although they knew they were embarking down their "own road" when they applied, they do sometimes wonder what they're missing. There's a surrealness to Hilltop; it can feel, according to Henry, like "neutral between high school and life." At Hilltop, students learn things that can feel a little "superfluous"—"esoteric" theories and the academy's "exclusionary" language—and, Daniel suspects, they might leave with less "concrete knowledge" than they had when they arrived. They watch their classmates "form these really, really strong opinions, just to connect with other people, when there isn't really much other basis for it." They sit through classroom discussions that can seem "condescending," making Sebastian want to respond, "Look, we are twenty, and we are entitled to nothing, and we have done nothing, so let's just relax for now." At home, where "street smarts" matter more than "book smarts" and the work is more "physical" than "mental," things sometimes feel more "real."

But this unreality is also what attracted them to Hilltop. They came for its unbelievable abundance of resources: its rigorous courses and beautiful campus and good reputation. They came, Ethan's mother knows, for the "opportunity and awesome life experiences that he is not going to get here." They came for that distance.

Distance and Judgment

Throughout their years at Hilltop, the students stay remarkably attached to their families and homes—as do many underrepresented students.[5] They continue to call, to text, to Skype. Those who live nearby still return regularly, sometimes to work jobs and other times just to visit. They keep turning to their parents for guidance, too, especially for "emotional stuff" or "life advice." Still, as they spend more time at college, home begins to feel a little more distant—and for some of them, more complicated.

Like John, Amelia spends a lot of time at home. During her first year, home was an "escape," a place to go when the drinking and the stress and the general "grossness" of Hilltop became too much. She remains close to her parents throughout her college years, with routine calls and regular weekend visits. She's close to her extended family, too, running a local race with her aunt and frequently stopping in to see her grandmother. She makes this trip—from Hilltop to home, from home to Hilltop—often and, it seems to me, naturally. So I ask her about these worlds, whether they feel similar or different.

"Completely separate," she answers. As evidence, she explains that her best friend from home has never visited her at Hilltop: "I don't think she would like it here." Her friend "was not a Hillary supporter" and didn't vote in the election, Amelia says, and "she's pretty ignorant in the things she says." Amelia is beginning to realize how "sheltered" her hometown is. She continues, "Everyone was pretty much White Catholics . . . [and] some people from my high school definitely were kind of White supremacists, even though they wouldn't say it like that. . . . It was honestly kind of a close-minded place." She loves her hometown—it "will always be like a little piece of heaven" to her—but she describes coming from there as "a disadvantage": she's had a lot of learning to do at Hilltop.

But while John stays closely tied to home, Amelia finds herself growing distant—still close to family but drawing some boundaries. By her senior year at Hilltop, she says, "I've definitely distanced myself a lot from a lot of the people I used to spend time with in high school." When she goes home, "a lot of them are stuck right in the same place, and they don't talk about their majors and stuff." I ask what she means by "stuck," and she explains, "They are going to live in our hometown for the rest of their lives, and I just think, 'How many times can you do the same thing and not want more?'"

It's also about staying in the same "emotional place": "They're dating the same people, and they have no desire to see the world." She finishes, "Everyone tries to ignore that anything has changed, and I can't ignore these last four years." She's different now, and she just can't relate to them anymore.

She sees differences emerging with her parents, too. Often, these are political differences "about stuff they don't view the same or just aren't educated in a particular subject." But it's also about priorities, goals, talents. Her parents see her as "a thinker." "She is more book smart than she is technically," her mom explains. "She is kind of a geek. I mean, how many people read the *New York Times* at twenty-two?" Actually, many Hilltop students do, but they don't know that; what they do know is that "she could go a lot of places." Her mother is clear: "She is not going to be a physical worker, not like [her father] and I."

Over the years, I watch Amelia struggle with this: what it means to be "a thinker" from a family of "physical workers," what it means to be "a rural kid" from a place that feels a "little close-minded." At Hilltop, she's a premed psychology major: she's carved out as preprofessional a path as possible while studying a subject that fascinates her. She's done a lot of learning—learning, too, that her home is "a disadvantage."

And so, she finds that it's just easier if she doesn't invite her best friend to campus.

This distance between the students and their parents began emerging during their first years, as the students discovered that their parents couldn't fully understand their Hilltop lives. They start to learn what they can turn to their parents for and what they can't, and as their college years stretch on, that second list—what advice their parents can't give, what they don't understand—is getting longer. Academics become harder to discuss: their parents just don't know how to register for courses or write a thesis, and they're not reading the books or watching the movies or hearing the lectures their children are. Their parents recognize this and mostly leave their children to figure things out. They do continue to worry about careers: some of them fear that their children's majors offer little practical relevance or employable skills, others want more specificity in their children's career plans, and they all worry that any delay in employment or graduate school might result in "getting stuck" at home. The students share these concerns, but they're also hearing a vastly different message at Hilltop, where meandering career paths are the norm. And so they just don't talk to their parents about classes or careers much anymore.

Politics, especially around the election, is another area of silence or, for some families, argument. The students' families are politically diverse, but on the whole, the students are "left" of their parents— even those, like Henry or Sebastian, who find themselves "right" of Hilltop. For these politically split families, politics become a point of contention. Some families argue about candidates, usually Trump, and others argue about issues, like gun rights or campus politics. For many of the families, these are new disagreements. "She is learning all of her own stuff," Amelia's father explains. He recounts one recent argument: "When she came home from college, she was like, 'If you vote for Trump . . .' I'm like, 'Honey, I'm a gun owner, and that stuff is important to me. The Democrats are not supporting that.' 'Well, I just can't stand him.' I'm like, 'OK, so we can have a difference of opinion on politics.'" This kind of "difference of opinion" isn't surprising: like many college students, the students are learning how to think for themselves. But the election seems to add a sharpness to this independence, and for a few families, the disagreements grow "very heated." "Our neighbors must really love us," Ethan's mother confesses, "because we get going and it is instant." Other families just agree to disagree—and stop talking. Either way, these political divides are difficult.

The students, I notice, aren't trying to bridge these divides between home and college, between home and them. They learn which topics to avoid with their parents. They resign themselves to political differences. And they rarely invite home friends to Hilltop or Hilltop friends home; "I don't think his friends knew that he had parents," says Daniel's mother. Sometimes, it's as if the students want some distance between home and Hilltop.

The students are also growing more critical of home. These critiques are less about their parents: aside from the occasional comment on a specific political issue, they mostly avoid evaluations of their parents, their views, or their choices. Instead, it's their hometowns that get the brunt of their critique. In part, this is political: they just don't agree with their neighbors on some issues anymore. But they also seem to see and hear things differently now: they tell me about the racism and sexism they've witnessed back home—the jokes, Sylvan says, that he now knows are "not OK." And although most of them once had little to say about the Whiteness of their hometowns, they have come to describe it as a limitation. People there are "sheltered," they report: "They don't really understand what people go through, especially in terms of racial inequality and things like that," John says. I also hear more about some of the other issues in their hometowns: drugs, teen pregnancy, suicide. And even their once-defended hometown high schools are seen by most as "rinky-dink."

It's as if, after a few short years at Hilltop, the students have come to see their hometowns in a new way. Home is still beautiful, still a place of refuge and love, still "a little piece of heaven," but they now talk about their hometowns differently, using words like *uneducated* and *sheltered* and *ignorant*. As Hunter says, "I realize that some of the people back home are a little bit backwards."

Part of this shift is due, no doubt, to being in a (somewhat) more diverse environment, a place where, for the most part, overt racism is not tolerated. They're forced to reevaluate the norms, assumptions, and conditions of home—the backdrop of their younger lives. But I also notice that their critiques often parallel the narratives about rural places permeating the media—and Hilltop—after the election: that rural America is bigoted and backward. I wonder about some of the words they use—*backward*, especially, which conveys a paternalistic kind of contempt that I'm not sure the students understand. And I wonder why the students now feel licensed to make these kinds of judgments and if it has something to do with Hilltop. As Sebastian tells me, "I kind of look down a little on people now. . . . My initial reaction is that I went to Hilltop, I went to a private institution, I know what I'm talking about."

Maybe, then, they know exactly what *backward* means.

Outsiders

These nine students came to Hilltop for its abundant resources—for the "opportunity and awesome life experiences" not available back home. And they take advantage of these opportunities, developing who they are and what they want to do. But as the election made clear, not everyone belongs at Hilltop. "Access," the sociologist Anthony Abraham Jack writes, "is not inclusion," and increasingly, it seems like they're among those excluded, even though they don't always see these boundaries or their effects.[6]

Access...

There's no denying the extensiveness of Hilltop's resources. Most classes are small and intimate, led by professors who, as Hilltop's website boasts, are at the "top" of their fields. Labs are outfitted with state-of-the-art equipment. A ceramics studio occupies the basement of the arts building, and an observatory sits atop the science center. The college's career center helps students write résumés, and it uses the Hilltop name and its extensive alumni network to connect them with jobs across the globe. The school recently built several new dorms with spacious rooms, large flat-screen TVs, and comfortable couches. The indoor ice arena converts to turf in the fall and spring. A new boathouse sits on a river several miles from campus. Students can go rock climbing using equipment borrowed from one of the hundred student clubs, or they can pitch an idea to the Ventures club for the chance to win ten thousand dollars. Weekends are filled with college-sponsored parties, dances, and concerts. This is a school, their parents note, "with options."

And the students enjoy these options: they join clubs, compete on teams, perform on stage, write papers, hang out with friends, meet faculty, stay up late, take interesting classes, and participate in campus traditions. Most continue with the activities and extra-curriculars they began their first year; by senior year, John is a foot-ball captain, Amelia manages budgets for the student government, and Sebastian's band is headlining campus shows. Hunter quits the swim team but joins the power-lifting club. Daniel spends some time on the rugby team. They grow more accustomed to Hilltop's party scene: by sophomore year, they all drink, though the extent varies, some use drugs recreationally, and their weekend social cal-endars are full.

But like many working-class and first-generation students, they're not at Hilltop for its ice rink or rock-climbing equipment; they need a career.[7] So they enter their second year "more focused," settling into majors, tying them to careers, making their studies "practical." And they use Hilltop's vast resources to do this, too.

Like all art majors, Hunter has a studio space in the basement of the art building. His is filled with a table, a sketch pad on an easel, and a variety of pens and Sharpie markers, some as fat as rolling pins. His drawings hang on the walls, and tonight—an open-studio night for junior art majors—he's working on a large one covering the table. They are striking: detailed half-animal, half-human forms rendered in stark black lines with a few swaths of color. His work is inspired by comics, although, as he explains, "I'm bringing more of a gothic kind of look and not quite as bright colors as you would usually see." He's also experimenting with imagery of violence and innocence; in one, a horned, muscle-bound character holds a small blue teddy bear. Between his drawings, he has tacked magazine photographs of humans and tigers and spiders, both for inspiration and for reference.

The open-studio night marks the end of his junior year, a year with a lot of change and growth for Hunter. It was the first time—since he was little—that he didn't swim competitively; instead, he joined the weight-lifting club and took saxophone lessons. During the fall, supported by financial aid, he studied abroad in Prague, taking classes in psychology, film, and European architecture. He also made a big decision: he decided to become a graphic novelist.

Unlike the other students, Hunter entered Hilltop without any ideas about a career he might pursue. During our first interview, he explained to me, "I know that having a college education will definitely help me in almost any career path that I choose, but I truthfully don't really have a career path in mind right now." Through coursework and extracurriculars, though, he began to find that path. His interest in people and personality led him to take some psychology classes, and by the end of his first year, he was planning on a psychology major, but he told me, "I have always liked drawing comics, so I might try to find a little bit of a side thing in that." In his sophomore year, he enrolls in more art courses and then adds a studio art major. And junior year, as he sits in his psychology classes, he begins to have some "doubts," realizing "I don't want to spend my entire life just doing this." Drawing, though, is different: "It never got stale to me." "This," he starts to understand, "is probably what I should be doing." So he drops his psychology major, decides to focus on studio art, gets a studio, and begins writing a graphic novel.

He's realistic: he knows he'll need an income as he works on his novel. Through Hilltop, he secures a summer internship as an assistant curator in a California art gallery, and he loves it. Now he's planning a life as a graphic novelist and a job as a curator. His parents support his plans. "They wanted me . . . to find what I really want," he says, and he did. His father, who's "more type A" about financial stability, "is nervous," his mother admits, but she's not—she's thrilled. And whether nervous or thrilled, both of them are beginning to see him as an artist.

And so is he. "I came into college looking to get a psychology degree," he explains. "At the time, I didn't really find it viable to do art for myself." But Hilltop changed that.

The students use many of Hilltop's resources well. They find opportunities that are useful, applied, practical—like Hunter's open-studio night, his study abroad, and his summer internship. Sylvan, Amelia, and Liliana get EMT-certified through a class run by the local ambulance dispatch service. Ethan practices public speaking DJing for the campus radio station. Sebastian learns how to book gigs through a cappella and his band. Liliana and Amelia, like Hunter, find a summer job through Hilltop's extensive internship program, which advertises unpaid internships, helps students apply for them, and then, if they secure the internships, provides the students with funding. For the students, these experiences are profound, connecting academics to career, developing their personal and professional identities, changing their futures. These experiences open doors.

But some of Hilltop's opportunities are out of reach.

. . . with Limits

Sylvan's face is fuzzy on my computer screen, and he's whispering: there's a five-year-old asleep in the next room. Spending his junior fall in Rome, Sylvan is living with an Italian family. It's after 11:00 p.m. his time, and he's just returned from watching the movie *It* in Italian with two of his tutors, so we don't talk long. But even with the muffled, hurried blurriness, this much is clear: Sylvan loves being in Rome, loves learning Italian, loves studying abroad.

Sylvan is picking up the language quickly. He's enrolled in several Italian classes, a language he's always wanted to learn. He can't travel as much as the other students in his program—"they are literally made of money"—but that's OK: he's one of the few doing a homestay, which gives him lots of time to practice his Italian. "I'm focusing on immersing myself," he says, and he uses every opportunity he can to speak the language, talking to his host family and his tutors and "just random people on the streets." And he's "doing really, really well," telling me, "I get complimented a lot." He's surprised by how quickly he's adapted to living in Rome: "Honestly, I thought that the hardest part would be transitioning to a city because I had never been on a public bus before and never been on a tram before. . . . [But] it just seemed to click really easily." He's proud of himself, and he shares, "the last couple of months have felt really big for me."

Sylvan went to Rome "for a fun break from science," one that would help him finish his Latin minor. But instead, this experience has led to "an existential crisis . . . about the whole premed thing." As he explains, "I'm worried that the two things that I have been most passionate about the past few years have been science and language, and right now all I'm doing is language, and I am loving it." It's not just Rome, though. His questioning, he admits, is probably also tied to a recent rejection from a prestigious program that fast-tracks premed undergraduates into medical school. It offered early acceptance, substantial financial aid, and clinical support, and the rejection stung. So here he is: "I am still enamored with the idea of being a doctor . . . but I don't know if I can see myself doing it or if I really want to do it." Although he doesn't need to figure out his entire career on this particular October night, he does need to register for winter classes tomorrow, which will require some decisions about premed requirements. "I'm terrified," he admits.

I stop interviewing and start advising. I tell him that now is probably the right time for this "crisis": college—not medical school—is meant for questioning assumptions and exploring passions. Try to set aside the rejection. Part of the hurt is its unfamiliarity—he hasn't failed at much. Class schedules can be changed, and medicine and language aren't necessarily mutually exclusive careers. For now, just enjoy Rome.

Sylvan ends up not completing his premed requirements. For a while, I attribute this simply to a new experience forcing a reconsideration of old plans. It's only later that I see the other factors that shape his decision. Sylvan knew that he would have a hard time fitting in all the requirements while at Hilltop, and so he considered taking one or two of them during the summer, like many premed students do. But the costs were prohibitive—nearly $10,000 when factoring in room and board. And he was rejected from that fast-track medical school program not because he wasn't academically competitive but because he didn't have enough applied experience—experience that comes from job shadows or other unpaid volunteer work, experience that's hard to get if you don't live in a place with a lot of hospitals or if you have to spend your time making money. So Sylvan doesn't finish his premed requirements, and he no longer plans to go to med school. And this may be the right choice. But it's also hard to call it a choice, exactly, because so many other factors matter, too.

Sylvan is certainly aware of his family's financial position and can always quickly tally the checks coming in and the expenses piling up. He works throughout his time at Hilltop, retail or service jobs on campus during the week and bartending at home many weekends. Aside from one summer as a lab assistant, he prioritizes high-pay summertime work, like waiting tables at a restaurant near home, over poorly-paid-but-important internships or résumé-boosting volunteering. He's careful to buy his books used, and his financial realities also shape his social plans: he avoids expensive Hilltop Outing Club trips and pricey off-campus dinners. He's also beginning to notice how his wealthy classmates gravitate toward one another, because they can afford "the spring break trip to a resort in Florida" or "a trip to Mexico." "I don't think Hilltop is institutionally segregating people by class," he's careful to note, "but at an institution where there are people with such different classes, it just kind of happens."

Some people just have more options—more choice—than others.

Like Sylvan, the students work hard to capitalize on every opportunity, but oftentimes, their "Hilltop experience" isn't the same as their classmates'. These missed opportunities started early. Most of them struggled academically in their first years, and they're now beginning to understand that it wasn't because they procrastinated or studied the wrong material or hate math. They weren't prepared— and their prep school classmates were. Classroom discussions were hard for John, for example, because "in my high school we were never encouraged to talk." But, he says, "a lot of my friends that went to prep schools, they were really encouraged in participation." Ethan, too, notes: "My high school didn't teach me to write well." He continues: "I realize now why private schools are called prep schools. . . . I think they learn liberal arts college-style writing sooner than I did. . . . It probably took me all of freshman year to get the hang of it." The students do "get the hang of it," but they missed out during that first year—on skills, on learning, on confidence—as they struggled to catch up. And the stress sticks around.[8]

Other barriers relate to the hidden costs of college.[9] These costs, not covered by tuition, aren't required, but they're necessary for full participation at Hilltop—and the students are learning that they can't afford them. One is the pricey summer course that would have allowed Sylvan to finish his premed requirements; unable to pay for the course, he can't complete the requirements and enter medical school. Studying abroad is another hidden cost. Five of the students—Sylvan, Amelia, Daniel, Hunter, and Liliana—enroll in international study programs, most of them using financial aid to cover the costs, and even though they can't afford the extra travel their wealthier peers can, the programs are among their most impactful college experiences. While John and Sebastian aren't interested in studying abroad, Ethan and Henry are, but with their particular aid packages and their families' limited resources, they can't. Textbooks are also an expense, and at the beginning of the semester, a few of the students, like Sylvan, will go weeks without books, waiting for their delivery from a used-book seller. To help cover books and spending money, most of the students have jobs—waiting tables, stocking books at the campus bookstore, working the front desk at the science building—but these keep them from studying or hanging out with friends.

Like other first-generation college students, the students also often can't access Hilltop's faculty.[10] Most of them don't attend faculty office hours. They're not sure *how* to go to office hours—several ask me what to do—or why they'd even want to go. It just feels "superficial," Daniel explains; good grades should be tied to performance, not relationships. Sylvan tries once: "I went there, didn't have a specific question, and [the professor] said, 'If you don't have a specific question, get out of my office.' I never went to office hours again." So most of them, even those in smaller majors with smaller classes, don't develop relationships with faculty; Henry, Hunter, and Daniel can't tell me a single professor they're close to. And more generally, they're not likely to ask for help or seek guidance, even from other college staff. "He's not a reacher-outer," as Daniel's mother puts it, and "I don't think he really had a heck of a lot of advice." The students may not know what they're missing—and what their more-connected prep school classmates are enjoying[11]—but their parents worry: about their children's choices of majors, about their job prospects, about what happens when that first loan payment comes due. Without these relationships, the students have little help picking classes or tying academics to careers, and later, they won't have the strong networks and letters of recommendation they'll need to start those careers.

And despite all their work to make their studies "useful," they still miss out on some important experiences and connections. The need to work sometimes prevents students from getting the kind of training that's attractive to graduate schools and employers. Ethan, for example, turns down a summer research assistantship for a more lucrative job painting dorm rooms at a university near home, and Daniel spends his final summer digging ditches—and making good money—instead of securing a business-related internship. These choices can have long-term consequences, like Sylvan's rejection from the medical school program or, after graduation, students' difficulty finding work. Although a few of the students access jobs through Hilltop's internship program, the others don't; "I really don't know a lot about the program," Henry tells me. Most of their limited experiences are arranged through their families, like Amelia shadowing a local dentist and Henry installing internet for a company owned by a friend of his stepfather. These are good experiences, but they aren't the connections—"the gateways into the world"—they came to Hilltop to find.

These hidden costs and missed opportunities aren't just academic: the students also sometimes find themselves on the margins of Hilltop's social life. "Hilltop," Ethan notes, "is a place that to do well outside of the classroom you have to have a lot of money." They can't afford the alcohol, the concert tickets, or the "five-thousand-dollar spring break trip"—and those are the experiences that define the social scene. Their wealthy classmates share a certain "lifestyle," and these students don't, so sometimes they're "bored-sad." It may not be intentional, as Sylvan points out, but the campus is segregated, separated by the ability to pay.[12]

I ask the students about these exclusions—why they exist and what they mean for them. Their classmates are "rich kids from wealthy families," they tell me; "everybody, even some of my friends I hadn't really thought about, [is] fucking loaded," Sylvan says. These classmates can afford the summertime classes and the trips to Mexico—and they can't. Their parents see this gap, too. "Pretty much all of Amelia's friends are rich," Amelia's mother tells me—"different opportunities." Several students quote a statistic to me: at Hilltop, 45 percent of students receive financial aid. In their first year, this number was a testament to Hilltop's generosity. Now, after more time at Hilltop, they see—and explain—this number differently. While they scramble to pull together loans and grants, more than half of students can afford to cover the full cost of tuition and fees. It's that 55 percent that enjoys access—*full* access—to a Hilltop education.

And so their doubt—the lingering suspicion that they don't fit in—has grown. In their first years, when they talked about their classmates' wealth, they mostly said it didn't matter; now, they think it does. Although they're still quick to assure me that they have friends and stay busy, they're also more likely to admit they sometimes feel "different," a difference made up of luxury bedsheets and Canada Goose jackets. And that difference is hard. "You can get really into your head wanting to impress people," Liliana says. Or they feel a little "jealous": how is it, Ethan wonders, that "I'm smarter than you and I work harder than you and you drive an Audi?" A few of the students are grateful. As Henry says, "A lot of my friends come from wealthier families. . . . Thanks to most of these kids, it is why I can go here without paying full tuition." But gratitude isn't uncomplicated, and it's not the same as feeling like you belong.

So they know there's a wealth gap, and they understand many of its effects. But some effects, I notice, they don't see. They don't understand their reluctance to attend office hours as related to affluence, for example, overlooking how their prep school peers have been taught to pursue relationships with faculty and leverage these connections for jobs and other opportunities. And although they talk about loneliness and stress, they don't connect those feelings to "the rat race," as Ethan puts it, of trying to belong at a campus community with considerable disposable income while worrying about a parent's lost job.

I also notice that it's almost always wealth to which they attribute any feelings of otherness—never place, never to being rural. This surprises me: after all, they know that their classmates and professors have "never experienced rural America." They're cautious about who they bring home or invite to campus, and they tell me about the occasional rural-specific slight, like being teased for the way they talk. And the election and its aftermath certainly showed them the "disconnect" between Hilltop and home, that rurality, specifically, doesn't belong at Hilltop. But I suspect that they're still making sense of what it means to be a "rural kid" at an elite school, especially at a time when rurality is so charged.

That rurality is also racialized—and that racialization is charged, too. Racially, the White students very much belong at Hilltop: their friends are mostly White, and the Whiteness of campus culture feels familiar. After White childhoods spent at White schools in White towns, though, they're just beginning to understand the advantages that Whiteness confers—for "White girl Amelia," Amelia tells me, "it was easy to assimilate socially." Sebastian, who's biracial but looks more like his White father than his Asian mother, mostly assimilates, too; race, he tells me, has "no relevance" to his life—although I know it's likely more complicated than that. Even with this apparent comfort, the students seem hesitant when talking about race, racism, and privilege. It's unfamiliar terrain, a conversation rarely had—or at least rarely had openly—back in their segregated rural hometowns.[13] I think they're scared of offending or hurting someone or, maybe, ashamed of their ignorance. Only Liliana, a proud Latina, talks easily—and often—about race and racism, and she remains disappointed with the lack of diversity at Hilltop. Even so, she also notes, "I feel more comfortable around White culture because of where I grew up and the school that I went to." Hilltop's Whiteness, then, may be disappointing, but it is familiar.

It's a tricky arithmetic for these rural students, balancing the ledger of advantage and disadvantage that comes with race and place and class. Wealth may just feel more comprehensible—and after the election, less fraught. And so while they might sometimes feel as if they don't belong, they can't always articulate why. They're also reluctant to hold Hilltop responsible. It's no one's fault; exclusion "just kind of happens."

Disenchanted

The students are, though, beginning to question Hilltop, albeit cautiously. Yes, they still want to belong, and so most of them still party—a few, more than they really want; several swallow their more conservative political views; and a couple of them dress differently. But they're experiencing a new kind of doubt. It's no longer just about choosing the right major, navigating the distance home, finding their place on campus—it's also about Hilltop. Maybe Hilltop doesn't set some sort of universally desirable standard. Maybe that standard isn't just unreachable but also flawed. Maybe belonging at Hilltop isn't everything.

Selectively Belonging

Daniel is sitting at a table in a small classroom in Rabat, Morocco. He's wearing a blue Hawaiian shirt, and occasionally a classmate—in a college sweatshirt or a brightly colored hijab—passes across my computer screen. Daniel is on the second of three study-abroad programs he'll complete while at Hilltop. This one is a semester long and filled with seminars on human rights and classes in Arabic; the other two are shorter, a few weeks at the end of the spring semester, one to Vietnam and the other to China. He went to Vietnam first. He'd always been interested in the country, and he was "just ready for a break from Hilltop." He chose the program in Morocco for similar reasons: "I felt like just to go to a very different culture would be important to change my perspectives." He signed up for the China trip while still abroad in Morocco, "anticipating coming back and being disenchanted," which, he later tells me, "was pretty much true."

Daniel enjoys learning about other places. When he was little, his mother would find him up late at night, reading a world atlas. Traveling was something "he always wanted to do," she says, and through studying abroad, he learned a lot: how to use a squat toilet, how to survive food poisoning, how to escape the locked bathroom of your tiny Moroccan apartment (for the last: call your mother, who will call your aunt, who will explain how to pick the lock). He knows that he "wouldn't have been too happy just staying at Hilltop." "I just felt the need to do something else," he says. "Those [abroad programs] are the best parts of my Hilltop experience."

The "need to do something else" drives Daniel. He joins the rugby team his sophomore year—new to the sport and without any real interest in it—to "be more involved" on campus. He sometimes goes to Hilltop's Hillel—as a non-Jew—because it's "pretty cool" and "they have good food." The summer before his senior year, he works a "hard labor" construction job—good pay but not something he wants to do again—and learns about immigration and politics from the mostly Mexican crew. Many of his experiences during college are like this: he gets an idea, thinks "I might as well just try it," and does. And he's grateful to Hilltop for these extracurricular and off-campus opportunities; aside from the construction job, which his father helped him get, all come through Hilltop. He explains, "If you are on financial aid like myself and your parents don't make that much money, Hilltop will throw you a lot of bones."

But it's not just the "need to do something else" that motivates Daniel. It seems he also wants to escape Hilltop. While he's happier than he was his first year, he's never found a real community at Hilltop. He doesn't like his economics major. He chose it, after abandoning psychology, with "a flawed mindset"—that it would support his interest in business—but, he says, "I'm not the best at it." He gets frustrated with the dogmatism of campus: "I feel like I've encountered some perspectives at Hilltop that are more judgmental or closed off than people who you wouldn't think [would be open-minded], like my friends back home, [which] is definitely a lot less diverse." And his mother shares, "Some of the kids really flaunted their money in the way they dressed and the way they spent," which is "hard" for Daniel. All this leads to a kind of pressure. "The culture of Hilltop pushes you to do certain things," he tells me. Like partying: "I partied a lot sophomore and junior year, and . . . I was like, 'Why did I do that?' I would have never done that outside of Hilltop, just because there is this weird pressure here to do a lot of different things that I'm not really into in the real world."

So, although he does occasionally succumb to the "pressure" of Hilltop, he also wants to escape it, to "do something else," to leave this "very insular environment." And he does: through extracurriculars, through work, through studying abroad. When he gets too "disenchanted," he just leaves.

Membership at Hilltop is not only something that's granted. It is also something that's chosen, and sometimes the students opt out. Daniel goes abroad—not just once, but three times. John enjoys weekends with his girlfriend—and then fiancée—off campus. Liliana finds a small group of friends who take academics seriously, and they plan low-cost weekends away, hiking and camping and exploring. Henry stays on campus but spends most of his time with his girlfriend, and his senior year, he works long hours for a marketing company. Sylvan, Sebastian, Amelia, Hunter, and Ethan participate more fully in the Hilltop culture, but even they occasionally choose not to: Sylvan spends many weekends back home with a new hometown girlfriend; Sebastian busks off campus for good money; Amelia regularly returns home to see her parents and "escape"; Hunter quits varsity athletics; and Ethan nearly withdraws. All the students remain close to family, search for "practical" jobs and experiences, grow skilled at code switching as they move between their different worlds.[14] And they enjoy, at least occasionally, questioning Hilltop norms: they challenge the groupthink, resist its political orthodoxy, catalog the moral failings of their wealthy classmates.

So while they use its resources and attend its parties, they often distance themselves from Hilltop: they "do something else." As Henry says, with some pride, "I don't feel like I'm assuming the identity of the majority." Their parents notice this independence, too. "He became his own person," Daniel's mother tells me. "He is challenging every thought, everything in the world, every person." And it's this distance that might sustain them—providing them with necessary supports, protecting them from rejection, helping them maintain a healthy skepticism.

The Hilltop Bubble

Liliana's parents always told her to "educate yourself so you can help others." "There is always going to be people who are less fortunate than you," her dad would say, and you should "try to help." By the end of her junior year, Liliana is planning to become an immigration lawyer.

She arrived at Hilltop wanting to be a doctor but abandoned the premed track her first year—telling me then that she "didn't really enjoy" the classes, recognizing in hindsight that she found it "elitist." She picks up a double major in politics and Spanish and goes abroad to Nepal, studying the impact of the 2015 earthquake on landless Nepalis. She learns that "the government of Nepal is not really doing anything for these people even though it is saying it is" and realizes that, as a lawyer, she "can help people access justice and equality." Her plans are also tied to her family's experiences as Mexican immigrants in a mostly White, very rural, overwhelmingly conservative state. After the election of Trump, with his racist rhetoric and hard-line immigration policies, the stakes feel higher, and she begins to work toward law school.

She's grateful for the opportunities Hilltop has provided, like funding to study abroad and an immigration policy internship with an advocacy group for Latino rights. Yet I can see her dissatisfaction with parts of Hilltop growing. From her first weeks on campus, Liliana has noticed the gap between Hilltop's rhetoric of diversity and its reality, and when working for the admissions office, she watches the gap widen: "It's definitely gotten Whiter, wealthier." And, she says, "We talk about race as Black or White. We exclude Asian populations, Native American populations, Hispanic populations." Her mostly White friends don't get it. Race is "a very touchy subject in our group. . . . It is a non-PC conversation, and then that gets heated, and everyone gets mad." There's also no political diversity on campus, and even though she considers herself liberal—or at least she did before coming to Hilltop—she leans conservative on a few issues, and sometimes, in the face of so much liberal opposition, she finds herself inching rightward. As "a rural kind of kid," she chafes at the "very negative" rural stereotypes she hears on campus: rural communities painted as uneducated, gun toting, and politically extreme. I suspect that Liliana sometimes feels that there isn't a space for her—a rural Latina with complex political perspectives—at Hilltop; she knows she doesn't fit in.

But something happens to Liliana while she's abroad: she stops caring. Maybe it was living in a remote Nepali village for a month, but she's become more sure of herself and her priorities. When we meet that spring after she returns, she tells me, "After abroad, I feel more comfortable at Hilltop, I think because my personal confidence has gone up, and I think that has enabled me to really enjoy Hilltop more." She abandons the need she had as a first-year to "impress people," stops worrying about her appearance and clothing, finds her "niche." She starts to "separate a little" from her "play hard" friends, knowing, she explains, that "I have a lot on my plate and different priorities."

As Liliana nears graduation, she begins to recognize that Hilltop is "very much a bubble"—a bubble that doesn't have to define her. As grateful as she is for Hilltop, she's ready to leave the bubble.

Everyone calls Hilltop a bubble, both students and faculty. Depending on its context, the term can be a compliment, a reference to the endless possibilities and opportunities of a Hilltop education, or a critique, a comment on the "unreality" of Hilltop. But as the students are finishing up their years at Hilltop, I hear them use the term only in its more critical capacity. To them, Hilltop is a political bubble—a club of unthinking liberals. It's a wealth bubble—a school for the 1 percenters. And it's an academic bubble—an ivory tower unfettered by practical concerns.

Bubble, then, is a reference to Hilltop's isolation but also to its elitism. Hilltop isn't open to everyone, and that exclusivity creates a social and political homogeneity—or, at least, the appearance and experience of uniformity—that fails to match the reality of the world beyond campus. It's an understated elitism, packaged in a "down to earth" cover, but it is still an elite school. This elitism was once a draw: they were chosen to attend Hilltop and enjoy its resources and promises, and few people are. But now they are beginning to understand the limitations of elitism, even Hilltop's more restrained variety—that it fuels a pressure to conform, that it creates a distance with their families and homes, that it makes for an unreality that may not prepare them for life after Hilltop.

And so as much as this bubble offers, it also disappoints. They're no longer sure what it means to "earn" entry into Hilltop or what, exactly, a Hilltop education promises them.

5

Leaving

NOWHERE TO GO

It was the Tin Man that sold Sebastian on musical theater. For much of college, Sebastian wrestled with what he wanted to do with his life. His first year, he struggled to find a major, and then, after settling on rhetoric, he wasn't sure how he'd use it. He considered broadcasting, film, possibly writing. But then, during the spring of his junior year, he played the Tin Man in *The Wizard of Oz*. After that, there was no going back. "I couldn't envision anything else," he explains. He loves it all—the singing, the acting, the energy, the attention.

He tells me this at the beginning of his senior year. He spent the summer at home, writing for a music website, busking in a nearby seaside town, and working on his voice. He also pondered his career options, and by the end, he had reached a decision: musical theater. He's ready "to live paycheck to paycheck in New York City."

This decision isn't too surprising. He's now performed in several musicals. His band regularly plays at weekend parties and local bars and even won a statewide talent competition, and his a cappella group has toured the country. He's taken classes on composition and performance and directing. He's writing his thesis on the movie *American Beauty* and how it "challenged the typical genre theory." There's no doubt that Sebastian loves music and theater.

But he also loves—and, he admits, "romanticizes"—New York City. New York is "just so different, and it is so happening. . . . I mean, it's New York, the greatest city in the world." The contrast between New York and his hometown couldn't be starker: "Everything in New York is so competitive and so fast moving and just dirty and very straight-forward. You hear about it all the time, people in New York having a certain attitude. . . . Coming from a place that is just so wholesome, folky, and 'nice New England' . . . New York is just this whole other beast. . . . I'm just so drawn to New York City." New York isn't whole-some and nice, and that's its appeal. It's also a complete reversal for him: when he entered Hilltop, it was his sister who was drawn to "the big city type of environment, that kind of meeting-people-every-day, this fast-moving kind of thing." "That's not really for me," he told me then. After Hilltop, though, it is.

Sebastian realizes the risks of this path. "I mean, it is the most competitive field in the world, doing entertainment," he tells me. "It is ridiculous how many people go and just completely fall flat on their face and have to go back home." He's also "broke," and after spend-ing some time looking at New York City rent, he knows he might need to find some other kind of work first; maybe he'll return to his job bagging groceries at home, save up, and then head to New York. And he's never lived in a city before—that will be new for him. His parents are worried about his plans, too. Although they "don't want to squash any kind of dream," his dad has warned him, "the odds are very slim; a lot of times it is who you know." With me, his dad is more candid: "I'm nervous for him. I have no idea where his life is going."

But Sebastian has to try. He admits, "It's terrifying saying I'm going to be an actor. . . . [But] I'm ready to go all in on this." He feels like he's been "teased a little bit" being at Hilltop, "getting to expe-rience that elite thing." He says, "It is like, 'If you want this life, now you have to come earn it.' That is probably why I'm being drawn to go to New York. I got a taste of what that could be like. . . . That is where I belong now." So that's where he's headed: to New York City, to that place where he belongs now.

The students' last year at Hilltop mirrors their first: filled with expec-tation and anxiety. After four years of Hilltop, though, the stakes feel higher because now it's time for the "real world." They have to make choices and reckon with their consequences. So for them, the transi-tion out of Hilltop is just as difficult as the transition in—or perhaps even more.

The students spend the year planning. Like Sebastian, they have high hopes—for new jobs and new schools and, especially, new places—but they must square these ambitions with real demands and real pressures and real uncertainties. They graduate proud but anxious, ready to leave the Hilltop bubble but nervous for what comes next. And what does come next is hard. A few months after graduation, the students are facing debt, bills, and loneliness; even now, they wonder where they want to be and how to get there. They're more critical of Hilltop, not entirely sure what their degree is worth, disappointed by its substantial costs—but still proud.

Planning Ahead

Senior year is at once immediate and aspirational, as students simultaneously wring out every last moment on campus and scramble to prepare for what comes after graduation. It's a year of preparation. The students remain engaged with coursework—which, at Hilltop, includes writing a thesis or completing a capstone project in their major—but they're also thinking to the years beyond. And as they wrestle with what they want to do and how they want to do it, they're also struggling with *where* they'll do it.

Whether to return home is a complicated question for many underrepresented students.[1] The social costs of four years away keep some from returning; for others, it's the cultural distance that's emerged between them and their families. For these rural students, though, there's another imperative: at home, there are few jobs for college graduates and limited opportunities for further education.[2] Since birth, they've been told to leave, told that "success" is found in urban places.[3]

So they can't go home. But, as they try to reconcile their career plans with the stark realities that will accompany graduation, they're finding it hard to go anywhere else either.

Postgraduation Goals and Aspirations

After years of preparing for a career, the students regard graduation as its start. Most begin the year with career plans: for Sebastian, it's musical theater; Henry wants to go into marketing; Ethan hopes to take a corporate job for a few years and then head to law school; John plans to practice law; Sylvan is thinking about a career in biotech, although he hasn't ruled out becoming a physician's assistant; Amelia will go to dental school; Liliana wants to become an immigration lawyer; and Hunter plans to write a graphic novel, supporting himself with work in a gallery. Only Daniel remains undecided. These plans are, of course, just plans, and they change throughout the year and in the months beyond. But these are not plans made hastily. They are clear, thoughtfully considered, honed by their experiences over the past three years.

For the students, the plans are about more than jobs: they signify who they are and who they have become. Sebastian is now a musician and an actor; he can't *not* perform. These plans are tied to who their families are, too: Liliana is pursuing immigration law because, she says, "my parents were immigrants, and it has always been ingrained to help them." For some of the students, these plans also reflect a desire for a salary that can support new lifestyles. Several students—and parents—mention newly acquired, more expensive preferences, like Ethan's "champagne taste." Hilltop, as Sebastian puts it, was an opportunity "to experience that elite thing"—and some want careers that will sustain that kind of life. And their parents want this for them. As Hunter's father told me the summer before Hunter's first year, "I would like him to step better than me"; this mobility is what a Hilltop education promised. The students, then, are now looking for jobs of a particular sort: jobs that can launch their careers, that align with their identities, that will allow them to "step better."

Daniel is unlike the others; he doesn't really have a plan. He doesn't pretend to have one either, telling me in the fall of his senior year, "I feel like I'm not really going to figure it out by the end of this year, so I'm not going to stress too much over it and going to just try to enjoy the year for what it is. . . . I don't have a lot of anxiety over it." It's not just that he doesn't have a plan for the year after graduation. He also doesn't have longer-term career goals. He knows he wants to be self-employed, but he says, "Like a specific career, I feel like I could pick something now, and it would definitely change." Unlike most of his classmates that senior fall, he hasn't applied for many jobs yet, just a couple halfhearted attempts for positions in finance. He'd like to teach abroad at some point, but he can't figure out how to make it work financially. Student loans are a big concern, one his parents are especially worried about, and both are telling him, "You need to get a job to make some money and pay down this debt." He acknowledges that he got a little "spoiled" by all the travel he did through Hilltop: "Now that I have had a taste of traveling places, I feel like doing it. It is not super realistic for me, but it's something I still want to do." He's regretting his economics major—it was hard, and employers don't seem to care what he's majoring in—and the "professional connections or networks" that he hoped to gain at Hilltop just aren't there. "It still remains to be seen how much Hilltop was worth it or not," he reports. His mother is getting frustrated. She wants him to "get a job anywhere and then keep looking," telling him, "You can make really good commission working at Saks and be a leading shoe salesman." But she reports that he "won't settle." So, no, he really doesn't have a plan.

He does know one thing, though: he does not want to return home. He has made this clear from our very first interview during the summer before his first year: he won't go back. He needs a "more vibrant community," he told me then, and his complaints about his hometown are much the same today: lots of old people, few jobs, "nothing there." Getting out is a "huge priority." He's focused on someplace "definitely urban," like Boston or New York. He's not sure how he'll make rent and loan payments, but he is sure that he won't go home or to any place like it.

At first, I believe Daniel when he says that he's not worried about not having a job or even a plan; he's always been comfortable with himself and happy to forge his own path. But when I ask how he's feeling about graduation, he confesses: "It is anxiety provoking. It forces you to think about your life and what you want to do. I guess it will be the first time I really have no direction in my life. . . . I guess it is a little overwhelming." Then he reassures himself: "I think it will be cool. It is going to have to be cool."

He'll figure it out, he says; he'll make it "cool"—just as long as he's in a city.

Daniel is unusual, the only student without a plan. But one aspect of his thinking is consistent with the others': he has strong opinions about where he wants to live. Since admission to Hilltop, the students have often tied their postgraduation aspirations to place. As they approach graduation, questions of place grow even more urgent. These are lonely questions. Their parents also sometimes have feelings about where they want their children to live—feelings that create pressure and sometimes don't align with their children's plans. And there's a placeless quality to the guidance of Hilltop's career center staff; for all their career advice, they give little consideration to where these careers might be located. Students, then, typically wrestle with these questions by themselves.

By the fall of their senior year, eight of the students—all except for Henry—plan to move to a city after graduation. For Daniel, Sebastian, Ethan, and Hunter, an urban location is a major priority in their planning for after graduation—a long-standing priority for Daniel, Ethan, and Hunter, a new one for Sebastian. Sylvan, Liliana, John, and Amelia have more mixed feelings about location: none of them identifies as a "city person," but they all assume their career plans will require moving to one. The students haven't spent much time in cities. Hunter attended an urban high school, and a few studied abroad in cities, but mostly, their urban experience is limited to their relatively sheltered time in Millston. They still have clear ideas about cities, though, typically describing them as "exciting," "happening," and "vibrant." Even the supposed grittiness of cities—"fast moving and just dirty"—is a draw. They see cities as filled with "opportunities" for socializing and recreation—the restaurants and bars and night clubs—but more importantly, for work and education: the law firms and universities and Broadway theaters. Cities are a part of "that elite thing" they got to experience at Hilltop; it's where they "belong now." And their parents agree. "The opportunities are in the big cities and the experiences are in the big cities," explains Sylvan's mother, so they support—even push—these urban plans.

Although some of the students are drawn to cities for clear and specific reasons, they're also avoiding rural places. Their hometowns are "boring" and "backwards," just abandoned mills and Trump supporters, and they generalize these qualities to other rural places, too. They don't want to move home or to any place *like* home. So they seek out its "vibrant" opposite: the city.

Their avoidance of rural places sometimes manifests as a very specific anxiety: fear of "getting stuck" in their rural hometown after graduation. "It is such a thing that people go back to their small-world hometowns and get stuck there," Ethan says. "It feels very scary to me, knowing so many people just never leave." Even Henry, who wants a rural life, doesn't want to return home; he can't "end up stagnant." Their parents worry about this, too. Ethan's mother tells me: "I'm afraid he is going to get stuck here because that is what happened to me. He is too talented and he is too smart, and I don't want that to happen." Their children know and understand their parents' fears, making them even more anxious to leave.

Even those students less fearful of "getting stuck" report few opportunities for young college graduates in rural places. There are no large corporations, no networks for young professionals, no graduate schools. "I love rural," Liliana says, but "rural isn't where the policy is." They also think about their future families; John tells me that he is concerned about the quality of rural schools, explaining that "the opportunities aren't necessarily there for all kids." Their parents note the lack of rural employment and education options, too, worrying about the "upward mobility" of jobs in more rural locations.

Although most of the students entered college planning to leave rural America, they also link Hilltop to this desire. "I just couldn't graduate Hilltop," Daniel says, "and then go to back home and apply to jobs on the computer." For Ethan, it relates to his new identity: "It is more of an image of myself. I did not see the narrative of my life, after working so hard to be successful at as good of a school as Hilltop, to be the kid that is moving home to the middle of nowhere." After Hilltop, these students see themselves differently: they're too "successful" to return. They have to leave.

Postgraduation Pressures and Constraints

It's October of senior year, and Henry is stressed out. "Slammed since the first day," he tells me. He's taking only three classes, but two are upper-level seminars, and the third is his psychology thesis;

he's running Psych 101 students through a self-designed experiment examining the effects of color on purchasing preferences. He also just joined a club to learn to code. "I don't think a psych major alone will get you everywhere," he explains. "You have to have something else."

Then there's his job: he's still working ten hours a week for Maple Marketing, where he interned over the summer. He began the summer without work but, two weeks in, found the position at Maple near his mom's house. He was responsible for "website health," and he enjoyed the work and liked the company. In fact, he tells me, "If I had found Maple in my freshman year of college, I don't know if I would've finished." Few Maple employees have college degrees, and "I just don't see how it's necessary for this line of work." But he's gone too far now: "It would've been a gigantic waste of money for me not to finish." So he is finishing, but when Maple asked him to stay on part-time, he did, figuring it would be good "to get something on my résumé to show that I can do this sort of thing." They wanted him to work twenty hours a week, but he knew that, with school, ten would be the most he could handle—and even that's proving challenging.

He's also spending long hours looking for a job for next year. He thinks Maple will offer him one, and he loves its rural location, but it would be hard for his hometown-then-Hilltop girlfriend—an aspiring accountant—to find work there. And he needs to think about his loan payments. He's going to owe about ninety thousand dollars, and the debt is looming over his plans for next year; it's "overwhelming," his mother reports. So Henry wants a job that will allow him to pay off his loans, be with his girlfriend, work in marketing, *and* "live somewhere in the mountains"—an impossible combination, it seems.

I see Henry again at the end of May, just a few days before graduation, and he's feeling relieved. A few weeks earlier, he had found another marketing job, this one located right in Millston. After three interviews, he was hired, for the time being as an unpaid intern, but with plans for a paid internship in the summer and then full-time, salaried work in the fall. So he quit Maple, finished his classes, moved with his girlfriend to a small town outside of Millston, and began his new job. The location isn't ideal: he doesn't like working in the city, and they're living in an "in between," not-really-rural, not-really-urban kind of place. The salary isn't great either. Even when he's full-time, he'll be relying on his girlfriend's income to pay most of their living expenses; she's graduating with a good job and no debt. But he's glad he's finished with Hilltop. "It's nice to know that this is behind me," he says. "I'm happier now, not even being paid yet, living in my own place, going to work, happier now than I have been in quite a while." He's done, and that's what matters.

He acknowledges that it's been an "apprehensive" transition out of Hilltop, juggling "bills, fending for yourself, finding a job." He's also spent much of the year questioning his Hilltop education: "Did I really need to go to college to be where I am? I don't think so. And it's kind of depressing." He thinks back to all the rhetoric about the value of an elite degree, and he's frustrated. "That seems like a bunch of hogwash now."

Still, the degree is something. The "thinking, writing, researching"—maybe he could have developed those skills anywhere, but he learned them at Hilltop. And he made it. "I guess I did it on my own, right? . . . Being able to be the first one in your family to go to college and graduate—that's kind of nice, right?"

Intense emotions characterize these students' senior years—and for those who graduate without a job, their summers and falls. It is, as Henry puts it, an "apprehensive" time. Reality is casting its long shadow, and they describe the search for work or further education as "terrifying," "scary," "anxiety provoking." They're feeling pressured, "this huge pressure," Daniel says, "to go somewhere and do something." They want to find a job or pursue training that fits their career goals, that supports their lifestyle, that is located in the right— usually urban—place, that makes their education worth it. But these are tough demands for a first job or graduate school, and these students are also facing a whole host of other challenges that limit their possibilities.

The first—and, for most, the largest—burden is financial. Debt has lurked throughout their Hilltop years, as it does, disproportionately so, for many rural students.[4] "I have had these nightmares," Henry tells me. "During the day when I'm thinking about these things, I will call my mom and be like, 'Hey, what is the situation going to be like? Am I going to be like $120,000 in debt?'" As they graduate, they're learning just how much they will owe. Amelia, Liliana, and Sylvan owe nothing: Amelia didn't need to borrow, Liliana received a full financial scholarship, and Sylvan, who got "great financial aid" from Hilltop, is able to pay off his few loans while he's still a student. The rest, though, owe anywhere from ten thousand to ninety thousand dollars, with Henry and John facing the largest bills. These looming loan payments weigh heavily on them, shaping their job options. Even those with little or no debt detail the financial pressures influencing their decisions: rent, utilities, gas money, insurance, grad school tuition. It's a math they became familiar with during college, but now the calculations are even more complex and consequential.

Another challenge is a lack of connections: like many working-class students, they don't have the social networks that can help them find jobs.[5] These connections were a major reason they chose Hilltop, and over the years, the students and parents repeatedly, if vaguely, referred to the "network" that's supposed to come with a Hilltop degree—"a network . . . that's really powerful and can get you pretty high-level places in the world." But as they graduate, most don't have such connections. The jobs they held during college didn't provide them: they were often blue-collar jobs back home, just the kind of work they had been trying to escape. Their professors couldn't help. The students avoided office hours and never served as teaching or research assistants; Ethan was offered a research assistantship one summer but turned it down—the pay was too low. By graduation, then, they don't have the kind of faculty relationships that can lead to a job. And although some of them have wealthy friends, those relationships lead to few interviews or offers—perhaps because they also never led to a spot on the family vacation to Cabo either. Their friends' families don't know the students, and so the networks—the kind that deliver you to "high-level places"—never materialize.

Some also lack experience relevant to the jobs they are pursuing—a little ironic, given their focus on gaining "practical" experience. But they needed to make money, and so they painted dorm rooms instead of serving as research assistants. With their advisers more focused on helping them complete academic requirements than finding them jobs, they didn't know how important these summertime experiences were. For Liliana, Hunter, and Amelia, all of whom secured internships through Hilltop's paid program, these experiences are helpful—relevant training and an important line on their résumés. The others, though, didn't know about the program or, without good advising, didn't understand its significance, and they missed out. "That internship was key for this next year," Daniel says, "and I don't have it." Hilltop has a career center, but none of them goes to it. They tell me it's "kind of useless," and maybe it is. Or maybe it's another support they believe they shouldn't need, or one that won't solve their specific problem: how to realize their locational aspirations when their résumés are spotty, their networks are limited, and their loan payments are looming.

The pressure heightens their anxiety. It's often generated by their parents. This postgraduation world is unfamiliar to them, with higher stakes than even the world of college, and they know that they can't rescue their children with a job offer or a rent check or good advice. As graduation approaches, they grow more and more concerned about their children's plans—concerned that all of the money and the time and the work won't amount to anything—and so they sometimes weigh in. Some press their children to take a job, like selling shoes at Saks, just to pay the bills. Others push graduate school and worry that any "time off" from school will mean never returning. The parents also share their thoughts on place, mostly discouraging their children from coming home or considering rural jobs. Even the students whose parents aren't pushing feel pressure: their parents have made "sacrifices" for this degree, and they're afraid to disappoint them. And it's not just parents. Back home, there's an entire town waiting to see what happened to the kid who went to that elite school.

The pressure comes from classmates, too. There's a new "competitive" vibe on campus, the students report, a pressure to land jobs at big-name firms in big-name cities. And their classmates are landing them. "What's really hard," Liliana says, "is most of my friends have jobs, and they all have apartments and cool things." But their classmates—all of them, it sometimes seems—are living in a different reality. They aren't weighed down by debt. They have networks for getting hired and parents for cosigning on leases. They can even return, with a job, to their urban homes—without shame or stigma or even the need to really think about it. The students are watching this and, sometimes, quietly "seething."

The dean reads Ethan's name and then pauses as Ethan, negotiating a broken foot, two crutches, and his graduation robes, hobbles across the stage. Ethan exchanges an awkward half-handshake, half-hug with Hilltop's president, gives his diploma to the graduate behind him to hold, and then, red-faced and sweaty, makes his way back to his seat. I hear his family cheering for him across the crowd, and Ethan does look pleased—and kind of irritated. He was "annoyed," he tells me later, annoyed that he broke his foot three days before graduation, annoyed that he had to navigate the traditions of Senior Week on crutches, annoyed that his family didn't understand his frustration, annoyed that this was the somewhat ignoble end to his years at Hilltop.

But mostly, I think, he is annoyed—and scared—because he is returning home without a job after graduation. I talked with Ethan a few days earlier and asked what his plans were for the summer and following year. "That's a good question," he responded. "I'm moving home in a week and a half, which is disappointing." There are some benefits: he won't have to pay rent, and he can get a "normal-paying" job and put most of his salary toward paying off loans. But, he said, "There are not a lot of lucrative jobs there, so I am scared definitely about the trap sort of thing." He continued, "I would not care about moving home if my parents lived in the suburbs of New Jersey"—but they don't. And so he's worried: "Will I ever leave? Or will I ever get a job?" This isn't how Hilltop was supposed to end.

Ethan is graduating magna cum laude. He has a 3.9 grade point average. He completes an honors thesis. Still, it's not altogether surprising that he's moving home without a job. He desperately wants to move to a big city—really, to New York, with its "hustle and bustle" and "gay life"—but to both live in the city and pay off his loans before law school, he calculated that he would need a job that pays at least seventy-five thousand a year. He feels a little funny about that salary—it's nearly what his parents make combined—but even with it, money would be tight, and he wouldn't be living "a super fun New York City life." For him, the job search has come down to just two things: money and location.

Nothing works out. He looks into paralegal jobs: they don't make enough. He applies for some corporate jobs, even though it "goes against" his politics, rationalizing, "If anybody should be allowed to work at J. P. Morgan, it should be me because the jobs pay so well." And although he gets some interviews, he isn't hired—because, he suspects, "I don't have the résumé that is very experience driven." He also doesn't have the connections he needs. "What has been so frustrating about this whole job process," he says, "is that whoever got this job is probably some . . . dude from Connecticut whose dad is a partner at the firm, you know what I mean? I don't have any of these connections in Boston or New York City." He is offered one job, but the salary isn't enough to make it worth it. He finally realizes a hard truth: the jobs he's qualified for don't make enough to live with student loans in a big city.

And so he is returning home without a job, to parents who don't know he is gay, to a town full of people who "don't know what it means to go to Hilltop College." He's "more scared of the lack of things"—jobs, friends, entertainment—than returning to the closet: it's the abundances of Hilltop that he grew so accustomed to, less so the being out. He also doesn't want going home to "cloud" what he's accomplished: "Looking to my hometown, I'm probably the most successful person that I can think of." His parents agree. "He went from being in a hole-in-the-wall town . . . with not a lot of opportunity . . . to this land of milk and honey where there are all these different cultures and all these different experiences and all these different doors that he can choose to go through," his mother says. "I am so stinking proud."

Right now, though, Ethan isn't seeing "all these different doors." He tells me about a friend of his, a rich friend whose parents are paying for him to spend the summer in Paris, who's then moving to his own apartment in a large city and working at his uncle's wealth management company, who had only "a 2.9 grade point average" at Hilltop. That makes Ethan a little angry: "the land of milk and honey" just seems to make the rich richer.

Fear marks the students' senior years. They fear failing—failing to get a job or to pay off loans or to get into grad school. They fear being forced to abandon career plans that are so closely tied to who they are and how they now define themselves. They fear being "the kid that is moving home to the middle of nowhere," they fear "getting stuck" there, but they also fear the distance from family and the loneliness that comes with new places.

By graduation, some students, like Henry, are more relaxed. They have found a job that will pay the bills and a home they can live with—the fear is subsiding for now. But for others, like Ethan, the job searches and grad school applications and apartment hunts continue, and the anxiety remains.

Life after Graduation

My last interviews with the students take place during the fall after graduation. For those still in New England, I drive to their homes or grad schools, or we meet at Hilltop or a coffee shop, or they come to my house. Three—Liliana, Hunter, and Daniel—are farther away, and we talk by phone or Skype. These conversations are long and bittersweet: they're finished with Hilltop, and they've moved on to new victories, new disappointments, and new goals.

Satisfactions and Dissatisfactions

That fall finds the students—alumni—in jobs, schools, and places both planned and unplanned. Ethan returned home and found work at a software company in a nearby suburb; he's "overqualified" for the position, and it's boring, but because he can live at home, he's able to make his loan payments. His parents still don't know he's gay, and he's still looking for a well-paying job in New York; after a few years, he plans to head to law school. Henry is enjoying his work at the marketing company in Millston; he's less satisfied living in an "in between" small town and still wants to be in the mountains someday. He and his girlfriend live on her salary while he works to pay off his loans. Daniel didn't graduate with a job and had to return home—exactly what he'd dreaded. As soon as he arrived, he "just started freaking out," so within a few weeks of graduation, he moves to Chicago, where a college friend lives, and through a temp agency finds work at a logistics company, selling freight to truckers. He's not using his Hilltop education, he doesn't want to remain in the job, and he's only got a six-month lease; he's not sure what he'll do when it ends. Sebastian realized that he wasn't ready for the New York theater scene yet, neither financially nor artistically, so he decided to spend a year at home, making money and auditioning for a nearby community theater. He's living with his dad, waiting tables at a diner, looking for local music and theater gigs, and also hoping to be in New York soon.

John's senior year was spent filling out law school applications; he got married a few weeks after graduation, and, in the fall, he begins his studies in state, attending a law school in its largest city. After finishing, he hopes to move to the suburbs, start a family, and practice law. At graduation, Sylvan was excited for a two-year position at an immunology lab in Boston and was planning an eventual graduate degree in biotech or bioengineering. By the fall, though, he's regretting that he didn't pursue a job at a lab near home and trying to reconcile his career plans with a newly realized desire to live somewhere more rural. After spending her senior year taking entrance exams and applying to dental schools, Amelia planned to take a gap year at home to work and finish up her premed requirements. She does this, getting a job at a psychology lab and enrolling in two classes at a nearby state school but, disappointed with her scores, decides to retake her exams and may delay dental school a second year. Eventually, she wants to have a family practice in the suburbs. Liliana's senior year was filled with applications for jobs working as a paralegal, and she hoped to work for a year or two before heading to law school. She didn't find anything by graduation and went home, but within a few weeks, she was hired as a paralegal doing immigration work for a firm in Washington, DC. She intends to start studying for the LSAT soon, and although she might move somewhere more rural "long, long term," she expects to live in a city for a while. After graduation, Hunter moved home to make money working at a casino; he and his girlfriend plan to leave for a year in Australia at the end of October. He wants to find a job at a gallery or museum there and then follow her to wherever she enrolls in med school—hopefully in a large city, where he'll continue to work in the art world and publish his graphic novel.

And so, just a few months after graduation, all the students have found employment or graduate studies. They all have places to live. They are paying their bills, and most are starting to pay off their loans. Some rely on their parents for housing, but all are, to some extent, employed and supporting themselves and planning for the future. They have succeeded—quite thoroughly.

But some are happier than others. That fall finds a couple of students excited by their new situations. The others seem less content: their postgraduation realities bear little resemblance to their aspirations, or their plans aren't as satisfying as they'd hoped.

John is carrying a large iced coffee. He's traded his Hilltop Athletics gear for a black shirt and black pants, and his backpack is stuffed with books. It's the fall after graduation, and we're meeting at the library of the law school where he's now enrolled. With his coffee and books, John certainly looks the part.

But getting here wasn't easy. Even though he was ready to leave Hilltop—"I was pretty well spent by the end of four years"—the transition out was hard. He spent his senior year writing his thesis, playing football, completing coursework, and applying to schools. "There are a lot of logistics out there," John told me in the fall of his senior year. And there were. He would be graduating with about eighty thousand dollars in debt, an amount that would only grow with law school. His hometown fiancée, Kristen, was applying to nursing schools, so they had to coordinate their applications to a handful of schools in state and in Boston, hoping to get accepted in the same city. They were also in the midst of planning a summer wedding. "When I start looking ahead," John said, "I just feel a wave of anxiety."

By May, though, the anxiety has diminished. He and Kristen were both accepted to in-state programs, ones they're each thrilled to attend. They were looking for apartments in the city and feeling ready for their wedding. He had finished classes and was working full-time as a waiter at a pub near his house. The job kept him from most Senior Week activities, and it was a little "weird" not spending the time with his friends, but, he said, "I need the money." He's thinking ahead to loan payments, to his and Kristen's tuitions, to rent and moving costs: "We'll have a very limited income. . . . It's going to hit me hard after school, but it's OK."

And after graduation, it is OK. In fact, it's more than OK: he seems happy as a new husband and law student, as a person who now lives within walking distance of a Starbucks. The wedding was "great"— rain and thunder gave way to sunny skies—and even though he's only a few weeks in, he's loving law school. "I'm learning a lot," he reports, "and it's fun." Once he and Kristen have children, they will likely move to the suburbs—for their well-resourced schools—but he's thrilled to be staying in state. "It's my community," John says. "It's the people I want to help. I can't see myself living anywhere else."

He's proud of himself. He graduated from "one of the best liberal arts schools in the country." He proved something to the high school math teacher who "couldn't believe" when he got into Hilltop: he showed that he could thrive at a place like Hilltop. As much as he loved college, though, he is leaving a little more critical. Yes, he learned "how to write effectively, speak effectively, interact with people, how to have empathy for others, and stuff like that." "But," he continues, "I think there's this sort of . . ." He pauses. "It's who you know, your connections. . . . Sometimes it's who your parents know. You can get a job way better than somebody that knows nobody." He saw this. He watched his Hilltop friends with connected parents and little experience get jobs right after graduation. For him, it was different. "I had to work pretty hard to get to where I am, I guess. And I have to continue to work hard."

As we're finishing up our conversation in the library, an older man wearing a Hilltop hat walks by. He's overheard us talking about Hilltop; "Great day to be a Huskie," he says. "Yes, sir," John replies. So no, John might not have the connections his peers do, and he probably can't get a job as easily as they can. But he is still a Hilltop Huskie— and a Huskie pretty satisfied with his opportunities and decisions.

Sylvan is less satisfied. It's not easy to tell when Sylvan's unhappy: he's charming and funny, even in his darker moments. We meet up when he returns to Hilltop for homecoming. He's wearing a Hilltop sweatshirt over a plaid button-down, and he's got a neatly kept beard. We pick up a long-running discussion: the pseudonym he'll select for this book. Since identifying one of the other students in the study his first year, he's joked that he'll choose that student's real name. I've vetoed a bunch of other options he's considered, too, including my name and my dog's. This time he's pondering names adapted from Italian or Latin phrases. He likes "Lucy Allorizzonte," a modified version of *luce all'orizzonte*, which means "light on the horizon"—perfect for "a really bright shining character and a shining beacon for hope in the future." But he can't take a name like that, he says. "How do you say 'total fuckup' in Latin?"

Sylvan is anything but a "total fuckup." He graduated summa cum laude, with a spot in Phi Beta Kappa. He received an award for exceptional achievement in organic chemistry and biochemical research. He spent his senior year studying a kind of bacteria that could be used to break down crude oil and clean up oil spills. It was a hard year. Classes, he said, were "kicking my ass," he was denied a Fulbright to teach English in Italy, he broke up with his girlfriend, a hometown relationship that spanned most of his junior and senior years, and from what I could tell, he was partying harder than years past. Still, his academic achievement was undeniably outstanding, and it paid off with a good job. He's working for a Harvard Medical School immunology lab at Boston Children's Hospital. He processes blood samples for a trial antibody therapy, and although "immunology is not really [his] thing," he's developing skills that will be transferable to other labs. And his parents are "stoked" about his Harvard email address.

But he's not happy. "I got this job because I knew a friend whose dad was an immunologist," he explains—the only student to leverage a Hilltop connection to find a job. "He was looking for somebody to work in his lab. I was still competing in the application process with a couple of great potential applicants, but I absolutely believe I had an in for that." He got the job, and he got it quickly—before he could finish interviewing for a position at a lab in a rural coastal town near home. "Oh, shit! Yeah, I'll take it!" he said. Later, he said, "Oops."

His parents hadn't wanted him to stay in the rural part of the state. They were "worried about the upward mobility of it" and excited for the people he would meet at Harvard. In Boston he'd find opportunities "to move up"; his mom, he says, "didn't feel that the people that I'd be working with at [the rural lab] would offer me all that much." He was also excited to try Boston. But by fall, when I ask how he likes living in a city, he responds, "I hate it." He misses long drives and "easy access" to the people he loves and the things he enjoys. And he's lonely: "I don't like being surrounded by so many people and still feeling like I have no one to talk to." He regrets leaving.

He's not sure what'll come next for him. "I'm kind of floating," he says. He's still working through a bit of an identity crisis now that he's not going to medical school. "My identity in high school," he says, "was that of 'I'm this driven kid that's going to be a doctor and do great things.' . . . Now my plans are to hopefully live through my twenties and not starve to death in a shitty apartment in Boston." He's feeling disconnected from his family, which, he says, "is weird because I was always very in sync with my parents." At Hilltop, he was busy, "developing friendships and figuring out my opinions and my worldviews and stuff; there wasn't a lot of room for calling my parents all the time." He's changed, and they haven't, and now, he says, "I'm kind of alone." He continues, "I am more likely to have a life like the people I went to Hilltop with. . . . Grow up in a nice town, go to a nice prep school, go to a nice college, have children. . . . There's definitely a part deep down that is afraid that that's going to just not make sense to my parents and is going to make it hard for me to connect with [them]. . . . It makes me very sad." He starts to cry.

We talk a while about work and home and parents, about his fears of disappointing or losing them, about the anxiety and depression he's feeling (and about therapy). If he does return to the rural coast, he's just not sure what he'll do. "It's a dreamy, dreamy place. This is where I want to be," he says. "I'm glad that I know that; I just don't know how to make it feasible. . . . There is very little here. If you don't have a specific career opportunity here, it is not a great place to be." There are not many jobs for people with a bachelor's in science, fewer still for those with a master's or PhD. So he's just "kind of floating," feeling like he's been educated out of the place he loves.

The fall after graduation finds John relatively content. Though worried about money, he's starting a family and a career, and he feels purposeful, becoming a lawyer to serve a state that he's committed to. Hunter also seems happy: having spent the summer with his parents at home, he's about to leave for a year abroad with his girlfriend—for now, his career goals are somewhat secondary. The others are less settled. Some contend with dissatisfactions they see as temporary. Amelia appreciates the free housing, but she doesn't seem happy spending a year at home preparing for dental school. And Sebastian, though pleased to be getting any performance work, would rather be landing higher-profile gigs in New York. But for Sylvan, the dissatisfaction seems more profound. He's struggling to define himself, worried about his relationships, not sure how to build a career in the place he loves.

Several themes run through the students' dissatisfactions. They're frustrated—frustrated that they don't have the skills and experiences that employers want or the connections and financial flexibility that classmates enjoy, frustrated that they don't feel more prepared for the "real world." For some, the gap between aspiration and reality seems discouragingly large: What will Daniel do when his lease is up? How will Sebastian get to Broadway? They're also lonely. Sylvan, Daniel, and Liliana are living in new cities, far from family and most Hilltop friends, while Amelia, Ethan, and Sebastian are home, near family but far from college friends or even same-aged peers. And for all of them, there's the cultural and social and political distance, separating them from home, that has emerged with four years at Hilltop—the ways in which, just as Henry's mother predicted, they have changed.

Location also features prominently in their disappointment: most feel like they're in the wrong place. Ethan, Sebastian, and Amelia are living in their rural hometowns, but they want to be somewhere else, somewhere more metropolitan—Ethan and Sebastian in New York, Amelia in the suburbs. They're anxious, worried about getting "stuck," educated out but with nowhere else to go. Several of those living or working in cities aren't so satisfied, either. Job opportunities and family pressure led Liliana and Sylvan to large cities, where neither is happy—an anticipated disappointment for Liliana, a surprising regret for Sylvan. And Henry, working in a city and living in an "in between" kind of place, also wants a more rural, more remote home.

Location is, of course, changeable, and the students are just starting to figure out their ambitions and their commitments and what each might require. Their goals might change, especially as the costs of leaving grow clearer and more real. They might remain unsettled, by choice or by necessity. As these rural students are learning, though, for them, location will always mean trade-offs: jobs for family, education for relationships, opportunity for home.

Still Planning

Amelia's mother, Cindy, is worried. It's early September, and a "Congratulations, Graduate!" sign still stands near the driveway. June's graduation was emotional. Cindy wasn't always sure it was going to happen—"there were a couple of times I thought she wasn't going to make it." But, Cindy says, "she stuck it out . . . [and] kept her head above water." Cindy is definitely the proud mother of a Hilltop graduate.

Still, she's worried. Amelia is home, and she isn't working, just studying for the dental school entrance exams. Cindy hopes she'll take them next month, but she doesn't know what'll happen after that or when she'll go to grad school. "I thought she would be a little more aggressive," Cindy explains. "We need a backup plan." Cindy knows Amelia wants a break from school, but she continues, "I don't want her resources to wear out. I mean, [what] if she waits two years and then they say, 'I don't remember even who she is?' I want her to do the right thing, but I want her to do something." She worries, too, that, if Amelia delays graduate school, she won't get out "until [she's] thirty"—and what does that mean for starting a family?

The more we talk, I realize that Cindy's fears are, at least in part, a reflection of her own life. "If you are in a job that you hate, if you have an education . . . you can muddle your way through a lot of places and find something that you like. I'm uneducated, and I'm stuck where I am." Cindy doesn't want Amelia to get "stuck," and so she worries: she worries that Amelia needs to get started, to go to graduate school, to get a "backup plan." "Hopefully she figures it out," she says, probably more to herself than to me. "She just needs to have that kick in the rear, right?"

So when I meet Amelia a month later, I'm expecting to find her a bit aimless, in need of a plan and a "kick in the rear." I quickly discover, though, that Amelia has plans; in fact, she has plan after plan after plan. Having studied all summer, she's signed up to retake her entrance exams in two weeks. She's enrolled in anatomy and physics at a nearby state school and has a twenty-hour-a-week job in its psychology lab. This is actually the third job she has gotten; she rejected two offers she received when applying her senior year, worrying they would have thrown off her graduate school plans. Her exam scores will determine her next steps. If she does well, she'll delay dental school by a second year and take a few more premed courses, hoping to boost her grades and get into a more competitive program; if she doesn't, she'll start applying to schools and enter the following September. She's got a long list of schools she's thinking about, with detailed reasons for and against each. Eventually, she wants to have a family practice and live somewhere suburban—rural places are too far from anything, but she's "not an in-the-city kind of gal."

So Amelia most definitely has plans. But she needed this gap year, or two. She was exhausted: Hilltop was hard for her. She realizes that she "had a lot of anxiety stuff that . . . raised hell during college." She often wondered whether she'd chosen the right school, she says, "because Hilltop was really academically challenging for me, and I certainly wasn't prepared, not for the level of rigor, not for the exams, not for so much of it." She needed a break—from studying, from grades, from working so hard to catch up.

Amelia knows that her mom is worried that "there's not a clear trajectory" for her career and life. "I think that that's typical for people my age," she says, "especially coming from Hilltop—no super straight path to anywhere." "At my age," she continues, "my mom was getting ready to get married. . . . I feel no pressure by these landmarks." Amelia explains, "I think she really wants me to go on and get on with a career that I can see myself doing forever. And I want that, too, but I don't know that I want it so badly that I want to compromise on the quality." So with her mother, "there's definitely a disconnect there."

Even with that "disconnect," her mother is the reason she's being so careful. Her mother feels stuck, and that, Amelia says, is "just something I really want to avoid." So she won't hold herself to the traditional "landmarks." Instead, she'll keep studying hard, weighing her options, earning her degrees—just like her mother taught her.

During these last conversations, I hear about new jobs and new responsibilities. The students tell me about their bills and how they'll pay them. They explain where they are and where they want to be. They talk about their parents and the pressure they feel and, harder still, the "disconnect," as their lives continue to diverge. They share stories of victories and frustrations, of new friends and terrible bosses and interesting work assignments and mice in apartments.

But across all these conversations, I also hear these students' agency. They acknowledge the constraints and disappointments, and then they keep going. They're working hard to bring their realities a little closer to their aspirations, for who they will become and where. Their lives will be complex and dynamic and nuanced—because there's "no super straight path to anywhere."

Looking Back

Poll after poll shows that Americans fundamentally believe in the idea of meritocracy—that talent and effort are rewarded with success.[6] Education, in this ideology, acts as a "great equalizer": by developing talent and recognizing effort, it gives everyone the opportunity for social mobility. This faith is the foundation of the American education system, and it motivates the college admissions process. It's why high schoolers apply to elite schools like Hilltop: acceptance is both a reward in itself—affirming innate ability and hard work in high school—and a path to greater rewards in the future, like security and status.

The students bought into this narrative, too. Hilltop is a "good school," they knew, a school that accepts few applicants. So they applied, and their strong grades, outstanding extracurriculars, and stellar applications won them a spot. They trusted that they—and their new classmates—*earned* it. And they believed that the education they would receive at Hilltop, at this kind of "good school," would pay off, with good careers and good salaries and good lives. Their parents also trusted this ideology: "This is the school," Sebastian's parents said, "that ... you can do whatever you want. This is the place." This ideology didn't always serve the students well; when they struggled, its individualistic dogma—*you* earn your rewards—led to feelings of guilt and shame. Still, though, they bought in.

But gradually, they began to lose some of their faith. The transition into Hilltop was challenging, and some of them noticed that their wealthier classmates were better prepared than they were. Not all of the opportunities of Hilltop are available to all of its students, they learned. Not everyone can study abroad or take summertime premed courses, and not everyone belongs in a campus culture defined by ski trips and Louis Vuitton purses. The system isn't so fair, they began to see. It's not just about merit; it's also about who your parents know and where you went to high school and how much money you have. Hilltop itself also lost some of its luster, as they learned that a Hilltop degree won't get you "whatever you want."

By graduation, their faith had mostly evaporated. All the rhetoric? It's "hogwash." Hilltop isn't "as fair and nice as it seems." They were beginning to see the whole notion of a meritocracy for the myth that it is—and they weren't sure what to do with that.

Liliana's job, she acknowledges, was something of an impulse decision. She'd been home for just two weeks and had a few job interviews lined up, but, as soon as she was offered this one—as a paralegal in DC—she took it. So, less than a month after graduation, she is back on the East Coast, working long hours and living alone in a small studio apartment.

Her father is the first to tell me about her job. "I feel that she is doing so well," he says when we talk that summer. "To work hard and then move to DC with only two weeks off from school and just spending two weeks with me—I feel that she is going to gain a lot of benefit from the job." Hilltop was "100 percent" worth it, he feels, "because they gave a better education and more chances to be like where she is right now." For him, a job at a DC law firm—and a plan to attend law school in a year or two—is confirmation of Liliana's determination and skills, their family's sacrifices, and Hilltop's superior quality.

But Liliana is a pretty measured person, not one for quick decisions. When I talked with her a few days before graduation, she was still applying for jobs and preparing for the thirty-seven-hour drive home with her parents. "There's a lot of uncertainty," she acknowledged; "I'm a type A person, and this is not type A." It was difficult to be heading home while her friends were getting jobs and searching for apartments. "I just have to be OK with where I'm at and stop comparing myself to other people, which is really hard, especially at Hilltop."

It's this pressure that led to her impulse decision: taking a job that, she's discovering, means long hours filling out immigration forms. When we finally catch up one evening in September, she explains, "I was really OK at the beginning not comparing myself to other individuals, but when all of my friends had jobs [and] Mom and Dad were constantly telling me that I needed a job, I was very quick." Now she's frustrated with herself now. "Instead of waiting for other jobs, I jumped on board with [this firm]. It's always twenty-twenty hindsight, right?"

Liliana still likes law, still feels passionately about immigrant rights, still plans on law school. Although she misses the outdoors and finds that people are "a little more disconnected between each other" in a city, she knows where the career opportunities are, and she's resigned herself to city life, at least for now. But this job, helping wealthy clients file immigration paperwork, has been "very frustrating." She's already thinking about finding a new job.

I've caught Liliana on a bad day. Work was, like usual, long and hard, and she just watched a cockroach crawl up the wall of the restaurant where she picked up takeout. Her frustration is more than that, though. She's exhausted from her last job search and really doesn't want to think about starting another. She also sounds disappointed with Hilltop. It's not that she's not happy she went to college or to an elite school or even to Hilltop. "I can't imagine myself anywhere else," she says. But when I ask her if she thinks that college provides equal access to opportunity, her response is emphatic: "No, I do not." She explains, "It's sort of a 'sink or swim' kind of thing. I feel like a lot of my really, really wealthy friends did really well, got tutors, went on vacation every single time there was a break or things like that. . . . I heard the phrase, 'Oh, you may not be privileged outside of Hilltop, but now you are here and therefore you are just equally as privileged.' And I don't necessarily think that's true."

After this interview, I find myself thinking back to our very first conversation. When I asked why she decided to go to college, she talked about her parents and how they explained to her and her brothers, from a very young age, the importance of an education. A college degree, they said, means "more opportunities." It's also a challenge to all the stereotypes that equate being Hispanic with being uneducated. "It has always been a goal of mine to prove people wrong," she had said. Her impulsivity, why she took the job so quickly, makes sense: there is a lot of hope and expectation hanging on this degree. She can be critical of Hilltop and the entire elite education enterprise—but still, this degree *needs* to mean something.

Before we hang up, I ask Liliana how she's navigated this unequal terrain. After all, she double majored, wrote two senior theses, graduated, and got this job—all without tutors or vacations or parents' connections. "Grit and perseverance," she says. "I think for what I had and continue to have, I'm trying to do the best I can." And, she acknowledges, "there's a very nice feeling of being able to get a job on your own merit."

So a Hilltop degree may not mean as much as Liliana had hoped it would. And Liliana had to work harder than many of her classmates to get that degree. And it may come with some costs, like loneliness. But what she has achieved, she earned. And there's satisfaction in that.

Leaving Hilltop seems to sharpen students' doubts about the school and everything an elite degree is supposed to promise. Perhaps that's because, right now, it doesn't seem to promise all that much. Like many underrepresented students, they are struggling to find jobs and pay bills; these rural students are also struggling to make lives in the right places—and to mitigate the costs of their choices.[7] And they're disappointed. Daniel says: "Initially, I thought, 'I go to Hilltop, I'm set.' No, it's an entirely different reality from that." For most of them, Hilltop doesn't mean deep networks and high salaries and countless graduate school acceptances. Instead, it's job scarcity, social isolation, financial stress, and a kind of limbo—they can't go home, but they can't go anywhere else either.

This reality is also calling into question the entire narrative they'd written about themselves and their lives. None of them wanted to be "kind of floating." The fears of their senior year haven't really gone away. They're still scared—scared they won't live up to parental expectations, scared those doubting math teachers were right, scared they'll fail their own hopes and aspirations. They're also angry, as they realize that "some people are just always going to have an advantage over others."

I put the question to some of the students directly: Is college the great equalizer? Their answers vary in the details, but all reply much like Liliana: No. Amelia tells me about a wealthy friend who could afford a tutor for the dental exam—and will now have a more competitive application. Henry describes "legacy kids"—the connections that can get you into Hilltop—and the connections that "influence what you do after." Sylvan says, "People who came from different backgrounds"—"from super elite prep schools . . . and from public schools"—"don't have necessarily the same footing."

Their answers surprise me. Yes, they had been growing more critical of Hilltop and elite education for a while, but I had taken more of them for believers. In some respects, they still are, at least partially. They still hold some hope their elite degree will pay off. Most of them still trust the fairness of the admissions process. Some still seem wedded to the eliteness of an elite education and the cachet of the Hilltop name. A few are scrambling for high-status careers, the reward assumed by an achievement-oriented culture. And Henry tells me that it's "the individual that levels the playing field." This sounds like a bit of meritocratic evangelism, until he begins listing the disadvantages that he faced in getting to Hilltop, including "coming from a rural background—I guess I'm not expected to necessarily go on and exceed."

So their new doubt is still somewhat imprecise and incomplete. They realize there's an opportunity structure, but they're not sure where to locate themselves within it. It's also not clear to them exactly why they might not have some of the same advantages as their peers. They suspect it might be about class: they quite regularly cite the things their peers can afford and they can't. Occasionally they mention being the first in their families to attend college and the effects of that—but more often, they don't. After all, their parents supported their college aspirations, and three of them attended private schools; these resources, they suspect, aren't things that "first-gen kids" have. A few of the White students also recognize the privilege—the ability to "assimilate"—that comes with their Whiteness, a privilege that, they seem to think, should insulate them from any other kind of disadvantage. And even as they struggle with the spatial realities of graduation—the availability of jobs, the location of graduate schools, the cost of urban apartments, the loneliness of new lives and new lifestyles—it's only rarely that they see where they're from as a factor shaping opportunity.

Their faith in the American educational structure is eroding, but they're still fumbling for a plausible explanation for its inequality.

I call Hunter in early fall. He's been working room service at a local casino all summer, making "good money and good tips," saving for a year in Australia with his girlfriend; they leave in just a few weeks. I'm curious about the trip: how he'll pay for it, what he'll do, where he'll go afterward. Hunter dutifully answers my questions. His girlfriend has a job at a branch of her mother's company. He'll find work once he gets there, some kind of position in an art gallery or museum— he's not too worried. After Australia, she'll head to medical school, hopefully in a big city somewhere, and he'll go, too, and find another museum or gallery job. Throughout it all, he'll continue to work on his graphic novel. "That's basically the plan," he concludes, in his typical, understated way.

Then I ask about graduation, and his assessment is similar in its restraint: "It was definitely nice to get that kind of accomplishment and the diploma." It was more than "nice," I know. I remember seeing him on graduation day. It was hot, and by the end of the ceremony, most robes were unzipped and faces were slick with sweat and tears. Families gathered under the shade of trees, clutching balloons and flowers, searching for their graduates. I found Hunter and his parents standing in the cool shadow of Hilltop's massive library. Despite the heat, Hunter still had on his graduation hat and gown. Draped across his chest was a white sash that read First Generation Student; of the nine students, only he chose to wear one. He hugged me and told me about Senior Week—mostly, that he didn't really take part, wanting to be "alert" for graduation. When he walked across the stage, he explained, he became the only one in his family—the "first Lawrence"—with a college degree. In that moment, I could read through Hunter's restraint: he is proud.

In her recollection of graduation, Hunter's mother is as animated as he is muted: "Graduation was just so awesome. It was great. It was just so incredible, and we were so proud of him. It was just the proudest day of my life." As we talk, she recounts the long journey to graduation: the decision to pull him from his "overcrowded and underfunded" elementary school, the years of driving down the mountain to good schools in the city, his dad's long hours in the truck making tuition money, Hunter's "hellish" first year at Hilltop. Like Hunter, she's proud: "He made it, and he made it in four years"—the vast majority of Hilltop students do—"and he did well despite obstacles. It has made him into a very confident, fine young man."

This "very confident, fine young man" agrees. "It was certainly a good learning experience," he tells me. Like the other students, though, he's no longer totally sold on the idea of an educational meritocracy. "I think that [college] kind of elevates certain people and helps them more than others." Who? I ask. "I'd say, if you're an incredibly talented athlete, you're kind of given a lot of opportunity that maybe some other people that are not as athletic would be given." He continues, "But I definitely do think that it offers an opportunity for a lot of people to become more than they could have if they didn't have college." It's a telling response, especially for a first-generation student, on a lot of financial aid, who left college athletics. Hilltop gave him that opportunity—at least, some of that opportunity—and for that, he's grateful.

After our last conversation, I run across an artist statement posted on Hilltop's website. It's a short audio recording in which Hunter explains his interest in graphic novels and the motivations for his senior thesis. "I always wanted to be Superman," he begins. When he was little, it was because Superman was strong, but as he got older, he realized it was more about what Superman symbolizes: "he stands for hope." He's drawn to the optimism of comic books because, ultimately, they're about characters overcoming challenges.

So this is Hunter, too. He's quiet, a little inscrutable, but he's optimistic, more likely to see Hilltop for what it gave him than what it didn't. And he's proud—proud of all he's overcome to become the first Lawrence with a degree.

Proud is a word I hear again and again and again when talking to these students' parents. They're still proud that their children were accepted to Hilltop, and they're proud they made it through to graduation. They acknowledge it wasn't easy, and they credit their children's determination. "I know he was struggling," says Daniel's mother, "and he just stuck it out, and I'm proud of him for that." Or as Sebastian's father explains, "Just to stick it out no matter what, of course you are proud of him for that." Some of the parents do wonder what "sticking it out" will mean for their children. "Hopefully, someday that will pay off for her," Amelia's mother says. But they never question this: that their children *earned* that Hilltop degree.

These parents didn't have the opportunity to go to college, and they occasionally wonder if deep pockets can gain admittance to elite schools. But still, they seem to retain more faith in an American meritocracy than their children: their children are, in fact, proof that hard work pays off. That diploma, as Liliana puts it, "validates the sacrifices that they've made."

The students know that their parents are proud. "My parents are definitely really proud of me," Ethan says. "I think they are prouder of me than I am of me." Their pride serves as a source of motivation for the students—they often cite it as a reason they worked so hard at Hilltop. Now, though, it might also increase the pressure they feel. If they don't land that job or get into that law school, will their parents have sacrificed for nothing?

The students themselves seem a little more circumspect about their degree, perhaps because of this pressure. Or now that they know that the education game is rigged, a degree may feel a little less special. Or maybe this is one of the luxuries of being a college graduate— the privilege to downplay its meaning.

But it does mean something. As Henry says, "I guess I did it on my own, right? . . . Being able to be the first one in your family to go to college and graduate—that's kind of nice, right?" With "grit and perseverance" they got through, and so they just signal their pride more subtly—with robes that stay on after the graduation ceremony and a stubborn desire to prove themselves.

Leaving Hilltop brings a mix of emotions. Sadness to leave friends. Relief they made it. Appreciation for the education they received. Regret for the opportunities they missed. Anxiety about the future. Hope for the future. Distrust of society's grand myths. Gratitude for their families' sacrifices.

And pride.

6

Educated Out

"I'll prove you all wrong."

Rural, first-generation students aren't expected to go to colleges like Hilltop. But these nine students got in, they made it through, and they earned a Hilltop degree. They proved everyone wrong—a high school math teacher, but also school counselors, college admissions staff, and a public convinced of rural ignorance and committed to rural undereducation.

In many respects, they thrived at Hilltop. They relished the intense classes, competitive teams, and professional theater productions. They discovered new passions, made new friends, and found new love. And they learned. They learned Arabic and the psychology of marketing. They learned CPR and coding. They learned how to be a DJ and what makes for a compelling graphic novel and why oil spills are so hard to contain.

But they also learned this: that this "land of milk and honey" wasn't always theirs to enjoy. And they learned that their degree came with costs—to them and to their families and communities.

These rural students are no longer rural students—they're rural college graduates. That rurality shaped college for them. It determined why they went and, also, why they stayed, what they learned, how much it cost. And I suspect that it's not just *their* plans and opportunities that place influenced; place likely influences the plans and opportunities of other students also underrepresented on college campuses.

College, these rural students learned, is not just about merit. It's about money, it's about race, it's about your parents' education. And although it's not often talked about, college is also about where you're from. When colleges and policies fail to account for that geography, a degree not only becomes less attainable; it also loses some of its promise.

Rural at Hilltop

These students were the exceptions: they were rural students who enrolled at an elite liberal arts college. They were different from their high school classmates. They stood out academically, they wanted to attend college, they chose an elite school—and mostly, their families encouraged this. They were also different from their college classmates, and that difference mattered, too.

Here, I look across their experiences at how rurality—and the inequities tied to it—affected their college education. I focus on place, but I talk about class and race, too. Class and racial structures—like income inequality and segregation—are also spatial structures, and these students don't experience their various identities singly: they are rural, but they are not only rural.

Still, though, their rurality is significant. It shaped their hopes and plans for education. It determined their access to education. It offered resources for navigating their education. And it influenced the outcomes of that education—what was gained and what was lost.

What They Hoped

Although some studies suggest that a rural background might limit students' educational aspirations, these students' college aspirations were largely a product of their rurality.[1] In their rural hometowns, industries are changing: mills have closed, and farms are disappearing; or, as tourists arrive and suburbs creep closer, taxes are rising, and affordable housing is evaporating.[2] The students have seen jobs go and families follow. They watched their parents put in long hours at low-wage, physically demanding jobs. After school and during breaks, the students often worked these jobs, too, stocking shelves and sweeping floors—they knew the work was hard. They also knew that, without college degrees, their parents and neighbors were "stuck."[3] So these students' rurality shaped their aspirations: it pushed them to college.

This geography also caused the adults around them to support their college aspirations. Again, contrary to much of the research and assumption about rural parents, college was an expectation for most of these parents.[4] No matter the current debates about the necessity of college, their faith was unshakable—their children were going. Rural jobs are disappearing, the parents knew all too well, at least the ones that offer good wages and good benefits. They wanted their children to have more than they did—more money but also more stability, more flexibility, more satisfaction. They believed—and most research shows—that today, that kind of work requires a degree.[5] It wasn't uncomplicated to want these things for their children; they knew that college likely meant they wouldn't return. It's a high price to pay, and many of their friends and neighbors won't—or can't—accept that cost. But to these families, it felt necessary and possible, and so they pushed it. The students' high schools did, too, for the same reason their parents did: a shifting labor market, one that offers little locally and, elsewhere, requires further education. And the students listened—to their parents, to their teachers, to the slow silence of industries in decline—and so they planned for college.

Their rural contexts led the students to look to Hilltop specifically: Hilltop met their needs and spoke to their values—needs and values that were shaped by where they were from. Most had attended small local high schools, where they felt seen and known, and they looked for a college with this same kind of "communal feel." Close to their parents and families, they also wanted to stay near home, and most limited their searches to colleges within a couple of hours of their hometowns; it was only the scarcity of colleges in the rural West that forced Liliana and Hunter to look farther afield.[6] The students were tired of the Whiteness of their rural settings, and so they wanted a college that was racially diverse and inclusive, and they would need financial aid. They also wanted an elite school—not pretentious, not too far from the down-to-earth sensibilities of home, but elite enough to promise "connections," "an impressive résumé," an escape from the economic frustrations of home. So they aspired, not just to college, but to Hilltop, for its community and location and possibilities.

The economic context of their rural hometowns—little development, low wages, few jobs, and even fewer careers—didn't just push the students to Hilltop. It also influenced how they hoped to use this education: they were at college for a career. Despite Hilltop's academic breadth, then, they focused. While their classmates explored new disciplines and programs—exploration Hilltop's professors encouraged—these students gravitated toward the known: they took familiar classes and quickly chose majors. Their parents encouraged this focus. They wanted their children to find practical majors that promised good careers and more stable, more certain futures; this education, they reminded their children, needed to mean something. And their children listened to their parents' advice. They mostly chose majors that seemed, to them, to translate into jobs, jobs as doctors and lawyers and business owners, jobs recognizable back home and a "step better" than their parents'. They maintained this professional focus as their first year turned into a second and a third and a fourth, seeking out "practical" experiences that would make them employable and their studies useful. Then, after graduation, it was work that most of them chased: they came to Hilltop for employment, and that's what they left looking for, too.

The geographic asymmetry of employment, with few rural jobs for college-educated workers, meant that this career required an urban location—or at least it seemed to.[7] They couldn't return home, nor could they move to another rural place: they had to hope to leave. For some of them, the leaving was, in part, why they chose college, why they chose an elite school, why they chose Hilltop: they wanted somewhere "more vibrant," "more civilized," more urban than home—Hilltop was a way out. For the others, it was a slower, harder understanding, more of a reckoning, a recognition that they would have to leave. But all were afraid of "getting stuck" at home, stuck stocking shelves or waiting tables, stuck like their parents. These parents pushed them to leave, too: "The opportunities are in the big city and the experiences are in the big city," they'd say. They'd also grown up in a national culture that frames "rural" as lesser and equates "urban" with success, and Hilltop reinforced the message, too, through the location of its alumni networks and the jobs it advertised and the postgraduation plans of its students.[8] At Hilltop, the rural students came to have urban expectations: "This is where I belong now," said Sebastian.

What They Faced

Place—and more specifically, the spatial unevenness of resources—also shaped and oftentimes limited the students' college opportunities. Their rurality presented some barriers to applying and gaining admission. Most adults in their lives had never been to college—not their parents or their friends' parents or their neighbors—so the students knew little about college, like how to apply or how to pay or how to choose.[9] Elite schools were especially remote. No one at home had attended an elite school or knew anyone who had. Elite degrees were expensive, they assumed, and pretentious. Community colleges and state schools were the expectation, and they were closer: rural areas have fewer four-year options than cities, and many rural communities are located in what researchers call "education deserts," places with limited or no college choices.[10] The students also knew all the stereotypes around rurality and education and mobility: they knew they were "not expected to necessarily go on and exceed." In going to college, they were breaking with tradition, challenging expectations, venturing into unfamiliar territory.

The supports they relied on as they applied varied, a reflection of their particular rural contexts and positions within it. Those graduating from private schools and urban or suburban public schools had strong college advising—a kind of spatial privilege, as they were fortunate to live in rural places with private schools and financial support or with school choice and close, well-resourced metropolitan schools. Those attending rural public schools, though, had little postsecondary guidance, one product of a public funding system dependent on local property tax revenue.[11] Admissions officials also rarely traveled the long distances to visit their schools; they never saw the staff of elite colleges.[12] Like many rural public school students, they had scant SAT preparation, limited AP courses, and fewer extracurricular options to bolster their applications.[13] Their access to counselors, especially those who had the time, knowledge, and resources to offer sound guidance on college applications and decisions, was especially restricted.[14] And none of these students had the private SAT tutors or college consultants that many of their future classmates would use to reach Hilltop; they don't exist in most rural places, and even if they did, they wouldn't have been able to afford them. Despite all the college talk, then, these rural students—especially those attending rural public schools—faced rural-specific inequities as they planned to attend.[15]

Inequities continued to shape their access, even after they'd been admitted to college. Their high schools—public and private—didn't have the abundant resources of the prep schools that many of their new classmates attended, and so they entered Hilltop less prepared, without some of the skills, like writing research papers and participating in discussions, that Hilltop assumes.[16] They also didn't ask for help. They didn't know how—they hadn't needed it during high school—nor did they know why—they hadn't been coached on its importance. And they might have been scared to ask, for that would just prove the stereotype: that a "rural kid" isn't meant for a place like Hilltop. Socially, too, they struggled to participate in this new world of Canada Goose jackets and alcohol-infused parties and intense self-interest, a culture markedly different from that of home.[17] They also weren't used to navigating this new, more racially diverse space, and they weren't accustomed to the size and anonymity of campus. Slowly, the students acclimated, but it came with costs for some of them: self-doubt, low first-year grade point averages, changes in career plans.

The barriers stretched into their second and third and fourth years, when their limited financial resources often meant they couldn't afford the semesters abroad, the pricey summertime premed classes, or the weekend Outing Club trips. They needed to work, to cover tuition and buy books and keep up with the "pressure" to participate, but these jobs often kept them from campus, waiting tables and stocking shelves back home. This kind of blue-collar work, familiar and comparatively well paid, also filled their summers. When they could, they found jobs that were more career relevant, but those, too, were usually local, keeping them from building the "connections" they'd need—in the places they'd want to be—after graduation.[18] Without strong faculty relationships, they lacked the advising that could have helped them build résumés, lined with internships and job shadows and research assistantships, that would make them good hires in their intended fields. So, even though they attended Hilltop, geography and its inequities prevented full access.

It wasn't just access that these rural students were often denied; it was also inclusion.[19] Sometimes, they felt lonely or out of place, as if, although they'd been admitted to Hilltop, they didn't really belong there. They struggled to understand why: maybe it was about wealth and all the things they couldn't afford; maybe it was about education and the newness of college for their family; maybe it was, for some of them, about race or sexuality or politics. And it probably was. But even if they couldn't always articulate it, it was also about their rurality; rurality, specifically, didn't belong at Hilltop. They were one of just a handful of rural students on campus. They didn't have rural friends or rural classmates or rural professors. There were no rural affinity groups, no rural advisers. At first, it was mostly that rurality just wasn't considered; they felt out of place, but they suspected that it was mainly about money. But then came the 2016 election, and suddenly, rurality was the center of political and cultural debate. The narrative that accompanied the new attention—that bigoted, uneducated rural voters elected Trump—played on stereotypes, bred contempt, and invited pity. It quickly othered rural America, drawing a long, hard line between a righteously liberal Hilltop and the students' rural homes. For some of them, it also raised tough questions about race and class and place and their complicated intersections, about what it means to be rural. Their rurality, once not relevant, had become charged. It was too fraught to be rural, and so they kept quiet about that part of themselves, conflicted, aware that it wasn't welcome—and so maybe they weren't either.

What They Used

But place isn't only about limits and scarcity; it's also about resources. Family was one. Their parents prioritized education, trusting that a college degree would protect their children from a weakening rural economy and the trap of low-wage work, and they sacrificed for it, driving long distances to good urban schools and working extra hours and double shifts. They expected college, and—despite the assumptions of most admissions officials and guidance counselors and teachers—they believed that their children should attend a "good school." So they planned college visits and prayed the car wouldn't break down, because they wanted their children to have what they didn't: a degree, a promising career, a happier and more stable future. As their children entered Hilltop, the parents stayed close, through phone calls and video chats and visits, and they offered love, advice, and, perhaps most important, conviction. They never doubted that their children deserved a spot at Hilltop, that they could be successful there. These parents, then, flush with aspiration and faith, were a resource.[20]

Home offered other resources, too. The students often leveraged dense rural social ties.[21] These relationships led to most of their summer jobs, for example, jobs that, although they wouldn't build the urban networks the students would need after graduation, financed their education and sometimes shaped their professional paths. And amid all the low expectations, most of the students had at least one local adult—a teacher, a coach, or a Hilltop alum—who believed they should attend Hilltop.

Also, it seemed that rurality itself was sometimes a resource. No matter the politics, the isolation, the empty mills and factories, home is still "a dreamy, dreamy place." In between our conversations about roommates and classes and careers, they would tell me, with a casual kind of reverence, about the places they came from, places with quiet woods and clear lakes and open shores, places satisfyingly hard to get to and, sometimes, hard to leave. Throughout college, home remained a "refuge."

Their rurality fueled their determination, too—the "grit and perseverance" that got them to graduation. The same stereotypes and assumptions that they encountered as rural youth, the ones that told them they wouldn't "go on and exceed," also motivated them. "I'll prove you all wrong," they said, again and again, to the disbelieving math teacher, to the doubting neighbors, to the patronizing professor, to everyone who just didn't expect a kid from "a hole-in-the-wall town" to earn a Hilltop degree. They also didn't want to disappoint their parents, who had so badly wanted this for them, and they knew that loans would soon come due and that a half-finished education doesn't amount to much. This wasn't just an anxious determination, though. It was also a hopeful one: they were hopeful for all of the possibilities of a degree. And so they "stuck it out."

What They Gained and What They Lost

And this education—aspirations held, opportunities denied, resources used—had effects. They made it. They earned a degree, a degree from a "good school," a degree that many doubted they'd finish, a degree that, research suggests, will mean better jobs and greater earnings.[22] They left, ready and eager, with clear plans: dentistry, law, marketing, acting. Through it all, they learned—not just the academics but also that hidden social curriculum, mastering survival in an "ivy-covered" world filled with "preppy people."[23] They managed to remain connected to home, growing nimble, able to navigate the different politics and cultures of Hilltop and their rural homes—a skill they will undoubtedly use in the years to come.[24] And of this, of all of this, they were proud.

But even with this degree, they struggled. They looked for urban graduate schools and urban jobs—the ones that, everyone said, would use their college education and pay them well and make Hilltop worth it—but the realities of graduation were hard. They had few urban networks to leverage, and some didn't have the qualifications or experiences required by employers and graduate schools. Cities were expensive, and most of them were saddled with debt, a burden disproportionately carried by rural students.[25] They were anxious to start working, and they knew their parents were anxious for them to start, too, and so they were also stressed, frustrated, and, sometimes, a little jealous of their classmates—classmates who were urban and connected and employed. They went to college, did well, and graduated, and still they found it hard to find a job, make rent, and pay bills in a city. There's a geography to these realities, and it didn't favor these students.

Though they struggled to make it to the city, they couldn't go home either—or, really, to any other rural place. It was, as they'd been warned, also hard to find rural jobs. The "good" jobs—ones that would use their degrees and make enough for them to pay off their loans— are scarce, and they had little help finding them: few rural positions make it to the career center's list of job openings, and their parents' networks didn't include that kind of work. Most of them also didn't want a rural job. For some, this urban desire began years ago, well before Hilltop, shaped by the advice of worried adults and, perhaps, the urban bias of American media and culture; Hilltop only fueled it. For others, this desire was new. But for both, after Hilltop, home was less comfortable. They spent four years away, and they changed—politically, ideologically, personally. They developed new ideas, and a few found new identities—some of which weren't welcome at home. Most thought about their hometowns differently: whether the clarity of distance or the edge of stigma, there was a sharpness to its deficits and failings, and what they still appreciated was sometimes harder to see. Also, their parents sometimes felt distant. Despite the visits home and frequent phone calls, the students spent four years in a vastly different world, and that's not something they could easily explain. Most of the parents were also pushing their children away, pushing them to cities; worried about "the upward mobility" of rural work, they, too, wanted them to find urban jobs. These students, then, couldn't return. To come home was neither practical nor possible.

And so they were stuck, not at home, as they'd worried, but somewhere between the rural life they'd hoped to leave and the urban life they'd hoped to have. They were leaving—by the fall after graduation, they all had urban jobs or urban plans—but this leaving was slower and harder than they'd imagined. Some were back home, unhappily so, hoping to leave soon. Others were unsatisfied with their urban jobs, missing family and mountains and coast—something, they discovered, that even the most prestigious email address can't make up for. A couple of them wondered how they would maintain life in a city: soon, they'd owe more money than they'd make, and they didn't know what they'd do then. So, yes, they were leaving rural America. But they're not yet where they want to be.

College as Resistance

For these students, college was never an assumption. They grew up in rural places tied to industries that didn't require college, transitioning to economies that won't need them either. They were surrounded by adults who hadn't gone to college and by neighbors who questioned whether they should. The postsecondary messaging of their K-12 schools was uneven—"go to college" directives were often coupled with low expectations and little support. Popular media has made an industry out of rural ignorance: rural people are uneducated, the TV shows and movies and news anchors say, and they have little interest in getting educated.[26] Over and over, these students heard that college—especially the elite kind—isn't a place for rural youth: rural kids stay home, get rural jobs, do rural work.

But these students resisted. Not in the ways so often written about—that is, resisting education—but instead, resisting *through* education: they went to college.[27] For this group of high-performing, academically savvy students, college was an act of resistance. They were resisting an American economy that, despite restructuring, still depends on poorly compensated rural workers to pick produce, haul freight, clean hotel rooms. They were resisting the cultural messages that support this economy—the messages that tell them that they don't need a degree, that they shouldn't want one, that they aren't meant for anything but this kind of work. And they were resisting an education that is conflicted, caught between its loftier ideals of equality and mobility and its darker charge of vocational sorting.[28] It's not just that rural students aren't expected "to go on and exceed"; there's a vast economic system dependent on them not going. But these students did. They went to college—and to the kind of college that seemed the strongest guarantee against a lifetime of low-paid, undervalued rural work. And they finished that college, learning all the strategies (hiding, passing, code switching) and using all the resources (family, home, stubborn determination) to graduate.[29]

The costs of that resistance, though, were high. Despite their talent and hard work, they didn't receive a full Hilltop education. Access was only partial, belonging was often conditional, and promises were sometimes empty. They paid an emotional toll, too: loneliness and disappointment but also the pressure of big expectations, the worry of losing an increasingly distant home, the conflict and doubt and questions wrapped up in their rurality. For some, there was also regret—they didn't want an urban life, after all—and there was fear—it's too late, and they can't return. And these weren't just *their* costs. Their parents felt them, too. These college decisions weren't uncomplicated for them. There was the anxiety: the practical concerns of loans and bills and FAFSA forms, but also the apprehension that comes with sending a child to a place you don't know and a world you don't understand.

And there was the prickly reality that this departure would likely be not just four years but, instead, permanent. Their rural towns would also pay this price in the form of lost human capital, lost tax dollars, lost potential. So college was costly, for these students and for those who love and depend on them.

Research suggests that, as rural youth consider their futures, they face a hard choice: between college, for the opportunities it offers, and home, for its relationships and community.[30] These students felt that tension, too, and four years later, it sometimes seemed as though college came at the price of home.

But the students, I notice, never described that decision as a binary choice, even later, as the costs became more real. College was never just about the opportunities—at least, opportunities of the individualistic sort. For them, college was about their parents and *their* hopes and dreams. It was about stereotypes and the chance to disprove them. And it was about resistance: refusing to participate in rural undereducation and exploitation. College, then, wasn't only—or even mostly—about them; it was also about their families, their friends, and their communities. They went to college for them, too, so that higher education and its opportunities wouldn't seem so remote. These students weren't choosing opportunity over home; they were choosing both.

Now, after graduation, they're doing everything they can to hold on to each. Most of them didn't get the opportunities they were promised: the shiny résumé, the powerful connections, the "good job" in the city. And they can't return home: there's little work for them, and four years away has changed things. But they're not yet willing to let go of either, and so they're still holding on, still resisting.

The Spatial Inequities of Underrepresentation

It might not be just rural students whose college opportunities and experiences are shaped by geography. Other students underrepresented on college campuses—Black students, Latinx students, Indigenous students, international students, and low-income students—are also often from isolated, underresourced places: segregated city neighborhoods, reservations, and developing nations.[31] Although it's little recognized, the spatial marginality of these places might determine these students' college access and experiences, too.

Like these nine rural students, other underrepresented students might also see college as a way out—a way out of blue-collar work or poverty but also, for some, a way out of the places they're from.[32] Yet they, too, typically have few college-educated neighbors or local postsecondary options, and they rarely encounter admissions officials at their high schools.[33] Like many rural schools, these schools are also often underfunded, which can limit college counseling and weaken academic preparation—they get to college in spite of, not because of, their high school training.[34] And when they arrive, those from similarly segregated places might find themselves unprepared for the racial diversity of a college campus, as some of the rural students did, and those from places with high unemployment and low wages will encounter many of the same financial barriers to full academic and social participation.[35] Though these students may also benefit from the motivation and support that comes with growing up in close-knit, geographically isolated places, their local networks likely lack the connections useful for securing professionally important internships and white-collar jobs, and given their limited resources and financial responsibilities, they might not develop these connections during college.[36] As graduation looms, they may encounter the same stark reality facing these nine rural students: there's no work for them at home, yet there's nowhere else to go.[37]

And just as it was for the nine rural students, attending college may be an act of solidarity and resistance—a defiant refusal to participate in the subjugation of their communities, a choice of both college *and* home.[38] But for them, too, the choice may be costly. Home may feel farther now, and they likely can't return—at least, not easily. They have also been educated out.

Certainly, some geographic influences may be specific to rural students and rural places, like the political dimensions of belonging on a college campus. There are spatial inequalities that might be more acute. The remoteness of many rural places can intensify their isolation; admissions officials, for example, are particularly unlikely to visit far-flung rural high schools, and rural areas might be especially lacking in college options.[39] The small size of rural schools can also present barriers that make it difficult to staff a guidance department or provide Advanced Placement classes.[40] For rural students, returning to a rural place after graduation might be especially challenging, as even employment *near* home might be an impossibility.

And of course, not every barrier an underrepresented student faces is related to geography. Class and especially race may influence a student's experience in ways apart from place, too. And place may interact with class and race in ways both complicated and complex.

But clearly, place itself matters, shaping the opportunities of many students underrepresented on college campuses. So it's not just that the experiences of these nine rural students resemble those of other underrepresented students—although they do, in all kinds of ways. Instead, place likely structures the opportunities of *all* students, granting some students distinct advantages and putting others—those from places, whether rural or urban, that are overlooked and exploited—at a disadvantage. Thus, what we commonly assume to be disadvantages of class and race might actually be—at least in part—disadvantages of place. College opportunity depends on geography.

A Geography Hidden

Yet, for the most part, we overlook this.[41] We consider geography in crude, easy-to-count measures, like states and countries represented, mainly at the point of admission—rarely anything more meaningful or more lasting. We offer a few "college promise" programs, with scholarships for youth from specific neighborhoods or cities, and provide some community-based college access programs, which help local youth navigate application and admission processes—important supports, but limited in scope.[42] And after the 2016 election, we certainly have shown more interest in rural students—little, though, that will fundamentally change the relationship between place and opportunity.[43]

Students also mostly miss this geography of opportunity. The nine rural students noticed it sometimes, like when chafing under the low expectations of teachers. But they didn't seem to fully understand the slights and challenges as spatial inequalities—as regular and systemic, as rooted in their rurality, as a kind of injustice.

And, honestly, this surprised me. They saw how hard it was to access an elite education, and, for four years, they navigated the inequalities of Hilltop. They grew more critical—of Hilltop, eliteness, and meritocratic "hogwash." So why couldn't they see how rurality mattered?

Maybe, though, I shouldn't be surprised. Their rurality was a part of their identity they hadn't much considered and then, after the 2016 election, a part harder to claim. So maybe they couldn't see the influence of geography because they were distancing themselves from rurality itself. And maybe it's unfair to question the students' critical capacities. Schools are good at hiding their injustices, and it's difficult, when living out the particularities of a single experience, to see how these particularities might be arranged in larger patterns of inequalities. That might be especially true when those patterns are geographic in nature. There exists, however limited and ineffectual, a public and critical discourse about racial and class injustice. But geography is an overlooked and undertheorized dimension of inequality. There is no discourse about place in which students can locate themselves; they don't have a vocabulary to talk about their experiences or a framework through which to understand them. So maybe they don't see the place-based inequalities of higher education, not because they don't experience them, but because we, as a society, refuse to acknowledge them.

This hiddenness compounds the costs of college for these students—and, likely, for other underrepresented students. Sometimes, they individualize what's systemic, blaming themselves for what's actually the product of much larger injustices. Sometimes, they distance themselves from home or buy into narratives about the "backwardness" and "failures" of home. And sometimes, they may overlook the possibilities—the ways they can, with some work and creativity, become college graduates that return. This hiddenness, then, feeds the loneliness and also the leaving.

If we can develop this language, though, and build a vocabulary for spatial injustice that is honest and critical, we can begin to reduce the costs of a college degree, for these students and for their communities.[44]

7

To College and Back

I've always been a college advocate. Like these nine students, my parents preached the value of a degree. Like these students, I went to college—an elite college—and then I continued on to graduate school. Now I teach at an elite college and study college access. I know well the benefits of college, and the benefits of elite degrees, and I can see how these impacts—the wage bump, the increased job security, the generational returns—might be especially important for rural students. I can also see how reducing the place-based educational gap might have important political and economic returns for society. It's what made me want the possibility of college for my third graders; it's what led me to these nine rural students.

These nine students were believers, too. During the summer before Hilltop, as they were standing at the edge of college, with bags packed and goodbyes said, I asked them about the value of college. College, they said, is "super important," "beneficial," "a very good thing." Without it, life is "tougher."

But if I'm honest, as I then watched these students navigate Hilltop, I sometimes questioned this faith, both mine and theirs. For these students, a Hilltop education came with costs: isolation, doubt, distance from family and friends. Belonging sometimes felt conditional, and its opportunities weren't always open to them. They graduated with debt, surprisingly limited job options, some worries, and regrets. It isn't clear yet if the oft-cited economic and social benefits of an elite education will materialize for them.

I also worried about the costs to rural America: these students were leaving. They had been educated to leave, prepared for urban life and urban work. This had certainly been a long and comprehensive preparation: both their parents and their high schools had nurtured urban aspirations. But Hilltop turned these aspirations into expectations and, for some, realities. In part, this education was about training: Hilltop groomed these students for jobs that are more difficult to find in rural places.[1] But it was also a matter of acculturation. For four years, the students had lived with roommates who weren't rural, had classmates who weren't rural, and made friends who weren't rural. They read books written by authors who weren't rural and studied theories developed by academics who weren't rural. They worked internships that weren't rural and studied abroad in places that weren't rural. During their senior years, they pored over advertisements for jobs that weren't rural and applied to graduate schools that weren't rural. This socialization was perhaps even more effective than the training itself: they expected— and were expected—to leave rural America for urban America. And I was pretty certain that, eventually, they'd make it there. Hilltop would empty rural America.

Hilltop will likely pay off for these students.[2] They will earn more than their high school classmates. They will attend graduate school and get promoted. They won't have to worry about money like their parents did. And they deserve this: after all, they are talented, hard-working, well credentialed, "gritty."

The problem with grit, though, is that it conceals the circumstances that demand it.[3] College shouldn't require grit. College shouldn't be some sort of endurance test against the injustices of geography. College shouldn't gut communities.

And so sometimes—many years into a career in higher education and a study on college opportunity—I found myself wondering whether college really was worth it, for these students or for their communities. Maybe the college critics were right. Maybe a degree isn't all that important; maybe it could do more harm than good. Maybe these students and their families had made the wrong choice.

The Wrong Debate

I knew that the students' faith was waning, too. They were, after all, in debt, hoping to move, still looking for jobs. They no longer trusted that the educational system rewards the most deserving, that Hilltop opens doors. They were learning just how much their Hilltop degree might cost them. As Daniel told me, "It still remains to be seen how much Hilltop was worth it or not." And so when I asked them the question that has dominated recent college debates and animated recent interest in rural students—should everyone go to college?—I expected to hear that doubt.

But instead, I heard anger—resistance. That's the wrong question, they told me, the wrong debate. "The controversy should be whether everyone has access to it or not, not whether everybody should go," Liliana explained. "That is the issue that we should be focused on: giving access to education—good education."

It's not up to me—or anyone else—to determine whether a student should go to college. The question itself limits options; it's more about politics and the economy than students' own hopes and dreams for themselves and for their communities. So we should stop asking it and instead focus on ensuring that all students, no matter where they live, *can* go to college if they want, and that they can choose where to go, and that this education doesn't come with qualifications or limitations or awful costs.

A Good Education

Right now, most rural students don't have that kind of access: the spatial inequities of college opportunity limit their options. Too often, they're underprepared and underfunded. They may be tracked into certificate or two-year programs that don't match their goals. They're sometimes unsupported and excluded. They're often pushed toward urban jobs and lives that they can't attain or can't afford or, sometimes, don't even really want. Place shapes opportunity, and place also suffers the consequences of that opportunity, and we—critics, advocates, administrators, policymakers, researchers—mostly ignore this. And so it continues: we debate who should go to college and why, and some of us even push rural students toward college, but we do it without also providing them the means to get there, to thrive there, and to leave there, for a job in a city or maybe back home.

I think about what access to "good education"—full, inclusive, useful anywhere—would look like for these nine rural students, for my third graders, for all the other children growing up in places made marginal. It would require, first, that policymakers and practitioners and researchers acknowledge that there is a geography to college opportunity, that they work to identify and document its impacts, and that they talk about these impacts with students and families. And then it would mean changing policies and practices. It would mean rethinking approaches to place diversity in college outreach and admissions, moving from more superficial markers of place, such as home state, to indicators of spatial marginality, such as remoteness or isolation. It would mean admissions visits to high schools in hard-to-reach places and creative virtual work-arounds. It would mean accounting for spatial injustice in admissions decisions, understanding, for example, that geography might prevent a student from taking ten AP courses or boasting a diverse array of extracurriculars, but also understanding that overcoming geographic barriers is, in itself, an indication of "achievement." It would mean laying to rest long-held myths about meritocracy and education and having honest, place-specific conversations about aspirations and educational options and job opportunities. It would mean including families—all families, from all places—in college advising and welcoming them on college campuses. It would mean building strong partnerships between community colleges and four-year schools, making transferring a viable option, and between elite schools located in rural places and their surrounding communities, making these schools more likely destinations. And then, once rural students arrive at college, it would mean support, inclusion, and opportunity. It would mean counting rural students as rural students—and urban students as urban students, and suburban students as suburban students—and tracking them and their experiences. It would mean changing curriculum, addressing place-based bias, so that rural and other geographically marginal students can see themselves, fully and authentically and accurately, in the texts they're reading and the theories they're learning—and so that geographically privileged students, and geographically privileged faculty, can see them, too. It would mean making campus culture more socially and politically inclusive and helping students navigate, with kindness and respect, their differences in knowledge and understanding and experience. And it would mean support: K-12 funding that sustains college preparatory coursework in rural schools, college counseling that honors students' and families' goals, financial aid that covers travel home and the other hidden costs of college, transition programming that attends to place and its intersections with race and class, career advising that accounts for limited career knowledge and centers students' locational aspirations and includes opportunities in a diversity of places, and generous investments by colleges in the economies and cultures of communities, both near and far.

Good education requires more than just changing schools, though. Right now, we present rural and other geographically underrepresented youth with a choice. Either they can go to college and live an adult life far from home, or they can stay, remain close to family, and get "stuck" in a low-wage job. The reality, of course, is complex: one faraway job doesn't have to mean a lifetime lived away, and some graduates do find that job and return home or to someplace like it. But to many students—to these nine students—this is the choice we offer: college or home. They resist, doing their best to have both, but the challenge of doing so only underscores the fact of the choice. And it is a terrible choice, an anxious choice, a choice that students and families shouldn't have to make.[4] It can keep kids from college, rupture families, siphon skills and wealth from rural and other marginal places. It maintains the undereducation of rural America.

And so we also need more degree-using, well-paying jobs in rural places. This will require policies and incentives that address the urban dependence on cheap rural labor, that support rural sustainability and self-determination, that end spatial systems of economic exploitation. It will also require complicating how we talk about "success"—so that "leaving" doesn't have to mean "forever" and that "making it" doesn't have to mean "in a city."

Maybe college isn't for everyone. But I suspect that it's for more than currently go, and I know that it doesn't have to be so costly. Rural students—and their communities—don't have full access to good education. And that, as Liliana explained, is what needs attention.

My students—these nine students, my former third graders—are grown now. They're working, making homes, having babies. And here's what I hope for them: I hope they're comfortable. I hope they like their jobs. I hope they're close to family—maybe not near, but still close. And I hope that, when it comes time for their babies to think about college, we give them more options than we did their parents.

Acknowledgments

This research was made possible by generous grants from the Spencer Foundation and the Roger C. Schmutz Fund for Bates Faculty Development.

I am grateful to the staff of Hilltop's Admissions Office and Registrar's Office, who were gracious with their time and insight and patient with me. I am also indebted to the manuscript's reviewers, whose feedback was both incisive and encouraging, as well as the entire team at the University of Chicago Press. This is a much stronger book for their thoughtful reading, coaching, and editing. A number of colleagues and friends read and edited early drafts, including Jill Reich, MK Montgomery, Jay Braunstein, Anthony Abraham Jack, and Tobie Akerley Gordon; their careful eyes, wise words, and gentle delivery kept me writing. Travis Palmer provided critical support and motivation throughout this project. Liliana Garces, Cynthia Gordon da Cruz, Ann Ishimaru, Sola Takahashi, and Amanda Taylor—these women have always been so much more than a writing group. Therí Pickens knew just what to say when. And I'm grateful to AJ, who, for twelve years, listened to me talk—and laugh and cry—about this project.

And, finally, I cannot begin to put into words my gratitude to Amelia, Daniel, Ethan, Henry, Hunter, John, Liliana, Sebastian, and Sylvan. Thank you for trusting me.

Appendix

This study was unlike any I've undertaken before. Young people would be the focus—not adults, not organizations, not places. I would spend more than four years with each of these young people. I would learn intimate details about their lives. I would have close contact with their families. And then I would render their lives—their young lives—in a book, leaving a permanent and public record. So I was careful—methodologically, ethically, relationally.

The Setting

I decided to work with students at a single school: I knew that understanding the students' experiences would require an intimate understanding of their college context, and focusing on a single site would provide that depth. I chose Hilltop for a few reasons. It is a selective liberal arts college (SLAC)—the kind of elite school that, research suggests, rural, first-generation students are particularly unlikely to attend. Its admissions process is highly competitive, with an acceptance rate of less than 20 percent, and its name is well-recognized, even beyond college students and families. And its tuition is expensive: about $65,000 a year (including room and board) when these nine students were attending, above $85,000 today. I also had contacts at the school: I knew that its registrar's office would help me reach out to students, that its admissions staff would allow me to accompany them as they hosted events, and that I would have a dog-friendly place to conduct interviews.

Hilltop also shares many other qualities that are typical of SLACs. It is small, with a student body of a couple of thousand, and the vast majority of students live on campus. Although it has grown more racially diverse over the past couple of decades, it remains a predominantly White institution: only about 20–25 percent of the population identifies as domestic Black, Hispanic, Asian/Asian Pacific Islander, Native American, or multiracial. Although the school supports students' full financial need—at least, as determined by FAFSA—it is need aware in its admissions process, and more than half of students are full-pay. It also considers legacy status in admission. Only 5–10 percent of its students are first generation.

My focus on a single site limits the study's generalizability. The school does have its own idiosyncrasies, such as its test-optional admissions process, that may make some findings unique. However, because Hilltop is so typical of the SLAC genre, I trust that many of the findings are reflected at other SLACs, too. They might be less generalizable to larger, less competitive, or more career-oriented institutions or to those with more rural students.

The standard of rigor in portraiture, though, is not generalizability but authenticity—the kind of authenticity that exists in context-specific particularities.[1] And because all colleges are credentialing institutions that can provide access to jobs and opportunities, they are also all, to some degree, sites of negotiating belonging and mobility. Thus, I suspect that many of the stories resonate well beyond the rarefied atmosphere of elite education.

The Students

Far more difficult than choosing a school was finding participants. I needed rural students, and because rurality so often intersects with first-generation status, I wanted first-generation students. So I had to determine how I would identify Hilltop's incoming rural, first-generation students and invite them to join the study. First-generation status was relatively straightforward. I could use the

Common Application's definition of *first generation*—students for whom neither parent received a bachelor's degree. The application, which Hilltop uses, asks applicants for parents' education, and Hilltop records this information; its admissions office could easily pull a list of incoming first-generation students. But rural location was harder. The Common Application doesn't ask if students are from a rural place, and Hilltop doesn't track rurality in any kind of way. So I needed to figure out how to find the rural students. There are dozens of rural classification systems I could choose from, some tied to students' home address and others linked to the location of their K-12 schooling.[2] To protect students' anonymity, the registrar—understandably—limited my access to admitted students' information; I was given a list of the addresses of first-generation students, and I would learn students' names only if they opted into the study. Because I was interested in students' paths to college, I decided to connect students' addresses to local public schools—specifically, elementary schools, because some rural school districts don't have high schools—and identify potential participants based on the rurality of their schools. Focusing on school catchment areas also provided a finer-grained method of identification than many residential methods; county-based systems, for example, can overlook community heterogeneity within counties.[3] I knew that students may not have attended their local public schools, but that possibility seemed useful, allowing me to better capture the varied ways rural students arrive at an elite school like Hilltop.

Early in the summer of 2014, using students' home addresses and the locale codes issued by the National Center for Education Statistics, I identified the first-generation students assigned to schools located in rural areas or areas classified as "town remote"—that is, within a small town more than thirty-five miles from an urban area.[4] I wrote the students a letter, which Hilltop's registrar sent on my behalf. It described the study, explained issues like confidentiality and pseudonyms, and invited them to call me if they were, indeed, rural and first generation and willing to participate. I explained that the direct benefits of their participation were limited, but I was happy to serve as informal adviser—a possibility that, I later learned, calmed some parents' anxieties about college and led a few to encourage their children to sign up—and the study might contribute to our understanding of rural college opportunity and allow counselors and admissions officials to better support students.[5] After weeks of anxious waiting, I began receiving their (probably equally anxious) calls. I then repeated the processes in the summer of 2015. Ultimately, half of eligible students joined: three in 2014, from the class of 2018, and six in 2015, from the class of 2019.

Like with my choice of institutional settings, this method of selection limits generalizability. I reached students after they had already decided to attend Hilltop. Unsurprisingly, they were all among the top of their high school class, highly involved in numerous extracurricular activities, and excited to experience a small liberal arts college. Their parents were mostly college advocates and particularly strong advocates of Hilltop. The school's eliteness likely shaped the group in other ways, too. They were mostly men, which is somewhat unusual—a greater proportion of rural women typically attend college.[6] Because I don't know the genders of the students who declined to participate in the study, I cannot speak to the ratio of men to women for (or the presence of nonbinary students among) all rural, first-generation students at Hilltop. But research shows that rural girls may feel a greater sense of family responsibility than rural boys; if rural youth associate an elite degree with remaining away permanently, this might be one factor influencing the gender balance of these nine students.[7] Related to this, a not-insignificant portion of the students arrived at Hilltop intending to use their education to leave their hometowns.

So, yes, these students and their students represent a small fraction of rural families. But they are an important group precisely because of this unique position: their experiences at an elite school shed new light on the complex geography of college opportunity. These students also varied in their interests and abilities, and their parents varied in their levels of support—and I would discover, some of their feelings changed over time. These variations offer some insights into the broader diversity represented in rural populations. And again, the methodological standard for portraiture is authenticity, and I think that, in the details of these students and parents' perspectives and experiences, many readers will recognize broader truths of inequality and opportunity.

Data Sources

I came to know these nine students well, interviewing each of them twelve times and often hearing from them in between interviews. The interviews happened on Hilltop's campus, with a few exceptions: most of the first summertime interviews, when I drove to students' homes or, for those from places outside of New England, talked with them on the phone; a couple of conversations while students were abroad, which happened via Skype; and most of the final interviews, when we met at a variety of places, often close to their new homes. The interviews typically lasted thirty minutes to an hour but, with a few of the students, could run much longer. Although I asked about several topics every interview, such as their classes, their majors, their families and friends, and their extracurricular involvements, I developed protocols unique to each time (e.g., first-year fall, senior spring) and, often, with a few questions unique to each student. The protocols were informed both by prior conversations and the literature on college access, college opportunity, and rural college-going. After a while, the conversations started to feel familiar—to me and, I think, to the students, too—as we fell into regular patterns of updating and sharing and thinking; they became semiannual markers of the passage of time and, for all of us, reminders of the relative fleetingness of college.

I interviewed the students' parents, too. For six of the students, I interviewed both parents; this includes Sebastian, whose parents divorced while he was at Hilltop. I only interviewed Daniel's mother; his parents divorced when he was young, and he lived with his mother during high school and most college breaks. I also only interviewed Liliana's father; I cannot speak Spanish, and her mother speaks limited English—but I did meet and talk with her mother when I visited their hometown and joined her family for a meal. I interviewed Henry's mother and stepfather; Henry doubted his father would talk with me. I had three interviews with these parents. We met in their homes or on Hilltop's campus or, for those families living outside of the Northeast, we sometimes caught up by phone. Parents also occasionally reached out to me in between our formal conversations, typically looking for advice or guidance during their children's first year of college.

A few other data sources also informed this study. I regularly observed significant Hilltop events. Some marked important milestones in these students' lives, like graduation. Others were the more routine admissions events that pave many students' paths to Hilltop, like college fairs, campus tours, and recruitment dinners; with these, I usually didn't observe the specific sessions the nine students experienced. In addition, I read the students' applications and college essays, which offered demographic and schooling information and a useful window into their high school selves. Finally, the year before I began the student and parent interviews, I talked with a number of guidance counselors at rural high schools; college admissions officials at various institutions; and leaders of rural, college-focused community-based organizations. Together, these observations, applications, and community interviews helped contextualize the students' experiences and often provided a common reference point for later conversations.

As I completed interviews and observations, I took notes. I kept field notes of each interview, recording physical details, like clothing, gestures, and new beards or glasses; emotions and inflection points; and my own thoughts and reactions. I also recorded field notes during my observations or, for more public or immersive events, as soon as possible afterward; they focused on the details of the events—who, what, when, and where—but also on the complicated undercurrents of privilege and belonging. The field notes included reflections on emerging themes that I later fleshed out into more detailed memos. Finally, I kept a careful record of decisions related to design and methods, and I created several tables detailing students' background information.

Analysis

After more than six years of talking with the students and their families and attending Hilltop events and doing background interviews, I had mountains of data: thousands of pages of interview transcripts, plus the students' college applications and all the field notes. I first focused my analysis on the students individually, reading their transcripts, writing summary memos of their experiences, and identifying major themes and events for each. I then read across the students and developed a set of codes reflecting common ideas and experiences; the codes included concepts that the literature suggested might be useful (e.g., belonging) and others that emerged from the data (e.g., politics).[8] Using NVivo software, I coded the interview data and wrote memos on each code; the memos explored shared experiences, as well as nuances. I then divided the students' experiences into four time periods—their Hilltop aspirations and applications, their transitions into Hilltop, the experiences that filled their years at Hilltop, and their transitions from Hilltop. I looked within and across the coded material for common themes that defined each period. These themes became the framework for the four portraits.

For each portrait, I chose stories from the students that best represented the portrait's themes or highlighted important subtleties. As I wrote the portrait, I mostly used the students' words and experiences, although I sometimes incorporated parents' voices to add background or detail or to share their perspectives. I then stitched the stories together with my analysis.

After I completed the portraits, I turned to the question that motivated this study: how does place matter to rural students' college access and experiences? I examined the portraits but also reread transcripts and field notes, seeking to understand how students' rural backgrounds shaped their aspirations, their transitions, their experiences. Again, I looked for the patterns of their stories, as well as the divergences. I also consulted the literature on the college experiences of other underrepresented students, seeking to better understand how geography shapes opportunity more broadly, both during college and after graduation.

Relationships and Representation

This study was approved by my home institution's institutional review board (IRB). But the ethical considerations it raised seemed thornier and more complicated than those covered by most IRB reviews. So as I designed and carried out the study, I focused on the students' welfare and privacy.

Well-Being and Worry

My first priority was safety. As a college faculty member—and a former college student—I knew some of the situations and challenges they might encounter, and I soon learned of others. I worried about them, especially during their first years: I worried about bad roommates, I worried about poor academic advising, I worried about the pressures of the party scene.

I told the students that, if they ever shared anything with me that made me concerned for their physical safety or the safety of anyone else, I was obligated to share those concerns with Hilltop officials. No one did. But I did recommend counseling to a few, and I helped Sebastian access Hilltop's mental health services.

More frequently I'd offer advice. Usually it was somewhat generic advice, like how to juggle deadlines or what to include on a résumé. Not all the students wanted or needed this kind of guidance; I tried to identify and respect their needs, stepping in only when asked or when it was clear they wouldn't receive guidance elsewhere. More often, their parents sought my advice—or my reassurance—about classes or majors or the college social scene. Typically, they asked for this guidance in confidence, not wanting their child to feel as though they doubted them. I accommodated when I could, and I didn't share those moments with the students or identify them in this book. I was also honest with parents, both about my need to respect students' confidentiality and about the limitations of my expertise.

Certainly, sometimes the boundary between researcher and adviser grew blurry. Several students mentioned that our conversations had a cathartic or therapeutic quality, providing a space to process the events of the semester and a place to feel heard. I think this blurriness is instructive. It indicates the supports that students wanted but didn't always find, and I describe several of those moments in the portraits. But I don't think my listening or advising markedly altered any of their college paths. And the students were resourceful and proudly independent. So for the most part, my worries were quiet worries, worries that I didn't need to share.

Privacy and Respect

I tried to respect students' privacy, too. I hoped for a deep understanding of their experiences, but they needed the freedom to have those experiences, the space to falter and fail. So I carefully bounded my inquiry. I avoided questions that weren't relevant or necessary. I assured the students that I wouldn't tell their parents the details of their college lives, just as I told parents that I wouldn't share with students the information they disclosed to me. Only when I understood what information each knew—that, for example, Sylvan's parents were aware of his drunken night and trip to the hospital—did we discuss these events more freely. Occasionally these boundaries were awkward, but they were necessary for respecting the students' and parents' privacy.

I also didn't want the students to fear that the details of their college lives would be publicly and permanently affixed to them: these details should be theirs to own and to share. I let them choose pseudonyms (or opt to keep their real names, if they preferred). Hilltop is also a pseudonym, and in the book, I am intentionally vague about its location and some of its identifying characteristics. We invented names for the students' hometowns, too, and I kept their locations and details hazy.

I was selective in what I included in the portraits as well. I occasionally omitted identifying but nonessential information, and I sought explicit permission to include material they might not want shared with parents and others likely to identify them, even with pseudonyms. For example, Ethan and I discussed whether I would talk about his sexuality, especially because his parents don't know he is gay; he very much wanted me to, feeling it was an important part of his story—and, he noted, it was unlikely his parents would read this book. Likewise, Sylvan asked that I mention his struggles with mental health; he felt that it would help normalize depression and therapy, especially for rural men. When students had strong feelings about details they wanted included or removed, I honored those requests.

Responsibility and Review

The students qualified for this study because they were both "first generation" and "rural"—two labels that are fraught with meaning. They expressed some hesitation about the labels. Several told me that they didn't know they were considered "first generation" until my letter arrived. They were less surprised by "rural," but as I learned, most of the students had mixed feelings about the descriptor. I also noticed that they tended to avoid other labels that could apply to them. Most rarely used class signifiers, like *low income* and *working class*, and some were cautious in adopting racial descriptors, too. So in this book, these words are my words, labels that I, and other researchers, use—and not necessarily the labels the students would choose for themselves.

Still, I wanted to ensure that, in the end, I had captured, if not the words and stories they would write, something that felt truthful and honest. And so, after completing the portraits, I sent them to the students for review. I asked them to correct any factual errors and to share feedback, especially any themes or ideas that didn't reflect their experiences. Once again, I anxiously waited. Had I accurately and respectfully captured their experiences? Yes, I was reassured to learn. Their edits were few in number and minor in scope, mostly small details I'd misremembered or inaccurately assumed. A couple of students requested some small changes to provide a little more anonymity; others wanted me to remove some of the changes I'd made to protect their privacy and, instead, to include real names and places. I honored all their requests.

I also wanted to confirm that the portraits and these findings resonated with other rural students. So I hired a research assistant, an undergraduate at Bates College, my home institution, who was also rural, first generation, and working class. Travis read everything— outlines, chapter drafts, portraits—and offered his thoughts, with generosity and kindness. He provided another rural perspective, telling me where he saw himself in these stories and where he didn't and why. He also flagged flaws in my arguments, areas that needed detail, passages that could use some editing. For much of the book, he was the first reader, and what my eyes sometimes missed, his eyes often caught.

Positionality and Trust

I came to this study from a particular position: I am a White woman and a tenured member of the faculty at an elite college. I am a former rural teacher. I'm also the graduate of an elite college, the product of a mostly suburban public and private K-12 education, and the daughter of two first-generation college students, one of them rural. I am now raising my daughter in rural Maine, where we live on a dirt road and struggle to find child care but can drive forty minutes to the state's largest city.

These identities influenced my questions, my interpretations, and my writing. As I explain in the first chapter, I began this study because my rural third graders didn't go to college and I wondered why. I was curious about elite schools specifically because I understand—and have experienced—the benefits of an elite college degree. I focused on place-based inequities in access and opportunity because I saw evidence of them in my own classrooms and in the lives of those I loved; I suspected they existed, even if I did not yet grasp their extent or see their complexities. I was mindful of the potential bias these perspectives and experiences could introduce, and I routinely looked for disconfirming evidence and alternate interpretations by regularly revisiting the data; consulting with colleagues fluent in the research on college access, rural education, and structural inequality; and discussing my initial interpretations with family, friends, and students. Travis was also a useful check on my assumptions, and throughout the study, I often went to these nine students, ensuring I was accurately capturing their thoughts or asking for their perspective on themes or ideas.

Perhaps most consequentially, though, my various identities also shaped my interactions with the students and parents. First, there was the "professor" dynamic to contend with; I worried that the students and families would be cautious about opening up to a faculty member at an elite school—after all, I represented the elite world they were newly navigating. I also worried that they might assume that our worldviews might be too divergent for either of us to understand the other. To mitigate those barriers, I was clear about what was motivating this study: my experience as a rural teacher concerned about the opportunities my former students did not have. For the first summer interviews, I let parents and students choose where we'd meet—Hilltop's campus, their home, or by phone—allowing them to opt for the setting that felt most comfortable. For the interviews following graduation, I also met students at a variety of other settings—outdoors, coffee shops, graduate school campuses—places easy for them to reach, where we could talk out of the earshot of parents and beyond the confines of the Hilltop campus. Throughout the conversations, I was honest about my feelings about elite education—what I see as its advantages and what I see as its disappointments, failures, and shortfalls. I sometimes shared my own challenges navigating an elite school, never to equate mine to theirs but instead to normalize their difficulties. I tried to save my stories and opinions for the end of a conversation, so that they wouldn't influence the students' and parents' responses, but sometimes, as I describe in the portraits, it felt more ethical to abandon my role as researcher and relate as an adviser and friend. No matter when and how I shared, though, I was always careful to ensure my perspectives were adjacent to, rather than at the center of, a conversation. And finally, my dog Lulu often joined these conversations; for many of the students, she was a calming presence, a reminder of home, a point of connection.

That said, my relationships with students and parents varied in terms of the comfort, trust, and openness I was able to establish. Some students I would hear from quite regularly between our interviews, and even today I remain close to them. They often divulged information that went well beyond what I asked, and they sought my advice for everything from classes to dating to drinking. Some parents also reached out between interviews, and I regularly received invitations to visit to go canoeing or fishing or just have a beer. With others, our contact was more limited to our scheduled conversations and, with students, the occasional request for a reference or letter of recommendation. They often didn't share as much, and I didn't push them; I sought trust, not intimacy.

And I think I found that trust. After reading the portraits, the students told me that they are a faithful reflection of them, their parents, and their experiences. Because I had that trust, I could give them something accurate, honest, and respectful. Here's what Ethan wrote me: "This was an absolute joy to read, both in reviewing my own stories and experiences, tracing the ways that I have and have not changed, and in reading the narratives of the other participants, seeing that many of those exhausting and puzzling elements of my time at Hilltop and onward, the things I often struggled to put into words, were acutely felt by others. Put shortly, reading this made me feel like, for all of those years, I was not alone, even if it felt like it."

That, more than anything, has made all this worthwhile.

Notes

Chapter One

1 See, e.g., Autor, "Skills, Education, and the Rise of Earnings Inequality," 844.
2 Institute of Education Sciences, "Undergraduate Retention and Graduation Rates," 1; Carnevale and Rose, "Socioeconomic Status, Race/Ethnicity, and Selective College Admissions," 11; Jack, *Privileged Poor*, 7; Stevens, *Creating a Class*, 256.
3 Lee, "Elite Colleges and Socioeconomic Status," 794; Rivera, *Pedigree*, 32; Stevens, *Creating a Class*, 259.
4 Carnevale and Rose, "Socioeconomic Status," 11; Rivera, *Pedigree*, 31; Stevens, *Creating a Class*, 257. On earning more, see Witteveen and Attewell, "The Earnings Payoff from Attending a Selective College," 166.
5 U.S. Census Bureau, "2020 Census Urban Area Facts."
6 Institute of Education Sciences, "Condition of Education 2020," 125.
7 Aisch et al., "Some Colleges Have More Students from the Top 1 Percent."
8 See, e.g., Aries, *Race and Class Matters at an Elite College*, 170–74; Armstrong and Hamilton, *Paying for the Party*, 37; Feagin, Vera, and Imani, *Agony of Education*, 159; Goldrick-Rab, *Paying the Price*, 90; Jack, *Privileged Poor*, 190; Lee, "Elite Colleges and Socioeconomic Status," 788; Stuber, *Inside the College Gates*, 81; Zaloom, *Indebted*, 122–55.
9 Hillman, "Geography of College Opportunity," 988.
10 Peine, Azano, and Schafft, "Beyond Cultural and Structural Explanations of Regional Underdevelopment," 49–50; Tieken, "There's a Big Part of Rural America That Everyone's Ignoring"; Tieken, *Why Rural Schools Matter*, 7; Wray, *Not Quite White*, 50.
11 Thomas et al., *Critical Rural Theory*, 28.

12   Economic Research Service, "Educational Attainment Grew."
13   See, e.g., Carr and Kefalas, *Hollowing Out the Middle*, 20; Mahnken, "When College Grads Don't Come Back Home."
14   Koricich, Chen, and Hughes, "Understanding the Effects of Rurality and Socioeconomic Status," 293; Wells et al., "Narrowed Gaps and Persistent Challenges," 13; Yan, *Postsecondary Enrollment and Persistence*, 5.
15   Hu, "Educational Aspirations and Postsecondary Access and Choice," 7; Koricich, Chen, and Hughes, "Understanding the Effects," 293–94.
16   Byun, Meece, and Irvin, "Rural-Nonrural Differences in College Attendance Patterns," 275; Koricich, Chen, and Hughes, "Understanding the Effects," 294.
17   Pierson and Hanson, *Comparing Postsecondary Enrollment and Persistence*, 9; National Student Clearinghouse, "Persistence"; Yan, *Postsecondary Enrollment and Persistence*, 5.
18   Byun, Irvin, and Meece, "Predictors of Bachelor's Degree Completion," 431; Wells et al., "Narrowed Gaps," 19.
19   Fulkerson and Lowe, "Representations of Rural in Popular North American Television," 17–19, 21; Jicha, "Portrayals of Rural People and Places in Reality Television Programming," 52.
20   Tieken, "College Talk and the Rural Economy," 216–17.
21   Tieken, 216.
22   See, e.g., Haller and Virkler, "Another Look at Rural-Nonrural Differences in Students' Educational Aspirations," 177; Howley, "Remote Possibilities," 69; Hu, "Educational Aspirations," 4; Li, "Challenging Both Rural Advantage and Disadvantage Narratives," 10; Rojewski, "Career-Related Predictors of Work-Bound and College-Bound Status of Adolescents in Rural and Nonrural Areas," 153.
23   Brown and Schafft, *Rural People and Communities in the 21st Century*, 12; Cashin, *Place Not Race*, 19–40; Duncan, *Worlds Apart*, xvii; Galster and Killen, "Geography of Metropolitan Opportunity," 10; Galster and Sharkey, "Spatial Foundations of Inequality," 2; Lobao and Saenz, "Spatial Inequality and Diversity as an Emerging Research Area," 497; powell, "Race, Place, and Opportunity"; Sibley, *Geographies of Exclusion*, ix; Soja, *Seeking Spatial Justice*, 20.
24   Massey and Denton, *American Apartheid*, 13; Beaulac, Kristjansson, and Cummins, "A Systematic Review of Food Deserts, 1966–2007," 1.
25   Soja, *Seeking Spatial Justice*, 5.
26   Soja, 8–9.
27   powell, "Race, Place, and Opportunity."
28   Galster and Killen, "The Geography of Metropolitan Opportunity," 14.
29   Lobao and Hooks, "Advancing the Sociology of Spatial Inequality," 34; Hillman, "Geography of College Opportunity," 988.
30   On aspirations, see Chenoweth and Galliher, "Factors Influencing College Aspirations of Rural West Virginia High School Students," 10; Rowan-Kenyon, Bell, and Perna, "Contextual Influences on Parental Involvement in College Going," 571–72. On enrollment, see

Byun, Meece, and Agger, "Predictors of College Attendance Patterns of Rural Youth," 831; Demi, Coleman-Jensen, and Snyder, "Rural Context and Post-Secondary School Enrollment," 16; Sandefur, Meier, and Campbell, "Family Resources, Social Capital, and College Attendance," 546. On selectivity, see Pascarella et al., "First-Generation College Students," 264. On processes that college-educated parents engage in, see Choy et al., "Transition to College," 59; Rowan-Kenyon, Bell, and Perna, "Contextual Influences," 571–74.

31 Byun, Meece, and Irvin, "Rural-Nonrural Disparities," 431; Li, "Challenging Both Rural Advantage and Disadvantage Narratives," 10.

32 Byun, Meece, and Irvin, "Rural-Nonrural Disparities," 431; Demi, Coleman-Jensen, and Snyder, "Rural Context and Post-Secondary School Enrollment," 16; Wells et al., "Narrowed Gaps," 23.

33 Hotz et al., "Role of Parental Wealth and Income," 30; Wells et al., "Narrowed Gaps," 19.

34 U.S. Census Bureau, "Rural Median Household Income Remains about 25 Percent below the Urban Median"; Wells et al., "Narrowed Gaps," 19; McDonough and McClafferty, "Rural College Opportunity," 4; Rhoades, "Higher Education We Choose," 918–19.

35 Roscigno and Crowley, "Rurality, Institutional Disadvantage, and Achievement/Attainment," 289; Strange, "Finding Fairness for Rural Students," 10.

36 Goldhaber, Lavery, and Theobald, "Uneven Playing Field?," 304; Logan and Burdick-Will, "School Segregation and Disparities in Urban, Suburban, and Rural Areas," 214; Orfield and Lee, "Why Segregation Matters," 5–7; Byun, Meece, and Irvin, "Rural-Nonrural Disparities," 422; Wells et al., "Narrowed Gaps," 18–19.

37 Kolbe et al., "Additional Cost of Operating Rural Schools," 13; Sipple and Brent, "Challenges and Strategies Associated with Rural School Settings," 609–18; Strange, "Equitable and Adequate Funding for Rural Schools," 4–7; McDonough and McClafferty, "Rural College Opportunity," 8; Whiteside, "Becoming Academically Eligible," 216; Gagnon and Mattingly, *Most U.S. School Districts Have Low Access to School Counselors*, 2; Gagnon and Mattingly, *Limited Access to AP Courses for Students in Smaller and More Isolated Rural School District*, 1; Roscigno and Crowley, "Rurality, Institutional Disadvantage, and Achievement/Attainment," 283.

38 Turley, "College Proximity," 141. On school attendance and proximity to home, see Hillman and Weichman, *Education Deserts*, 3.

39 Turley, "College Proximity," 141.

40 Turley, 142; Hillman and Weichman, *Education Deserts*, 8.

41 Hillman, "Geography of College Opportunity," 1004.

42 Cramer, *Politics of Resentment*, 114; Gettinger, "Big Reason Rural Students Never Go to College"; Han, Jaquette, and Salazar, *Recruiting the Out-of-State University*, 17; McDonough and McClafferty, "Rural College Opportunity," 11.

43 England and Brown, "Community and Resource Extraction in Rural America," 317.

44 Duncan, *Worlds Apart*; Lyson and Falk, "Forgotten Places," 1–2; Ulrich-Schad and Duncan, "People and Places Left Behind," 62.

45 Corbett, *Rural Education and Out-Migration*, 53.

46 Fitchen, *Endangered Spaces, Enduring Places*, 215; Kang-Brown and Subramanian, *Out of Sight*, 6; Krishnaswami and Mittelman, *Clean Energy Sweeps across Rural America*; Reeder and Brown, *Recreation, Tourism, and Rural Well-Being*, 1.

47 Rembert, Osinubi, and Douglas, *The Rise of Remote Work in Rural America*, 8.

48 Laughlin, "Beyond the Farm."

49 Day, Hays, and Smith, "A Glance at the Age Structure and Labor Force Participation of Rural America"; Gould, "Cities, Workers, and Wages," 501; Marré, *Rural Education at a Glance*, 4; Reeder and Brown, *Recreation, Tourism, and Rural Well-Being*, 9; Schafft et al., "Busted amidst the Boom," 516; Smith and Tickamyer, *Economic Restructuring and Family Well-Being in Rural America*, 4; Willingham, "Rural Workers of Color Need a $15 Federal Minimum Wage."

50 Economic Research Service, "Rural Employment and Unemployment"; Johnson, "Rural America Lost Population over the past Decade for the First Time in History," 4; Johnson and Lichter, "Rural Depopulation," 7.

51 Johnson and Lichter, "Rural Depopulation," 4; Johnson, Winkler, and Rogers, *Age and Lifecycle Patterns Driving U.S. Migration Shifts*, 2. See also Gould, "Cities, Workers, and Wages," 501; Marré, *Rural Education at a Glance*, 4.

52 Carr and Kefalas, *Hollowing Out the Middle*, 1.

53 Young, *Middle-Skill Jobs*, 1.

54 Young, *Middle-Skill Jobs*, 1; Economic Research Service, "Educational Attainment Grew."

55 Ardoin, *College Aspirations and Access*, 35; Burnell, "The 'Real World' Aspirations of Work-Bound Rural Students," 108; Corbett, *Learning to Leave*, 237; Cox et al., "Practical Considerations," 180.

56 Corbett, *Learning to Leave*, 237.

57 Hektner, "When Moving Up Implies Moving Out," 12; Means et al., "Bounded Aspirations," 557; Petrin, Schafft, and Meece, "Educational Sorting and Residential Aspirations among Rural High School Students," 317; Puente, "Leaving La Puente," 9.

58 On the invisible minority, see Schmitt-Wilson and Byun, "Postsecondary Transitions and Attainment," 162. On practical reasons for pursuing a degree, see Armstrong and Hamilton, *Paying for the Party*, 12; Corbett, "No Time to Fool Around with the Wrong Education," 173; Cox et al., "Practical Considerations," 180.

59 On motivation, see Agger, Meece, and Byun, "Influences of Family and Place on Rural Adolescents' Educational Aspirations and Post-Secondary Enrollment," 2564; Cox et al., "Practical Considerations,"

178; Petrin, Schafft, and Meece, "Educational Sorting and Residential Aspirations," 317. On returning home, see Bryan and Simmons, "Family Involvement," 401; Means et al., "Bounded Aspirations," 557–58; Puente, "Leaving La Puente," 15; Wright, "Becoming to Remain," 9. On the challenges, see Bryan and Simmons, "Family Involvement," 401; Cox et al., "Practical Considerations," 180; Elder and Conger, *Children of the Land*, 54; Means et al., "Bounded Aspirations," 556; Petrin, Schafft, and Meece, "Educational Sorting and Residential Aspirations," 317.

60   On college aspirations, see Farmer et al., "Educating Out and Giving Back," 5; Heinisch, "Small Fish Out of Water," 25; McCulloh, "An Exploration of Parental Support in the Retention of Rural First-Generation College Students," Means et al., "Bounded Aspirations," 558; Nelson, "Rural Students' Social Capital in the College Search and Application Process," 275; Puente, "Leaving La Puente," 14; Whiteside, "Becoming Academically Eligible," 219. On general support, see Means et al., "Bounded Aspirations," 558; Nelson, "Rural Students' Social Capital," 262.

61   McCulloh, "An Exploration of Parental Support"; Nelson, "Rural Students' Social Capital," 273.

62   Sowl and Crain, "A Systematic Review of Research on Rural College Access since 2000," 25.

63   Rhodes, "Student Debt and Geographic Disadvantage," 18.

64   Rhodes, 18. On debt, see Bryan and Simmons, "Family Involvement," 399; Heinisch, "Small Fish Out of Water," 28; McCulloh, "An Exploration of Parental Support."

65   Nader, "Up the Anthropologist," 289–93.

66   See, e.g., Mykerezi, Kostandini, and Mills, "Do Rural Community Colleges Supply Unique Educational Benefits?," 417; Saboe, Ocean, and Condliffe, "Economic Impact of Rural Pennsylvania Community Colleges," 15.

67   In addition to using "Hilltop" as a pseudonym, I have also changed a few details about its defining programs.

68   See, e.g., Dryden-Peterson, "Refugee Education"; Gaztambide-Fernández, *Best of the Best*; Keene, "College Pride, Native Pride"; Lawrence-Lightfoot, *Good High School*; Wright, "On Jorge Becoming a Boy."

69   Lawrence-Lightfoot and Davis, *Art and Science of Portraiture*, 3.

70   Lawrence-Lightfoot and Davis, 3–16.

71   Bok, *Higher Education in America*, 15.

72   Kahler and Felton, *What's My Target?*, 4.

73   Bok, *Higher Education in America*, 19; Stevens, *Creating a Class*, 233.

74   Giancola and Kahlenberg, *True Merit*, 5.

75   Khan, "Education of Elites in the United States," 182–83; Ornstein, "Wealth, Legacy and College Admission," 338; Stevens, *Creating a Class*, 15.

76   Armstrong and Hamilton, *Paying for the Party*, 20; Geiger, "Ten Generations of American Higher Education," 63.

77   Fry and Cilluffo, *Rising Share of Undergraduates Are from Poor Families*, 3.

78   Johnson and Lichter, *Growing Racial Diversity in Rural America*, 1; Marré, *Rural Education at a Glance*, 3.

79   Agger, Meece, and Byun, "Influences of Family and Place," 2564.

80   Achieve, "Achieving the Possible," 1; Greenberg, "Survey: Conflicting Views of Higher Education"; Hacker and Dreifus, *Higher Education?*, 3; Kaufman, "Some Say Bypassing a Higher Education Is Smarter Than Paying for a Degree"; Mattioli, "Generation Jobless"; Mitchell and Belkin, "Americans Losing Faith in College Degrees, Poll Finds"; Obama, "Remarks by the President in a National Address to America's Schoolchildren"; Owen and Sawhill, *Should Everyone Go to College?*, 6; Professor X, "Anti-College Backlash?"; White House, "The Clinton Presidency."

81   Lincoln Project, "Public Research Universities," 2; Mitchell, Leachman, and Saenz, *State Higher Education Funding Cuts Have Pushed Costs to Students, Worsened Inequality*, 1.

82   Geiger, "Ten Generations of American Higher Education," 43.

83   On increased tuition, see Goldrick-Rab, *Paying the Price*, 2. On income, see DeNavas-Walt and Proctor, *Income and Poverty in the United States: 2014*, 5; Lobosco, "10 Most Expensive Colleges."

84   Hanson, "Total Student Loan Debt."

85   Arum and Roksa, *Academically Adrift*, 36; Clynes, "Peter Thiel Thinks You Should Skip College"; HR&A Advisors, "New York City Tech Ecosystem," 5; Associated Press, "Half of Recent College Grads Underemployed or Jobless, Analysis Says."

86   Deresiewicz, *Excellent Sheep*, 20; Hacker and Dreifus, *Higher Education?*, 63-76.

87   Pappano, "Colleges Discover the Rural Student."

88   Belkin, "For Colleges, a Rural Reckoning"; Marcus and Krupnick, "Rural Higher-Education Crisis"; Pappano, "Colleges Discover the Rural Student."

89   Brown and Mettler, "Sequential Polarization," 16; Kurtzleben, "Rural Voters Played a Big Part in Helping Trump Defeat Clinton"; Niskanen Center, "Explaining the Urban-Rural Political Divide"; Silver, "Education, Not Income, Predicted Who Would Vote for Trump."

90   Marcus, "If the Anger That Propelled Trump's Win Is Economic, Can Higher Education Fix It?"

Chapter Two

1   I gave students the option of choosing a pseudonym or using their real name. I have also excluded or, in a few cases, changed identifying details.

2   Carr and Kefalas, *Hollowing Out the Middle*, 27–52; Cox et al., "Practical Considerations," 178–80; Morton, *Moving Up without Losing Your Way*, 1–42; Rondini, "Healing the Hidden Injuries of Class?," 104–8; Sherman and Sage, "Sending Off All Your Good Treasures," 7–8.

3   On expectations, see Agger, Meece, and Byun, "Influences of Family and Place," 2564; Byun et al., "Role of Social Capital in Educational Aspirations of Rural Youth," 372; Gofen, "Family Capital," 115; Hossler, Schmit, and Vesper, *Going to College*, 23; Perna and Titus, "Relationship between Parental Involvement as Social Capital and College Enrollment," 507–8; Rowan-Kenyon, Bell, and Perna, "Contextual Influences on Parental Involvement," 571–74. On lower aspirations, see Byun, Meece, and Irvin, "Rural-Nonrural Disparities," 431; Gibbons and Borders, "Prospective First-Generation College Students," 204; Li, "Challenging Both Rural Advantage and Disadvantage Narratives," 10; Pascarella et al., "First-Generation College Students," 8.

4   Corbett, *Learning to Leave*, 220–21.

5   Byun et al., "Role of Social Capital," 372; Carr and Kefalas, *Hollowing Out the Middle*, 27–52; Glass and Nygreen, "Class, Race, and the Discourse of 'College for All,'" 3–4; Nelson, "Rural Students' Social Capital," 275; Tieken, "College Talk," 210.

6   Corbett, *Learning to Leave*, 9; Cox et al., "Practical Considerations," 178–80; Sherman and Sage, "Sending Off," 7–8.

7   Corbett, *Learning to Leave*, 92.

8   Petrin, Schafft, and Meece, "Educational Sorting and Residential Aspirations," 320.

9   Byun, Irvin, and Meece, "Rural-Nonrural Differences in College Attendance Patterns," 275; Koricich, Chen, and Hughes, "Understanding the Effects," 294.

10 Armstrong and Hamilton, *Paying for the Party*, 12; Corbett, "No Time to Fool Around," 173; Cox et al., "Practical Considerations," 180.

11 Stephens et al., "Unseen Disadvantage," 1192.

12 Turley, "College Proximity," 141.

13 Hillman and Weichman, *Education Deserts*, 6.

14 Holland, "Framing the Search," 387; Hossler, Schmit, and Vesper, *Going to College*, 26; Stevens, *Creating a Class*, 18–19.

15 Hillman and Weichman, *Education Deserts*, 10; McDonough and Calderone, "Meaning of Money," 1711.

16 Alvarado, "Role of College-Bound Friends in College Enrollment Decisions," 1340.

17 Gagnon and Mattingly, *Limited Access to AP Courses*, 1; Roscigno and Crowley, "Rurality, Institutional Disadvantage, and Achievement/Attainment," 283; Dougherty, Mellor, and Jian, *Relationship between Advanced Placement and College Graduation*, 9; Pilchen, Caspary, and Woodworth, *Postsecondary Outcomes of IB Diploma Programme Graduates in the U.S.*, 8–11; Schneider, "Privilege, Equity, and the Advanced Placement Program," 827.

18   Choy et al., "Transition to College," 59; Horn and Núñez, "Mapping the Road to College," 41-45; Nelson, "Rural Students' Social Capital," 265.

19   Alleman and Holly, "Multiple Points of Contact," 9; Coles, "Role of Community-Based Organizations in the College Access and Success Movement," 3; Wells et al., "Reconsidering Rural-Nonrural College Enrollment Gaps," 4.

Chapter Three

1   Melendez, "The Influence of Athletic Participation on the College Adjustment of Freshmen and Sophomore Student Athletes," 41.

2   Azpeitia et al., "'It's Easy to Feel Alone,'" 25; Dennis, Phinney, and Chuateco, "Role of Motivation, Parental Support, and Peer Support in the Academic Success of Ethnic Minority First-Generation College Students," 233; Tinto, *Leaving College*, 74. For rural youth and communities, Byun, Meece, and Irvin, "Rural-Nonrural Difference," 9; Elder and Conger, *Children of the Land*, 107-8; Heinisch, "Small Fish Out of Water," 26; San Antonio, "Complex Decision-Making Process," 256; Wilkinson, *Community in Rural America*, 63.

3   Kalsner and Pistole, "College Adjustment in a Multiethnic Sample," 104; Núñez, "Negotiating Ties," 109-11; Ricks and Warren, "Transitioning to College," 9; Winkle-Wagner, "Perpetual Homelessness of College Experiences," 26.

4   San Antonio, "Complex Decision-Making Processes," 258.

5   Wiggins, "'We Do Way More Than Just Clean Up Puke,'" 36.

6   Heinisch, "Small Fish Out of Water," 26; Jenkins et al., "First-Generation Undergraduate Students' Social Support, Depression, and Life Satisfaction," 137-38; Osborne, *Polished*, 63, 73; Ricks and Warren, "Transitioning to College," 7; Pascarella et al., "First-Generation College Students," 17-18.

7   Bryan and Simmons, "Family Involvement," 399-400; Winkle-Wagner, "Perpetual Homelessness of College Experiences," 14.

8   Bui, "First-Generation College Students at Four-Year University"; Osborne, *Polished*, 61-63; Reid and Moore, "College Readiness and Academic Preparation for Postsecondary Education," 251.

9   Byun, Irvin, and Meece, "Rural-Nonrural Differences in College Attendance Patterns," 270; Saw and Agger, "Stem Pathways of Rural and Small-Town Students," 599.

10   Heinisch, "Small Fish Out of Water," 26.

11   Covarrubias et al., "'You Never Become Fully Independent,'" 395-98; Heinisch, "Small Fish Out of Water," 26; Lee and Kramer, "Out with the Old, in with the New?," 30; Núñez, "Negotiating Ties," 109-11.

Chapter Four

1   Monnat and Brown, "More Than a Rural Revolt," 227.

2   Jadhav, "Was It Rural Populism?," 556–58; Tieken, "There's a Big Part of Rural America That Everyone's Ignoring."

3   Aries, *Race and Class Matters*, 172–73; Bryan and Simmons, "Family Involvement," 397; Covarrubias et al., "'You Never Become Fully Independent,'" 395–98; Feagin, Vera, and Imani, *Agony of Education*, 13; Jack, *Privileged Poor*, 25–78; London, "Transformations," 6; Morton, *Moving Up*, 62; Osborne, *Polished*, 3; Stephens et al., "Unseen Disadvantage," 1192; Vasquez-Salgado, Greenfield, and Burgos-Cienfuegos, "Exploring Home-School Value Conflicts," 296–98.

4   Brayboy, "Transformational Resistance and Social Justice," 204; Lee and Kramer, "Out with the Old," 30; Osborne, *Polished*, 47–79; Stephens et al., "Unseen Disadvantage," 1193.

5   Bryan and Simmons, "Family Involvement," 396–97; Covarrubias et al., "'You Never Become Fully Independent,'" 402; Roksa and Kinsley, "Role of Family Support in Facilitating Academic Success of Low-Income Students," 425.

6   For the quote, see Jack, *Privileged Poor*, 24. For exclusion of underrepresented students, see Aries, *Race and Class Matters*, 74–81; Armstrong and Hamilton, *Paying for the Party*, 11; Feagin, Vera, and Imani, *Agony of Education*, 7; Havlik et al., "Strengths and Struggles," 124; Jack, *Privileged Poor*, 27, 25–78; Stebleton, Soria, and Huesman, "First-Generation Students' Sense of Belonging, Mental Health, and Use of Counseling Services at Public Research Universities," 13; Stuber, *Inside the College Gates*, 33–85.

7   Armstrong and Hamilton, *Paying for the Party*, 12; Corbett, "No Time to Fool Around," 173; Cox et al., "Practical Considerations," 178–80.

8   Stebleton, Soria, and Huesman Jr., "First-Generation Students' Sense of Belonging," 14.

9   Coles, Keane, and Williams, "Beyond the College Bill," 4; Havlik et al., "Strengths and Struggles," 126–28.

10   Jack, *Privileged Poor*, 109–13.

11   Jack, 114–19.

12   Havlik et al., "Strengths and Struggles," 126–28.

13   Lensmire, *White Folks*, 25; Lewis, Ketter, and Fabos, "Reading Race in a Rural Context," 318; Tieken, *Why Rural Schools Matter*, 2; Tieken, "Making Race Relevant," 200.

14   Carter, *Keepin' It Real*, 13; Morton, *Moving Up*, 74; Osborne, *Polished*, 135.

Chapter Five

1 Brayboy, "Transformational Resistance and Social Justice," 206–7; Jackson, Smith, and Hill, "Academic Persistence among Native American College Students," 559–60; Lee, "Building Native Nations through Native Students' Commitment to Their Communities," 33; Morton, *Moving Up*, 50; Salis Reyes, "'What Am I Doing to Be a Good Ancestor?,'" 624–25.

2 For limited employment, see Brinkman, "Big Cities and the Highly Educated," 14; Marré, *Rural Education at a Glance*, 4. For limited educational opportunities, see Hillman and Weichman, *Education Deserts*, 8.

3 Creed and Ching, "Recognizing Rusticity," 17–18; Corbett, *Learning to Leave*, 17–22; Peine, Azano, and Schafft, "Beyond Cultural and Structural Explanations," 53.

4 Rhodes, "Student Debt and Geographic Disadvantage," 18.

5 Osborne, *Polished*, 70; Rivera, *Pedigree*, 53.

6 Reynolds and Xian, "Perceptions of Meritocracy in the Land of Opportunity," 134.

7 DeOrtentiis, Van Iddekinge, and Wanberg, "Different Starting Lines, Different Finish Times," 453; Fry, *First-Generation College Graduates Lag behind Their Peers on Key Economic Outcomes*, 4.

Chapter Six

1 See, e.g., Andres and Looker, "Rurality and Capital," 36; Haller and Virkler, "Another Look at Rural-Nonrural Differences in Students' Educational Aspirations," 174; Howley, "Remote Possibilities," 69; Hu, "Educational Aspirations and Postsecondary Access and Choice," 4; Rojewski, "Career-Related Predictors," 153.

2 Green, "Deindustrialization of Rural America," 15–18; Lyson and Falk, "Forgotten Places," 3–4.

3 Marré, *Rural Education at a Glance*, 2.

4 See, e.g., Byun, Meece, and Irvin, "Rural-Nonrural Disparities," 431; Tieken, "College Talk and the Rural Economy," 216; Yan, *Postsecondary Enrollment and Persistence*, 9.

5 Autor, "Skills, Education, and the Rise of Earnings Inequality," 844; Carnevale, Jayasundera, and Gulish, *Good Jobs Are Back*, 6.

6 Hillman and Weichman, *Education Deserts*, 6.

7 Brinkman, "Big Cities and the Highly Educated," 14; Marré, *Rural Education at a Glance*, 4.

8 Creed and Ching, "Recognizing Rusticity," 17–18; Corbett, *Learning to Leave*, 17–22.

9 For the educational attainment of rural adults, see Marré, *Rural Education at a Glance*, 2. For the supports offered by college-educated parents, see Rowan-Kenyon, Bell, and Perna, "Contextual Influences on Parental Involvement," 572.

10   Hillman, "Geography of College Opportunity," 1004; Hillman and Weichman, *Education Deserts*, 6–8; Rosenboom and Blagg, *Disconnected from Higher Education*, 5.

11   Gagnon and Mattingly, *Most U.S. School Districts Have Low Access to School Counselors*, 4; Kozol, "Savage Inequalities," 54–55; McDonough, "Counseling and College Counseling in America's High Schools," 14.

12   Salazar, Jaquette, and Han, "Coming Soon to a Neighborhood Near You?," 1287.

13   Byun, Irvin, and Meece, "Rural-Nonrural Differences in College Attendance Patterns," 275; Gagnon and Mattingly, *Limited Access to AP Courses*, 1.

14   Gagnon and Mattingly, *Most U.S. School Districts Have Low Access to School Counselors*, 2.

15   Seaman et al., "Youth Identity and Postsecondary Decision Making in a Rural State," 6; Tieken, "College Talk and the Rural Economy," 210.

16   Gaztambide-Fernández, *Best of the Best*, 10; Klugman, "How Resource Inequalities among High Schools Reproduce Class Advantages in College Destinations," 814–16; Roscigno, Tomaskovic-Devey, and Crowley, "Education and the Inequalities of Place," 2135; Strange, "Finding Fairness," 10.

17   Jack, *Privileged Poor*, 68; Stephens et al., "Unseen Disadvantage," 1192.

18   Rajkumar et al., "A Causal Test of the Strength of Weak Ties," 5; Wilkinson, *Community in Rural America*, 85–86.

19   Jack, *Privileged Poor*, 24.

20   Yosso, "Whose Culture Has Capital?," 77–78.

21   Byun, Meece, and Irvin, "Rural-Nonrural Disparities," 9; Elder and Conger, *Children of the Land*, 107–8; Wilkinson, *The Community in Rural America*, 63.

22   Brewer, Eide, and Ehrenberg, "Does It Pay to Attend an Elite Private College?," 119; Rivera, *Pedigree*, 30; Witteveen and Attewell, "Earnings Payoff," 166.

23   Jack, *Privileged Poor*, 86.

24   Carter, *Keepin' It Real*, 13; Morton, *Moving Up*, 74.

25   Rhodes, "Student Debt and Geographic Disadvantage," 26.

26   Fulkerson and Lowe, "Representations of Rural," 17–19, 21; Jicha, "Portrayals of Rural People and Places," 52.

27   See, e.g., Corbett, *Learning to Leave*, 13; Willis, *Learning to Labour*, 3.

28   Labaree, "Public Goods, Private Goods," 60–65.

29   Brayboy, "Hiding in the Ivy," 127; Carter, *Keepin' It Real*, 13; Morton, *Moving Up*, 74; Osborne, *Polished*, 135; Phelan, *Unmarked*, 6.

30   Cox et al., "Practical Considerations," 180; Corbett, *Learning to Leave*, 26–31; Elder and Conger, "Attachment to Place and Migration Prospects," 420; Hektner, "When Moving up Implies Moving Out," 11.

31   Cashin, *Place Not Race*, 23; powell, "Race, Place, and Opportunity," paras. 5 and 6.

32   Morton, *Moving Up*, 47; Suskind, *A Hope in the Unseen*, 21.

33 For lack of college-educated adults, see Hoxby and Avery, "Missing 'One-Offs,'" 24. For lack of institutions of higher education, see Dache-Gerbino, "College Desert and Oasis," 105; Olivas, "Higher Education as 'Place,'" 182; Rhoades, "Higher Education We Choose," 919. For lack of admissions officials, see Salazar, Jaquette, and Han, "Coming Soon to a Neighborhood Near You?," 1298; Stevens, *Creating a Class*, 67.

34 Gagnon and Mattingly, *Most U.S. School Districts Have Low Access to School Counselors*, 2; Hyman, "Does Money Matter in the Long Run?," 257; Jackson, Johnson, and Persico, "Effects of School Spending on Educational and Economic Outcomes," 212; LaFortune, Rothstein, and Schanzenbach, "School Finance Reform and the Distribution of Student Achievement," 32–33; Lautz, Hawkins, and Pérez, "The High School Visit," 110; Logan, Minca, and Adar, "Geography of Inequality," 296–97; Roderick, Nagaoka, and Coca, "College Readiness for All," 190–97.

35 For lack of preparation for racial diversity, see Park and Chang, "Understanding Students' Precollege Experiences with Racial Diversity," 356. For barriers to participation, see Armstrong and Hamilton, *Paying for the Party*, 155; Jack, *Privileged Poor*, 22; Stuber, *Inside the College Gates*, 81.

36 For strong social ties, see Aries, *Race and Class Matters*, 54–55; Briggs, *Geography of Opportunity*, 9; Small, *Villa Victoria*, 182; Warren, Thompson, and Saegert, "Role of Social Capital in Combating Poverty," 9. For lacking connections, see Armstrong and Hamilton, *Paying for the Party*, 216; Hirudayaraj and McLean, "First-Generation College Graduates," 97; Rivera, *Pedigree*, 107–8.

37 Jackson, Smith, and Hill, "Academic Persistence among Native American College Students," 560; Morton, *Moving Up*, 15; Salis Reyes, "'What Am I Doing to Be a Good Ancestor?,'" 607.

38 Brayboy, "Transformational Resistance and Social Justice," 194; Stephens et al., "Unseen Disadvantage," 1187.

39 Gettinger, "A Big Reason Rural Students Never Go to College"; Salazar Jaquette, and Han, "Coming Soon to a Neighborhood Near You?," 1287; Hillman and Weichman, *Education Deserts*, 8.

40 Gagnon and Mattingly, *Limited Access to AP Courses*, 1; Gagnon and Mattingly, *Most U.S. School Districts Have Low Access to School Counselors*, 2.

41 Hillman, "Geography of College Opportunity," 988; Singleton, *Educational Opportunity*, 186; Turley, "College Proximity," 126–27.

42 Coles, "Role of Community-Based Organizations," 3; Perna, *Delivering on the Promise*, 1; Perna, Wright-Kim, and Leigh, "Will College Promise Programs Improve or Reduce Equity?," 20–21; Ruiz and Perna, "The Geography of College Attainment," 100.

43 Pappano, "Colleges Discover the Rural Student."

44 Peine, Azano, and Schafft, "Beyond Cultural and Structural Explanations," 50.

Chapter Seven

1   Brinkman, "Big Cities and the Highly Educated," 14; Marré, *Rural Education at a Glance*, 4.
2   Dancy, Garcia-Kendrick, and Cheng, *Rising above the Threshold*, 7.
3   Gorski, "Poverty Ideologies and the Possibility of Equitable Education," 104; Love, *We Want to Do More Than Survive*, 78–79.
4   Hektner, "When Moving Up Implies Moving Out," 12; Means et al., "Bounded Aspirations," 557; Petrin, Schafft, and Meece, "Educational Sorting and Residential Aspirations," 317.

Appendix

1   Lawrence-Lightfoot and Davis, *Art and Science of Portraiture*, 14.
2   Cromartie and Bucholtz, "Defining the 'Rural' in Rural America," 29.
3   Hawley et al., "Defining and Describing Rural," 6.
4   Researchers often include town designations in the category of "rural" for the purposes of analysis. See, e.g., Petrin, Schafft, and Meece, "Educational Sorting and Residential Aspirations," 298; Agger, Meece, and Byun, "Influences of Family and Place," 2557.
5   I decided not to compensate the students monetarily. It was difficult to determine an adequate level of compensation for a project that would run more than four years, and I wanted our interactions to be relational, not transactional. However, if I were to do the study again now, with the benefit of hindsight and a better understanding of many of their financial positions, I would compensate participants.
6   Agger, Meece, and Byun, "Influences of Family and Place," 2564.
7   Agger, Meece, and Byun, 2563.
8   Saldaña, *Coding Manual for Qualitative Researchers*, 6.

Bibliography

Achieve. "Achieving the Possible: What Americans Think about the College-and Career-Ready Agenda." August 2010. https://www.achieve.org/files/AchievingThePossible-FinalReport.pdf.

Agger, Charlotte, Judith Meece, and Soo-yong Byun. "The Influences of Family and Place on Rural Adolescents' Educational Aspirations and Post-Secondary Enrollment." *Journal of Youth and Adolescence* 47 (2018): 2554–68.

Aisch, Gregor, Larry Buchanan, Amanda Cox, and Kevin Quealy. "Some Colleges Have More Students from the Top 1 Percent Than the Bottom 60. Find Yours." *New York Times*, January 18, 2017. https://www.nytimes.com/interactive/2017/01/18/upshot/some-colleges-have-more-students-from-the-top-1-percent-than-the-bottom-60.html.

Alleman, Nathan F., and L. Neal Holly. "Multiple Points of Contact: Promoting Rural Postsecondary Preparation through School-Community Partnerships." *Rural Educator* 34, no. 2 (2013): 1–11.

Alvarado, Steven Elías. "The Role of College-Bound Friends in College Enrollment Decisions by Race, Ethnicity, and Gender." *American Educational Research Journal* 58, no. 6 (2021): 1315–54.

Andres, Lesley, and E. Dianne Looker. "Rurality and Capital: Educational Expectations and Attainments of Rural, Urban/Rural, and Metropolitan Youth." *Canadian Journal of Higher Education* 31, no. 2 (2001): 1–46.

Ardoin, Sonja. *College Aspirations and Access in Working-Class Rural Communities.* Blue Ridge Summit, PA: Lexington Books, 2017.

Aries, Elizabeth. *Race and Class Matters at an Elite College*. Philadelphia: Temple University Press, 2008.

Armstrong, Elizabeth A., and Laura T. Hamilton. *Paying for the Party: How College Maintains Inequality*. Cambridge, MA: Harvard University Press, 2013.

Arum, Richard, and Josipa Roksa. *Academically Adrift: Limited Learning on College Campuses*. Chicago: University of Chicago Press, 2010.

Associated Press. "Half of Recent College Grads Underemployed or Jobless, Analysis Says." *Cleveland.com*, April 23, 2012. https://www.cleveland.com/business/2012/04/half_of_recent_college_grads_u.html.

Autor, David H. "Skills, Education, and the Rise of Earnings Inequality among the 'Other 99 Percent.'" *Science* 344, no. 6186 (May 23, 2014): 843–51.

Azpeitia, Jovani, Yasmin Meza Lazaro, Sergio A. Ruvalcaba, and Guadalupe A. Baccio. "'It's Easy to Feel Alone, but When You Have Community, It Makes [College] a Lot Easier': First-Generation Students' Academic and Psychosocial Adjustment over the First Year of College." *Journal of Adolescent Research* (2023): 1–38.

Beaulac, Julie, Elizabeth Kristjansson, and Steven Cummins. "A Systematic Review of Food Deserts, 1966–2007." *Preventing Chronic Disease* 6, no. 3 (July 2009). https://www.ncbi.nlm.nih.gov/pmc/articles/PMC2722409/.

Belkin, Douglas. "For Colleges, a Rural Reckoning." *Wall Street Journal*, December 1, 2017. https://www.wsj.com/articles/for-colleges-a-rural-reckoning-1512159888.

Bok, Derek. *Higher Education in America*. Princeton, NJ: Princeton University Press, 2013.

Brayboy, Bryan McKinley Jones. "Hiding in the Ivy: American Indian Students and Visibility in Elite Educational Settings." *Harvard Educational Review* 74, no. 2 (2004): 125–52.

———. "Transformational Resistance and Social Justice: American Indians in Ivy League Universities." *Anthropology & Education Quarterly* 36, no. 3 (2005): 193–211.

Brewer, Dominic J., Eric R. Eide, and Ronald G. Ehrenberg. "Does It Pay to Attend an Elite Private College? Cross-Cohort Evidence on the Effects of College Type on Earnings." *Journal of Human Resources* 34, no. 1 (Winter 1999): 104–23.

Briggs, Xavier de Souza. *The Geography of Opportunity: Race and Housing Choices in Metropolitan America*. Washington, DC: Brookings Institution, 2005.

Brinkman, Jeffrey. "Big Cities and the Highly Educated: What's the Connection?" *Business Review* 98, no. 3 (2015): 10–15.

Brown, David L., and Kai A. Schafft. *Rural People and Communities in the 21st Century: Resilience and Transformation.* Malden, MA: Polity Press, 2011.

Brown, Trevor E., and Suzanne Mettler. "Sequential Polarization: The Development of the Rural-Urban Political Divide, 1976–2020." *Perspectives on Politics* (2023): 1–29. https://doi.org/10.1017/S1537592723002918.

Bryan, Elizabeth, and Leigh Ann Simmons. "Family Involvement: Impacts on Post-Secondary Educational Success for First-Generation Appalachian College Students." *Journal of College Student Development* 50, no. 4 (July–August 2009): 391–406.

Burnell, Beverly A. "The 'Real World' Aspirations of Work-Bound Rural Students." *Journal of Research in Rural Education* 18, no. 2 (2003): 104–13.

Byun, Soo-yong, Judith L. Meece, and Charlotte A. Agger. "Predictors of College Attendance Patterns of Rural Youth." *Research in Higher Education* 58 (2017): 817–42.

Byun, Soo-yong, Matthew J. Irvin, and Judith L. Meece. "Predictors of Bachelor's Degree Completion among Rural Students at Four-Year Institutions." *Review of Higher Education* 35, no. 3 (Spring 2012): 463–84.

———. "Rural-Nonrural Differences in College Attendance Patterns." *Peabody Journal of Education* 90, no. 2 (2015): 263–79.

Byun, Soo-yong, Judith L. Meece, and Matthew J. Irvin. "Rural-Nonrural Disparities in Postsecondary Educational Attainment Revisited." *American Educational Research Journal* 49, no. 3 (June 2012): 412–37.

Byun, Soo-yong, Judith L. Meece, Matthew J. Irvin, and Bryan C. Hutchins. "The Role of Social Capital in Educational Aspirations of Rural Youth." *Rural Sociology* 77, no. 3 (September 2012): 355–79.

Carnevale, Anthony P., Tamara Jayasundera, and Artem Gulish. *Good Jobs Are Back: College Graduates Are First in Line.* Washington, DC: Center on Education and the Workforce, 2015. https://cew.georgetown.edu/cew-reports/goodjobsareback/.

Carnevale, Anthony P., and Stephen J. Rose. "Socioeconomic Status, Race/Ethnicity, and Selective College Admissions." Working paper, Century Foundation, New York City, 2003. https://files.eric.ed.gov/fulltext/ED482419.pdf.

Carr, Patricia J., and Maria J. Kefalas. *Hollowing Out the Middle: The Rural Brain Drain and What It Means for America.* Boston: Beacon Press, 2009.

Carter, Prudence L. *Keepin' It Real: School Success beyond Black and White*. New York: Oxford University Press, 2005.

Cashin, Sheryll. *Place Not Race: A New Vision of Opportunity in America*. Boston: Beacon Press, 2014.

Chenoweth, Erica, and Renee V. Galliher. "Factors Influencing College Aspirations of Rural West Virginia High School Students." *Journal of Research in Rural Education* 19, no. 2 (2004): 1–14.

Choy, Susan P., Laura J. Horn, Anne-Marie Núñez, and Xianglei Chen. "Transition to College: What Helps At-Risk Students and Students Whose Parents Did Not Attend College." *New Directions for Institutional Research* 2000, no. 107 (2000): 45–63.

Clynes, Tom. "Peter Thiel Thinks You Should Skip College, and He'll Even Pay You for Your Trouble." *Newsweek*, February 22, 2017. https://www.newsweek.com/2017/03/03/peter-thiel-fellowship-college-higher-education-559261.html.

Coles, Ann. *The Role of Community-Based Organizations in the College Access and Success Movement*. Washington, DC: National College Access Network, 2012.

Coles, Ann, Laura Keane, and Brendan Williams. "Beyond the College Bill: The Hidden Hurdles of Indirect Expenses." uAspire, June 2020.

Corbett, Michael. *Learning to Leave: The Irony of Schooling in a Coastal Community*. Halifax, NS: Fernwood Publishing, 2007.

———. "No Time to Fool around with the Wrong Education: Socialisation Frames, Timing and High-Stakes Educational Decision Making in Changing Rural Places." *Rural Society* 19, no. 2 (August 2009): 163–77.

———. "Rural Education and Out-Migration: The Case of a Coastal Community." *Canadian Journal of Education* 28, nos. 1–2 (2005): 52–72.

Covarrubias, Rebecca, Ibette Valle, Giselle Laiduc, and Margarita Azmitia. "'You Never Become Fully Independent': Family Roles and Independence in First-Generation College Students." *Journal of Adolescent Research* 34, no. 4 (2019): 381–410.

Cox, Genevieve R., Corinna Jenkins Tucker, Erin Hiley Sharp, Karen T. Van Gundy, and Cesar J. Rebellon. "Practical Considerations: Community Context in a Declining Rural Economy and Emerging Adults' Educational and Occupational Aspirations." *Emerging Adulthood* 2, no. 3 (2013): 173–83.

Cramer, Katherine J. *The Politics of Resentment: Rural Consciousness in Wisconsin and the Rise of Scott Walker*. Chicago: University of Chicago Press, 2016.

Creed, Gerald W., and Barbara Ching. "Recognizing Rusticity: Identity and the Power of Place." Introduction to *Knowing Your Place: Rural Identity and Cultural Hierarchy*, edited by Barbara Ching and Gerald W. Creed, 1–38. New York: Routledge, 1997.

Cromartie, John, and Shawn Bucholtz. "Defining the 'Rural' in Rural America." *Amber Waves*, June 1, 2008. https://www.ers.usda.gov/amber-waves/2008/june/defining-the-rural-in-rural-america/.

Dache-Gerbino, Amalia. "College Desert and Oasis: A Critical Geographic Analysis of Local College Access." *Journal of Diversity in Higher Education* 11, no. 2 (2016): 97–116.

Dancy, Kim, Genevieve Garcia-Kendrick, and Diane Cheng. *Rising above the Threshold: How Expansion in Financial Aid Can Increase the Equitable Delivery of Postsecondary Value for More Students.* Washington, DC: Institute for Higher Education Policy, 2023. https://www.ihep.org/wp-content/uploads/2023/06/IHEP_Rising-above-the-Threshold_rd4.pdf.

Day, Jennifer Cheeseman, Donal Hays, and Adam Smith. "A Glance at the Age Structure and Labor Force Participation of Rural America." *Random Samplings* (2016). https://www.census.gov/newsroom/blogs/random-samplings/2016/12/a_glance_at_the_age.html.

Demi, Mary Ann, Alish Coleman-Jensen, and Anastasia R. Snyder. "The Rural Context and Post-Secondary School Enrollment: An Ecological Systems Approach." *Journal of Research in Rural Education* 25, no. 7 (2010): 1–26.

DeNavas-Walt, Carmen, and Bernadette D. Proctor. *Income and Poverty in the United States: 2014.* Washington, DC: United States Census Bureau, September 2015. https://www.census.gov/content/dam/Census/library/publications/2015/demo/p60-252.pdf.

Dennis, Jessica M., Jean S. Phinney, and Lizette Ivy Chuateco. "The Role of Motivation, Parental Support, and Peer Support in the Academic Success of Ethnic Minority First-Generation College Students." *Journal of College Student Development* 46, no. 3 (May–June 2005): 223–36.

DeOrtentiis, Philip S., Chad H. Van Iddekinge, and Connie R. Wanberg. "Different Starting Lines, Different Finish Times: The Role of Social Class in the Job Search Process." *Journal of Applied Psychology* 107, no. 3 (2021): 444–57.

Deresiewicz, William. *Excellent Sheep: The Miseducation of the American Elite and the Way to a Meaningful Life.* New York: Free Press, 2014.

Dougherty, Chrys, Lynn Mellor, and Shuling Jian. *The Relationship between Advanced Placement and College Graduation.* National Center for

Educational Accountability, February 2006. https://files.eric.ed.gov/fulltext/ED519365.pdf.

Dryden-Peterson, Sarah. "Refugee Education: Education for an Unknowable Future." *Curriculum Inquiry* 47, no. 1 (2017): 14–24.

Duncan, Cynthia M. *Worlds Apart: Why Poverty Persists in Rural America.* New Haven, CT: Yale University Press, 1999.

Economic Research Service. "Educational Attainment Grew for Bachelor's Degrees and Higher. 2023." https://www.ers.usda.gov/data-products/chart-gallery/gallery/chart-detail/?chartId=106147#.

Economic Research Service. "Rural Employment and Unemployment." 2022. https://www.ers.usda.gov/topics/rural-economy-population/employment-education/rural-employment-and-unemployment/.

Elder, Glen H., and Rand D. Conger. "Attachment to Place and Migration Prospects: A Developmental Perspective." *Journal of Research on Adolescence* 6, no. 4 (1996): 397–425.

———. *Children of the Land: Adversity and Success in Rural America.* Chicago: University of Chicago Press, 2000.

England, Lynn, and Ralph B. Brown. "Community and Resource Extraction in Rural America." In *Challenges for Rural America in the Twenty-First Century*, edited by David L. Brown and Louis E. Swanson, 317–28. University Park: Pennsylvania State University Press, 2003.

Farmer, Thomas W., Kimberly Dadisman, Shawn J. Latendresse, Jana Thompson, Matthew J. Irvin, and Lei Zhang. "Educating Out and Giving Back: Adults' Conceptions of Successful Outcomes of African American High School Students from Impoverished Rural Communities." *Journal of Research in Rural Education* 21, no. 10 (2006): 1–12.

Feagin, Joe R., Hernán Vera, and Nikitah Imani. *The Agony of Education: Black Students at White Colleges and Universities.* New York: Routledge, 1996.

Fitchen, Janet M. *Endangered Spaces, Enduring Places: Change, Identity, and Survival in Rural America.* New York: Routledge, 1991.

Fry, Richard. *First-Generation College Graduates Lag Behind Their Peers on Key Economic Outcomes.* Washington, DC: Pew Research Center, 2021. https://www.pewresearch.org/social-trends/2021/05/18/first-generation-college-graduates-lag-behind-their-peers-on-key-economic-outcomes/.

Fry, Richard, and Anthony Cilluffo. *A Rising Share of Undergraduates Are from Poor Families, Especially at Less Selective Colleges.* Washington, DC: Pew Research Center, May 2019.

Fulkerson, Gregory M., and Brian Lowe. "Representations of Rural in Popular North American Television." In *Reimagining Rural: Urbanormative Portrayals of Rural Life*, edited by Gregory M. Fulkerson and Alexander R. Thomas, 9–34. New York: Lexington Books, 2016.

Gagnon, Douglas J., and Marybeth J. Mattingly. *Limited Access to AP Courses for Students in Smaller and More Isolated Rural School Districts*. Durham, NH: Carsey Institute, 2015.

———. *Most U.S. School Districts Have Low Access to School Counselors*. Durham, NH: Carsey Institute, 2016.

Galster, George C., and Sean P. Killen. "The Geography of Metropolitan Opportunity: A Reconnaissance and Conceptual Framework." *Housing Policy Debate* 6, no. 1 (1995): 10–47.

Galster, George, and Patrick Sharkey. "Spatial Foundations of Inequality: A Conceptual Model and Empirical Overview." *Russell Sage Foundation Journal of the Social Sciences* 3, no. 2 (2017): 1–33.

Gaztambide-Fernández, Rubén A. *The Best of the Best: Becoming Elite at an American Boarding School*. Cambridge, MA: Harvard University Press, 2009.

Geiger, Roger L. "The Ten Generations of American Higher Education." In *American Higher Education in the Twenty-First Century: Social, Political, and Economic Challenges*, edited by Philip G. Altbach, Patricia J. Gumport, and Robert O. Berdahl, 37–68. Johns Hopkins University Press, 2011.

Gettinger, Aaron. "A Big Reason Rural Students Never Go to College: Colleges Don't Recruit Them." *Hechinger Report* (2019). https://hechingerreport .org/a-big-reason-rural-students-never-go-to-college-colleges-dont -recruit-them/.

Giancola, Jennifer, and Richard D. Kahlenberg. *True Merit: Ensuring Our Brightest Students Have Access to Our Best Colleges and Universities*. Lansdowne, VA: Jack Kent Cooke Foundation, January 2016. https://www.jkcf .org/wp-content/uploads/2018/06/JKCF_True_Merit_FULLReport.pdf.

Gibbons, Melinda M., and L. DiAnne Borders. "Prospective First-Generation College Students: A Social-Cognitive Perspective." *Career Development Quarterly* 58 (2010).

Glass, Ronald David, and Kysa Nygreen. "Class, Race, and the Discourse of 'College for All': A Response to 'Schooling for Democracy.'" *Democracy & Education* 19, no. 1 (2011): 1–8.

Gofen, Anat. "Family Capital: How First-Generation Higher Education Students Break the Intergenerational Cycle." *Family Relations* 58: 104–20.

Goldhaber, Dan, Lesley Lavery, and Roddy Theobald. "Uneven Playing Field? Assessing the Teacher Quality Gap between Advantaged and Disadvantaged Students." *Educational Researcher* 44, no. 5 (2015): 293–307.

Goldrick-Rab, Sara. *Paying the Price: College Costs, Financial Aid, and the Betrayal of the American Dream.* Chicago: University of Chicago Press, 2016.

Gorski, Paul C. "Poverty Ideologies and the Possibility of Equitable Education: How Deficit, Grit, and Structural Views Enable or Inhibit Just Policy and Practice for Economically Marginalized Students." *Counterpoints* 523 (2018): 95–120.

Gould, E. D. "Cities, Workers, and Wages: A Structural Analysis of the Urban Wage Premium." *Review of Economic Studies* 74, no. 2 (2007): 477–506.

Green, Gary Paul. "Deindustrialization of Rural America: Economic Restructuring and the Rural Ghetto." *Local Development & Society* 1, no. 1 (2020): 15–25.

Greenberg, Susan H. "Survey: Conflicting Views of Higher Education." *Inside Higher Ed*, July 25, 2022. https://www.insidehighered.com/news/2022/07/26/public-support-higher-education-wobbling.

Hacker, Andrew, and Claudia Dreifus. *Higher Education? How Colleges Are Wasting Our Money and Failing Our Kids—and What We Can Do about It.* New York: St. Martin's Griffin, 2010.

Haller, Emil J., and Sarah J. Virkler. "Another Look at Rural-Nonrural Differences in Students' Educational Aspirations." *Journal of Research in Rural Education* 9, no. 3 (1993): 170–78.

Han, Crystal, Ozan Jaquette, and Karina Salazar. *Recruiting the Out-of-State University: Off-Campus Recruiting by Public Research Universities.* Chicago: Joyce Foundation, 2019. https://ozanj.github.io/joyce_report/#/title.

Hanson, Melanie. "Total Student Loan Debt." *Education Data Initiative*, November 30, 2021. https://educationdata.org/total-student-loan-debt.

Havlik, Stacey, Nicole Pulliam, Krista Malott, and Sam Steen. "Strengths and Struggles: First-Generation College-Goers Persisting at One Predominantly White Institution." *Journal of College Student Retention: Research, Theory & Practice* 22, no. 1 (2020): 118–40.

Hawley, Leslie R., Natalie A. Koziol, James A. Bovaird, Carina M. McCormick, Greg W. Welch, Ann M. Arthur, and Kirstie Bash. "Defining and Describing Rural: Implications for Rural Special Education Research and Policy." *Rural Special Education Quarterly* 35, no. 3 (2016): 3–11.

Heinisch, Benjamin P. "Small Fish out of Water: Rural First-Generation Student Experience at a Large University." *Journal of College Orientation and Transition* 24, no. 1 (2017): 21–33.

Hektner, Joel M. "When Moving Up Implies Moving Out: Rural Adolescent Conflict in the Transition to Adulthood." *Journal of Research in Rural Education* 11, no. 1 (Spring 1995): 3–14.

Hillman, Nicholas W. "Geography of College Opportunity: The Case of Education Deserts." *American Educational Research Journal* 53, no. 4 (2016): 987–1021.

Hillman, Nicholas, and Taylor Weichman. *Education Deserts: The Continued Significance of "Place" in the Twenty-First Century.* Washington, DC: American Council on Education, 2016. https://www.acenet.edu/Documents/Education-Deserts-The-Continued-Significance-of-Place-in-the-Twenty-First-Century.pdf.

Hirudayaraj, Malar, and Gary N. McLean. "First-Generation College Graduates: A Phenomenological Exploration of Their Transition Experiences into the Corporate Sector." *European Journal of Training and Development* 42, nos. 1–2 (2018): 91–109.

Holland, Megan M. "Framing the Search: How First-Generation Students Evaluate Colleges." *Journal of Higher Education* 91, no. 3 (2020): 378–401.

Horn, Laura, and Anne-Marie Núñez. "Mapping the Road to College: First-Generation Students' Math Track, Planning Strategies, and Context of Support." Washington, DC: US Department of Education, 2000.

Hossler, Don, Jack Schmit, and Nick Vesper. *Going to College: How Social, Economic, and Educational Factors Influence the Decisions Students Make.* Baltimore: Johns Hopkins University Press, 1999.

Hotz, V. Joseph, Emily E. Wiemers, Joshua Rasmussen, and Kate Maxwell Koegel. "The Role of Parental Wealth and Income in Financing Children's College Attendance and Its Consequences." Working Paper No. 25144, National Bureau of Economic Research. Cambridge, MA, 2018.

Howley, Caitlin W. "Remote Possibilities: Rural Children's Educational Aspirations." *Peabody Journal of Education* 81, no. 2 (2006): 62–80.

Hoxby, Caroline, and Christopher Avery. "The Missing 'One-Offs': The Hidden Supply of High-Achieving, Low-Income Students." Brookings Papers on Economic Activity, Spring 2013.

HR&A Advisors. "The New York City Tech Ecosystem: Generating Economic Opportunities for All New Yorkers." March 2014. https://www.hraadvisors

.com/wp-content/uploads/2014/03/NYC_Tech_Ecosystem_032614_WEB .pdf.

Hu, Shouping. "Educational Aspirations and Postsecondary Access and Choice: Students in Urban, Suburban, and Rural Schools Compared." *Education Policy Analysis Archives* 11 (2003). http://epaa.asu.edu/epaa/ v11n14/.

Hyman, Joshua. "Does Money Matter in the Long Run? Effects of School Spending on Educational Attainment." *American Economic Journal: Economic Policy* 9, no. 4 (2017): 256–80.

Institute of Education Sciences. "The Condition of Education 2020." Washington, DC: US Department of Education, 2020. https://nces.ed.gov/ pubsearch/pubsinfo.asp?pubid=2020144.

———. "Undergraduate Retention and Graduation Rates." Washington, DC: US Department of Education, 2022. https://nces.ed.gov/programs/coe/ indicator/ctr.

Jack, Anthony Abraham. *The Privileged Poor: How Elite Colleges Are Failing Disadvantaged Youth.* Cambridge, MA: Harvard University Press, 2019.

Jackson, Aaron P., Steven A. Smith, and Curtis Hill. "Academic Persistence among Native American College Students." *Journal of College Student Development* 44, no. 4 (2003): 548–65.

Jackson, C. Kirabo, Rucker C. Johnson, and Claudia Persico. "The Effects of School Spending on Educational and Economic Outcomes: Evidence from School Finance Reforms." *Quarterly Journal of Economics* (2016): 157–218.

Jadhav, Adam. "Was It Rural Populism? Returning to the Country, 'Catching Up,' and Trying to Understand the Trump Vote." *Journal of Rural Studies* 82 (2021): 553–69.

Jenkins, Sharon Rae, Aimee Belanger, Melissa Londoño Connally, Adriel Boals, and Kelly M. Durón. "First-Generation Undergraduate Students' Social Support, Depression, and Life Satisfaction." *Journal of College Counseling* 16 (July 2013): 129–42.

Jicha, Karl A. "Portrayals of Rural People and Places in Reality Television Programming: How Popular American Cable Series Misrepresent Rural Realities." In *Reimagining Rural: Urbanormative Portrayals of Rural Life,* edited by Gregory M. Fulkerson and Alexander R. Thomas, 35–58. New York: Lexington Books, 2016.

Johnson, Kenneth M. "Rural America Lost Population over the Past Decade for the First Time in History." Carsey Research National Issue Brief, Carsey School of Public Policy: University of New Hampshire, 2022.

Johnson, Kenneth M., and Daniel T. Lichter. *Growing Racial Diversity in Rural America: Results from the 2020 Census*. Durham, NH: Carsey Institute, 2022. https://carsey.unh.edu/publication/growing-racial-diversity-in -rural-america.

———. "Rural Depopulation: Growth and Decline Processes over the Past Century." *Rural Sociology* 84, no. 1 (2019): 3–27.

Johnson, Kenneth M., Richelle Winkler, and Luke T. Rogers. *Age and Lifecycle Patterns Driving U.S. Migration Shifts*. Durham, NH: Carsey Institute, Spring 2013. https://scholars.unh.edu/cgi/viewcontent.cgi?article=1191 &context=carsey.

Kahler, Jonathan R., and Clifford S. Felton. *What's My Target? Estimating College Costs*. Valley Forge, PA: Vanguard Group, 2022.

Kalsner, Lydia, and M. Carole Pistole. "College Adjustment in a Multiethnic Sample: Attachment, Separation-Individuation, and Ethnic Identity." *Journal of College Student Development* 44, no. 1 (January–February 2003): 92–109.

Kang-Brown, Jacob, and Ram Subramanian. *Out of Sight: The Growth of Jails in Rural America*. New York: Vera Institute of Justice Safety and Justice Challenge, June 2017. https://www.vera.org/downloads/publications/out -of-sight-growth-of-jails-rural-america.pdf.

Kaufman, Sarah. "Some Say Bypassing a Higher Education Is Smarter Than Paying for a Degree." *Washington Post*, September 10, 2010. https:// www.washingtonpost.com/wp-dyn/content/article/2010/09/09/ AR2010090903350.html.

Keene, Adrienne J. "College Pride, Native Pride: A Portrait of a Culturally Grounded Precollege Access Program for American Indian, Alaska Native, and Native Hawaiian Students." *Harvard Educational Review* 86, no. 1 (2016): 72–97.

Khan, Shamus Rahman. "The Education of Elites in the United States." *Troisième Série* 66, no. 1 (2016): 171–91.

Klugman, Joshua. "How Resource Inequalities among High Schools Reproduce Class Advantages in College Destinations." *Research in Higher Education* 53, no. 8 (2012): 803–30.

Kolbe, Tammy, Bruce D. Baker, Drew Atchison, Jesse Levin, and Phoebe Harris. "The Additional Cost of Operating Rural Schools: Evidence from Vermont." *AERA Open* 7, no. 1 (2021): 1–16. https://journals.sagepub.com/ doi/full/10.1177/2332858420988868.

Koricich, Andrew, Xi Chen, and Rodney P. Hughes. "Understanding the Effects of Rurality and Socioeconomic Status on College Attendance and

Institutional Choice in the United States." *Review of Higher Education* 41, no. 2 (Winter 2018): 281–305.

Kozol, Jonathan. *Savage Inequalities: Children in America's Schools.* New York: Harper Perennial, 1991.

Krishnaswami, Arjun, and Elisheva Mittelman. *Clean Energy Sweeps across Rural America.* New York: National Resource Defense Council, November 2018. https://www.nrdc.org/sites/default/files/rural-clean-energy-report.pdf.

Kurtzleben, Danielle. "Rural Voters Played a Big Part in Helping Trump Defeat Clinton." *NPR*, November 14, 2016. https://www.npr.org/2016/11/14/501737150/rural-voters-played-a-big-part-in-helping-trump-defeat-clinton.

Labaree, David F. "Public Goods, Private Goods: The American Struggle over Educational Goals." *American Educational Research Journal* 34, no. 1 (1997): 39–81.

LaFortune, Julien, Jesse Rothstein, and Diane Whitmore Schanzenbach. "School Finance Reform and the Distribution of Student Achievement." Working paper, National Bureau of Economic Research, Cambridge, MA, 2016.

Laughlin, Lynda. "Beyond the Farm: Rural Industry Workers in America." *Random Samplings* (2016). https://www.census.gov/newsroom/blogs/random-samplings/2016/12/beyond_the_farm_rur.html#:~:text=Rural%20America%20faces%20unique%20challenges%20and%20opportunities%20compared%20with%20urban%20America.&text=In%20fact%2C%20the%20largest%20segment,care%20and%20social%20assistance%20industry.

Lautz, Jessica, David Hawkins, and Angel B. Pérez. "The High School Visit: Providing College Counseling and Building Crucial K-16 Links among Students, Counselors and Admission Officers." *Journal of College Admission* (Winter 2012): 108–16.

Lawrence-Lightfoot, Sara. *The Good High School: Portraits of Character and Culture.* New York: Basic Books, 1983.

Lawrence-Lightfoot, Sara, and Jessica Hoffman Davis. *The Art and Science of Portraiture.* San Francisco: Jossey-Bass Publishers, 1997.

Lee, Elizabeth M. "Elite Colleges and Socioeconomic Status." *Sociology Compass* 7, no. 9 (2013): 786–98.

Lee, Elizabeth M., and Rory Kramer. "Out with the Old, in with the New? Habitus and Social Mobility at Selective Colleges." *Sociology of Education* 86, no. 1 (2013): 18–35.

Lee, Tiffany S. "Building Native Nations through Native Students' Commitment to Their Communities." *Journal of American Indian Education* 48, no. 1 (2009): 19–36.

Lensmire, Timothy J. *White Folks: Race and Identity in Rural America*. New York: Routledge, 2017.

Lewis, Cynthia, Jean Ketter, and Bettina Fabos. "Reading Race in a Rural Context." *Qualitative Studies in Education* 14, no. 3 (2001): 317–50.

Li, Xiao. "Challenging Both Rural Advantage and Disadvantage Narratives: The Effects of Family Factors on American Student College Expectations in the Early 2010s." *Journal of Research in Rural Education* 35, no. 5 (2019): 1–16.

Lincoln Project. "Public Research Universities: Changes in State Funding." Cambridge, MA: American Academy of Arts & Sciences, 2015.

Lobao, Linda M., and Gregory Hooks. "Advancing the Sociology of Spatial Inequality: Spaces, Places, and the Subnational Scale." In *The Sociology of Spatial Inequality*, edited by Linda M. Lobao, Gregory Hooks, and Ann R. Tickamyer, 29–61. Albany: State University of New York Press, 2007.

Lobao, Linda, and Rogelio Saenz. "Spatial Inequality and Diversity as an Emerging Research Area." *Rural Sociology* 67, no. 4 (2002): 497–511.

Lobosco, Katie. "10 Most Expensive Colleges." *CNN Money*, March 5, 2015. https://money.cnn.com/gallery/pf/college/2014/11/16/most-expensive-colleges/index.html.

Logan, John R., and Julia Burdick-Will. "School Segregation and Disparities in Urban, Suburban, and Rural Areas." *Annals of the American Academy* 674 (2017): 199–216.

Logan, John R., Elisabeta Minca, and Sinem Adar. "The Geography of Inequality: Why Separate Means Unequal in American Public Schools." *Sociology of Education* 85, no. 3 (July 2012): 287–301.

London, Howard B. "Transformations: Cultural Challenges Faced by First-Generation Students." In *New Directions for Community Colleges*, edited by L. S. Zwerling and H. B. London, 5–11. San Francisco: Jossey-Bass, 1992.

Love, Bettina. *We Want to Do More Than Survive: Abolitionist Teaching and the Pursuit of Educational Freedom*. Boston: Beacon Press, 2019.

Lyson, Thomas A., and William W. Falk. "Forgotten Places: Poor Rural Regions in the United States." In *Forgotten Places: Uneven Development in Rural America*, edited by Thomas A. Lyson and William W. Falk, 1–6. Lawrence: University Press of Kansas, 1993.

Mahnken, Kevin. "When College Grads Don't Come Back Home: New Numbers Show a Widening Urban-Rural Education Divide." *The 74*,

June 27, 2017. https://www.the74million.org/article/when-college-grads -dont-come-back-home-new-numbers-show-a-widening-urban-rural -education-divide/.

Marcus, Jon. "If the Anger That Propelled Trump's Win Is Economic, Can Higher Education Fix It?" *Hechinger Report*, November 9, 2016. https:// hechingerreport.org/anger-propelled-trumps-win-economic-can-higher -education-fix/.

Marcus, Jon, and Matt Krupnick. "The Rural Higher-Education Crisis." *The Atlantic*, September 27, 2017. https://www.theatlantic.com/education/ archive/2017/09/the-rural-higher-education-crisis/541188/.

Marré, Alexander W. *Rural Education at a Glance, 2017 Edition.* Washington, DC: Economic Research Service, US Department of Agriculture, 2017. https://www.ers.usda.gov/webdocs/publications/83078/eib-171.pdf?v =4802.6.

Massey, Douglas S., and Nancy A. Denton. *American Apartheid: Segregation and the Making of the Underclass.* Cambridge, MA: Harvard University Press, 1993.

Mattioli, Dana. "Generation Jobless: From Ivied Halls to Traveling Sales- man." *Wall Street Journal*, November 8, 2011. https://www.wsj.com/ articles/SB10001424052970203733504577024090027351410.

McCulloh, Edna. "An Exploration of Parental Support in the Retention of Rural First-Generation College Students." *Journal of College Student Reten- tion: Research, Theory & Practice* 24, no. 1 (2022): 144–68.

McDonough, Patricia M. "Counseling and College Counseling in America's High Schools." Alexandria, VA: National Association for College Admis- sion Counseling, January 2005.

McDonough, Patricia M., and Shannon Calderone. "The Meaning of Money: Perceptual Differences between College Counselors and Low-Income Families about College Costs and Financial Aid." *American Behavioral Scientist* 49, no. 12 (2006): 1703–18.

McDonough, Patricia A., and Karen A. McClafferty. "Rural College Opportu- nity: A Shasta and Siskiyou County Perspective." Los Angeles: University of California Los Angeles, 2001.

Means, Darris R., Ashley B. Clayton, Johnathan G. Conzelmann, Patti Baynes, and Paul D. Umbach. "Bounded Aspirations: Rural, African American High School Students and College Access." *Review of Higher Education* 39, no. 4 (2016): 543–69.

Melendez, Mickey C. "The Influence of Athletic Participation on the College Adjustment of Freshmen and Sophomore Student Athletes." *Journal of College Student Retention* 8, no. 1 (2006–2007): 39–56.

Mitchell, Josh, and Douglas Belkin. "Americans Losing Faith in College Degrees, Poll Finds." *Wall Street Journal*, September 7, 2017. https://www.wsj.com/articles/americans-losing-faith-in-college-degrees-poll-finds-1504776601.

Mitchell, Michael, Michael Leachman, and Matt Saenz. *State Higher Education Funding Cuts Have Pushed Costs to Students, Worsened Inequality.* Washington, DC: Center on Budget and Policy Priorities, October 24, 2019. https://www.cbpp.org/sites/default/files/atoms/files/10-24-19sfp.pdf.

Monnat, Shannon M., and David L. Brown. "More Than a Rural Revolt: Landscapes of Despair and the 2016 Presidential Election." *Journal of Rural Studies* 55 (2017): 227–36.

Morton, Jennifer M. *Moving up without Losing Your Way: The Ethical Costs of Upward Mobility.* Princeton, NJ: Princeton University Press, 2019.

Mykerezi, Elton, Genti Kostandini, and Bradford Mills. "Do Rural Community Colleges Supply Unique Educational Benefits?" *Journal of Agricultural and Applied Economics* 41, no. 2 (2009): 411–17.

Nader, Laura. "Up the Anthropologist: Perspectives Gained from Studying Up." In *Reinventing Anthropology*, edited by Dell Hymes, 284–311. New York: Pantheon Books, 1972.

National Student Clearinghouse. "Persistence" (2023). https://www.studentclearinghouse.org/dei-data-lab/research-data/persistence-data/.

Nelson, Ingrid A. "Rural Students' Social Capital in the College Search and Application Process." *Rural Sociology* 81, no. 2 (2016): 249–81.

Niskanen Center. "Explaining the Urban-Rural Political Divide." July 17, 2019. https://www.niskanencenter.org/explaining-the-urban-rural-political-divide/.

Nuñez, Anne-Marie. "Negotiating Ties: A Qualitative Study of First-Generation Female Students' Transitions to College." *Journal of the First-Year Experience and Students in Transition* 17, no. 2 (2005): 87–118.

Obama, Barack. "Remarks by the President in a National Address to America's Schoolchildren." September 8, 2009. https://obamawhitehouse.archives.gov/the-press-office/remarks-president-a-national-address-americas-schoolchildren.

Olivas, Michael A. "Higher Education as 'Place': Location, Race, and College Attendance Patterns." *Review of Higher Education* 28, no. 2 (2005): 169–89.

Orfield, Gary, and Chungmei Lee. *Why Segregation Matters: Poverty and Educational Inequality.* Cambridge, MA: Civil Rights Project, 2005.

Ornstein, Allan. "Wealth, Legacy and College Admission." *Society* 56 (2019): 335–39.

Osborne, Melissa. *Polished: College, Class, and the Burdens of Social Mobility.* Chicago: University of Chicago Press, 2024.

Owen, Stephanie, and Isabel Sawhill. *Should Everyone Go to College? Center on Children and Families at Brookings.* Washington, DC: Brookings Institution, May 2013. https://www.brookings.edu/wp-content/uploads/2016/06/08 -should-everyone-go-to-college-owen-sawhill.pdf.

Pappano, Laura. "Colleges Discover the Rural Students." *New York Times,* February 5, 2017. https://www.nytimes.com/2017/01/31/education/edlife/ colleges-discover-rural-student.html.

Park, Julie J., and Stephanie H. Chang. "Understanding Students' Precollege Experiences with Racial Diversity: The High School as a Microsystem." *Journal of College Student Development* 56, no. 4 (2015): 349–63.

Pascarella, Ernest, Christopher T. Pierson, Gregory C. Wolniak, and Patrick T. Terenzini. "First-Generation College Students: Additional Evidence on College Experiences and Outcomes." *Journal of Higher Education* 75, no. 3 (May–June 2004): 249–84.

Peine, Emelie K., Amy Price Azano, and Kai A. Schafft. "Beyond Cultural and Structural Explanations of Regional Underdevelopment: Identity and Dispossession in Appalachia." *Journal of Appalachian Studies* 26, no. 1 (2020): 40–56.

Perna, Laura W. *Delivering on the Promise: Structuring College Promise Programs to Promote Higher Education Attainment for Students from Underserved Groups.* Philadelphia: PennAHEAD Alliance for Higher Education and Democracy, October 2016.

Perna, Laura W., and Marvin A. Titus. "The Relationship between Parental Involvement as Social Capital and College Enrollment: An Examination of Racial/Ethnic Group Differences." *Journal of Higher Education* 76, no. 5 (2005): 485–518.

Perna, Laura W., Jeremy Wright-Kim, and Elaine W. Leigh. "Will College Promise Programs Improve or Reduce Equity? Understanding the Contextual Conditions That Influence Program Implementation." *Education Policy Analysis Archives* 29, no. 26 (2021): 1–31.

Petrin, Robert A., Kai A. Schafft, and Judith L. Meece. "Educational Sorting and Residential Aspirations among Rural High School Students: What Are the Contributions of Schools and Educators to Rural Brain Drain?" *American Educational Research Journal* 51, no. 2 (April 2014): 294–326.

Phelan, Peggy. *Unmarked: The Politics of Performance.* New York: Routledge, 1996.

Pierson, Ashley, and Havala Hanson. *Comparing Postsecondary Enrollment and Persistence among Rural and Nonrural Students in Oregon.* Washington, DC: Department of Education, 2015. https://files.eric.ed.gov/fulltext/ED556748.pdf.

Pilchen, Aliya, Kyra Caspary, and Katrina Woodworth. *Postsecondary Outcomes of IB Diploma Programme Graduates in the U.S.* Menlo Park, CA: SRI Education, December 2019. https://www.ibo.org/globalassets/new-structure/research/pdfs/us-postsecondary-outcomes-final-report.pdf.

powell, john. "Race, Place, and Opportunity." *American Prospect*, September 2008. http://prospect.org/article/race-place-and-opportunity.

Professor X. "An Anti-College Backlash?" *The Atlantic*, March 31, 2011. https://www.theatlantic.com/national/archive/2011/03/an-anti-college-backlash/73214/.

Puente, Mayra. "Leaving La Puente: A Critical Race Counterstory of Rural Chicana/Latina College Choice." *InterActions: UCLA Journal of Education and Information Studies* 16, no. 2 (2020).

Rajkumar, Karthik, Guillaume Saint-Jacques, Iavor Bojinov, Erik Brynjolfsson, and Sinan Aral. "A Causal Test of the Strength of Weak Ties." *Science* 377 (September 16, 2022): 1304–10.

Reeder, Richard J., and Dennis M. Brown. *Recreation, Tourism, and Rural Well-Being.* Washington, DC: Economic Research Service, US Department of Agriculture, 2005. https://www.ers.usda.gov/webdocs/publications/46126/15112_err7_1_.pdf?v=0.

Reid, M. Jeanne, and James L. Moore III. "College Readiness and Academic Preparation for Postsecondary Education: Oral Histories of First-Generation Urban College Students." *Urban Education* 43, no. 2 (2008): 240–61.

Rembert, Mark, Adenola Osinubi, and Dani Douglas. *The Rise of Remote Work in Rural America.* Hartland, VT: Center on Rural Innovation and Rural Innovations Strategies, 2021. https://ruralinnovation.us/wp-content/uploads/2022/01/Remote-Work_122721.pdf.

Reynolds, Jeremy, and He Xian. "Perceptions of Meritocracy in the Land of Opportunity." *Research in Social Stratification and Mobility* 36 (2014): 121–37.

Rhoades, Gary. "The Higher Education We Choose, Collectively: Reembodying and Repoliticizing Choice." *Journal of Higher Education* 85, no. 6 (2014): 917–30.

Rhodes, Alec P. "Student Debt and Geographic Disadvantage: Disparities by Rural, Suburban, and Urban Background." *Rural Sociology* 87, no. 1 (2021): 231–63.

Ricks, Jonathan R., and Jeffrey M. Warren. "Transitioning to College: Experiences of Successful First-Generation College Students." *Journal of Educational Research & Practice* 11, no. 1 (2021): 1–15.

Rivera, Lauren A. *Pedigree: How Elite Students Get Elite Jobs.* Princeton, NJ: Princeton University Press, 2015.

Roderick, Melissa, Jenny Nagaoka, and Vanessa Coca. "College Readiness for All: The Challenge for Urban High Schools." *Future of Children* 19, no. 1 (Spring 2009): 185–210.

Rondini, Ashley C. "Healing the Hidden Injuries of Class? Redemption Narratives, Aspirational Proxies, and Parents of Low-Income, First-Generation College Students." *Sociological Forum* 31, no. 1 (2016): 96–116.

Rojewski, Jay W. "Career-Related Predictors of Work-Bound and College-Bound Status of Adolescents in Rural and Nonrural Areas." *Journal of Research in Rural Education* 15, no. 3 (1999): 141–56.

Roksa, Josipa, and Peter Kinsley. "The Role of Family Support in Facilitating Academic Success of Low-Income Students." *Research in Higher Education* 60 (2019): 415–36.

Roscigno, Vincent J., and Martha L. Crowley. "Rurality, Institutional Disadvantage, and Achievement/Attainment." *Rural Sociology* 66, no. 2 (2001): 268–93.

Roscigno, Vincent J., Donald Tomaskovic-Devey, and Martha L. Crowley. "Education and the Inequalities of Place." *Social Forces* 84, no. 4 (2006): 2121–45.

Rosenboom, Victoria, and Kristin Blagg. *Disconnected from Higher Education: How Geography and Internet Speed Limit Access to Higher Education.* Washington, DC: Urban Institute, February 3, 2018. https://www.urban.org/research/publication/disconnected-higher-education.

Rowan-Kenyon, Heather T., Angela D. Bell, and Laura W. Perna. "Contextual Influences on Parental Involvement in College Going: Variations by

Socioeconomic Status." *Journal of Higher Education* 79, no. 5 (September–October 2008): 564–86.

Ruiz, Roman, and Laura W. Perna. "The Geography of College Attainment: Dismantling Rural 'Disadvantage.'" Washington, DC: Pell Institute and the Council for Opportunity in Education and the Alliance for Higher Education and Democracy, 2017.

Saboe, Matt, Mia Ocean, and Simon Condliffe. "The Economic Impact of Rural Pennsylvania Community Colleges." Harrisburg: Center for Rural Pennsylvania, 2020.

Salazar, Katrina G., Ozan Jaquette, and Crystal Han. "Coming Soon to a Neighborhood Near You? Off-Campus Recruiting by Public Research Universities." *American Educational Research Journal* 58, no. 6 (2021): 1270–314.

Saldaña, Johnny. *The Coding Manual for Qualitative Researchers.* 4th ed. Thousand Oaks, CA: Sage Publications, 2021.

Salis Reyes, Nicole Alia. "'What Am I Doing to Be a Good Ancestor?': An Indigenized Phenomenology of Giving Back among Native College Graduates." *American Educational Research Journal* 56, no. 3 (2019): 603–37.

San Antonio, Donna M. "The Complex Decision-Making Process of Rural Emerging Adults: Counseling Beyond Dualism." *Peabody Journal of Education* 91, no. 2 (2016): 246–69.

Sandefur, Gary D., Ann M. Meier, and Mary E. Campbell. "Family Resources, Social Capital, and College Attendance." *Social Science Research* 35 (2006): 525–53.

Saw, Guan K., and Charlotte A. Agger. "Stem Pathways of Rural and Small-Town Students: Opportunities to Learn, Aspirations, Preparation, and College Enrollment." *Educational Researcher* 50, no. 9 (2021): 595–606.

Schafft, Kai A., Erin McHenry-Sorber, Daniella Hall, and Ian Burfoot-Rochford. "Busted Amidst the Boom: The Creation of New Insecurities and Inequalities within Pennsylvania's Shale Gas Boomtowns." *Rural Sociology* 83, no. 3 (2018): 503–31.

Schmitt-Wilson, Sarah, and Soo-yong Byun. "Postsecondary Transitions and Attainment." In *The Bloomsbury Handbook of Rural Education in the United States*, edited by Amy Price Azano, Karen Eppley, and Catharine Biddle, 157–64. New York: Bloomsbury Academic, 2022.

Schneider, Jack. "Privilege, Equity, and the Advanced Placement Program: Tug of War." *Journal of Curriculum Studies* 41, no. 6 (2018): 813–31.

Seaman, Jayson, Andrew D. Coppens, Cindy L. Hartman, Erin Hiley Sharp, Sarah Jusseaume, and Molly Donovan. "Youth Identity and Postsecondary

Decision Making in a Rural State: Evidence of a *College for All* Master Narrative." *Frontiers in Education* (2023). https://doi.org/10.3389/feduc.2023.1257731.

Sherman, Jennifer, and Rayna Sage. "Sending Off All Your Good Treasures: Rural Schools, Brain-Drain, and Community Survival in the Wake of Economic Collapse." *Journal of Research in Rural Education* 26, no. 11 (2011): 1–14. http://jrre.psu.edu/articles/26-11.pdf.

Sibley, David. *Geographies of Exclusion: Society and Difference in the West.* New York: Routledge, 1995.

Silver, Nate. "Education, Not Income, Predicted Who Would Vote for Trump." *FiveThirtyEight*, November 22, 2016. https://fivethirtyeight.com/features/education-not-income-predicted-who-would-vote-for-trump/.

Singleton, Alexander D. *Educational Opportunity: The Geography of Access to Higher Education.* New York: Routledge, 2010.

Sipple, John W., and Brian O. Brent. "Challenges and Strategies Associated with Rural School Settings." In *Handbook of Research in Education Finance and Policy*, edited by Helen F. Ladd and Margaret E. Goertz, 607–22. New York: Routledge, 2015.

Small, Mario Luis. *Villa Victoria: The Transformation of Social Capital in a Boston Barrio.* Chicago: University of Chicago Press, 2004.

Smith, Kristen E., and Ann R. Tickamyer, eds. *Economic Restructuring and Family Well-Being in Rural America.* University Park: Penn State University Press, 2011.

Soja, Edward W. *Seeking Spatial Justice.* Minneapolis: University of Minnesota Press, 2010.

Stebleton, Michael J., Krista M. Soria, and Ronald L. Huesman Jr. "First-Generation Students' Sense of Belonging, Mental Health, and Use of Counseling Services at Public Research Universities." *Journal of College Counseling* 17 (2014): 6–20.

Stephens, Nicole M., Stephanie A. Fryberg, Hazel Rose Markus, Camille S. Johnson, and Rebecca Covarrubias. "Unseen Disadvantage: How American Universities' Focus on Independence Undermines the Academic Performance of First-Generation College Students." *Journal of Personality and Social Psychology* 102, no. 6 (2012): 1178–97.

Stevens, Mitchell L. *Creating a Class: College Admissions and the Education of the Elite.* Cambridge, MA: Harvard University Press, 2009.

Strange, Marty. "Equitable and Adequate Funding for Rural Schools: Ensuring Equal Educational Opportunity for All Students." *Nebraska Law Review* 82, no. 1 (2003): 1–8.

———. "Finding Fairness for Rural Students." *Phi Delta Kappan* 92, no. 6 (March 2011): 8–15.

Stuber, Jenny M. *Inside the College Gates: How Class and Culture Matter in Higher Education*. New York: Lexington Books, 2011.

Suskind, Ron. *A Hope in the Unseen: An American Odyssey from the Inner City to the Ivy League*. New York: Broadway Books, 1998.

Thomas, Alexander R., Brian M. Lowe, Gregory M. Fulkerson, and Polly J. Smith. *Critical Rural Theory: Structure, Space, Culture*. Lanham, MD: Lexington Books, 2011.

Tieken, Mara Casey. "College Talk and the Rural Economy: Shaping the Educational Aspirations of Rural, First-Generation Students." *Peabody Journal of Education* 91, no. 2 (2016): 203–23.

———. "Making Race Relevant in All-White Classrooms: Using Local History." In *Everyday Antiracism: Getting Real about Race in School*, edited by Mica Pollock, 200–203. New York: New Press, 2008.

———. "There's a Big Part of Rural America That Everyone's Ignoring." *Washington Post*, March 26, 2017.

———. *Why Rural Schools Matter*. Chapel Hill: University of North Carolina Press, 2014.

Tinto, Vincent. *Leaving College: Rethinking the Causes and Cures of Student Attrition*. Chicago: University of Chicago Press, 1987.

Turley, Ruth N. López. "College Proximity: Mapping Access to Opportunity." *Sociology of Education* 82, no. 2 (April 2009): 126–46.

Ulrich-Schad, Jessica D., and Cynthia M. Duncan. "People and Places Left Behind: Work, Culture and Politics in the Rural United States." *Journal of Peasant Studies* 45, no. 1 (2018): 59–79.

US Census Bureau. "Rural Median Household Income Remains about 25 Percent Below the Urban Median." July 20, 2017. https://www.ers.usda.gov/data-products/chart-gallery/gallery/chart-detail/?chartId=84389.

———. "2020 Census Urban Area Facts." February 9, 2023. https://www.census.gov/programs-surveys/geography/guidance/geo-areas/urban-rural/2020-ua-facts.html.

Van T. Bui, Khanh. "First-Generation College Students at Four-Year University: Background Characteristics, Reasons for Pursuing Higher Education, and First-Year Experiences." *College Student Journal* 36, no. 1 (2002): 3–12.

Vasquez-Salgado, Yolanda, Patricia M. Greenfield, and Rocio Burgos-Cienfuegos. "Exploring Home-School Value Conflicts: Implications for Academic Achievement and Well-Being among Latino First-Generation College Students." *Journal of Adolescent Research* 30, no. 3 (2015): 271–305.

Warren, Mark R., J. Phillip Thompson, and Susan Saegert. "The Role of Social Capital in Combating Poverty." In *Social Capital and Poor Communities*, edited by Susan Saegert, J. Phillip Thompson, and Mark R. Warren, 1–28. New York: Russell Sage Foundation, 2001.

Wells, Ryan S., Ling Chen, Genia M. Bettencourt, and Sarah Haas. "Reconsidering Rural-Nonrural College Enrollment Gaps: The Role of Socioeconomic Status in Geographies of Opportunity." *Research in Higher Education* 64 (2023): 1089–112.

Wells, Ryan S., Catherine A. Manly, Suzan Kommers, and Ezekiel Kimball. "Narrowed Gaps and Persistent Challenges: Examining Rural-Nonrural Disparities in Postsecondary Outcomes over Time." *American Journal of Education* 126, no. November (2019): 1–31.

White House. "The Clinton Presidency: Expanding Education Opportunity." https://clintonwhitehouse5.archives.gov/WH/Accomplishments/eightyears-05.html.

Whiteside, Jasmine L. "Becoming Academically Eligible: University Enrollment among First-Generation, Rural College Goers." *Rural Sociology* 86, no. 2 (2021): 204–28.

Wiggins, Yolanda M. "'We Do Way More Than Just Clean up Puke . . . We Connect with Students': Custodial Staff as Informal Mentors at a Large, Public University." In *Campus Service Workers Supporting First-Generation Students: Informal Mentorship and Culturally Relevant Support as Key to Student Retention and Success*, edited by Georgina Guzmán, La'Tonya Rease Miles and Stephanie Santos Youngblood, 32–47. New York: Routledge, 2022.

Wilkinson, Kenneth P. *The Community in Rural America*. New York: Greenwood Press, 1991.

Willingham, Caius Z. "Rural Workers of Color Need a $15 Federal Minimum Wage." *CAP 20* (blog), September 1, 2021. https://www.americanprogress.org/article/rural-workers-color-need-15-federal-minimum-wage/.

Willis, Paul. *Learning to Labour: How Working Class Kids Get Working Class Jobs*. New York: Columbia University Press, 1977.

Winkle-Wagner, Rachelle. "The Perpetual Homelessness of College Experiences: Tensions between Home and Campus for African American Women." *Review of Higher Education* 33, no. 1 (Fall 2009): 1–36.

Witteveen, Dirk, and Paul Attewell. "The Earnings Payoff from Attending a Selective College." *Social Science Research* 66 (2017): 154–67.

Wray, Matt. *Not Quite White: White Trash and the Boundaries of Whiteness.* Durham, NC: Duke University Press, 2006.

Wright, Christina J. "Becoming to Remain: Community College Students and Post-Secondary Pursuits in Central Appalachia." *Journal of Research in Rural Education* 27, no. 6 (2012): 1–11. http://jrre.vmhost.psu.edu/wp -content/uploads/2014/02/27-6.pdf.

Wright, Travis. "On Jorge Becoming a Boy: A Counselor's Perspective." *Harvard Educational Review* 75, no. 2 (2007): 164–86.

Yan, Wenfan. *Postsecondary Enrollment and Persistence of Students from Rural Pennsylvania.* Harrisburg: Center for Rural Pennsylvania, 2002. http:// www.rural.palegislature.us/Postsecondary_Ed.pdf.

Young, Justin R. *Middle-Skill Jobs Remain More Common among Rural Workers.* Durham, NH: Carsey Institute, 2013. https://scholars.unh.edu/cgi/ viewcontent.cgi?article=1195&context=carsey.

Yosso, Tara J. "Whose Culture Has Capital? A Critical Race Theory Discussion of Community Cultural Wealth." *Race Ethnicity and Education* 8, no. 1 (2005): 69–91.

Zaloom, Caitlin. *Indebted: How Families Make College Work at Any Cost.* Princeton, NJ: Princeton University Press, 2019.

Index